Workbook

AN INVITATION TO FLY

Basics for the Private Pilot

For further information about ordering or adopting this text or the accompanying material, write or call

The Continuing Education Division
Wadsworth Publishing Company
10 Davis Drive
Belmont, California 94002
(415) 595-2350

Accompanying materials:

Textbook
Telecourse Viewer's Guide
San Francisco Sectional Chart (partial)

The Wadsworth Continuing Education Professional Series

Power and Conflict in Continuing Education: Survival and Prosperity for All? Sponsored by Wadsworth Publishing Company and the National University Continuing Education Association

Administration of Continuing Education by George B. Strother and John P. Klus

The Wadsworth Series in Continuing Education

Are You a Target? A Guide to Self-Protection, Personal Safety, and Rape Prevention by Judith Fein

PCP, The Devil's Dust—Recognition, Management, and Prevention of Phencyclidine Abuse by Ronald L. Linder, Steven E. Lerner, and R. Stanley Burns

The Promotable Woman: Becoming a Successful Manager by Norma Carr-Ruffino

An Invitation to Fly: Basics for the Private Pilot by Sanford Gum and Bruce Walters

Viewer's Guide for an Invitation to Fly: Basics for the Private Pilot by Karen Bisgeier and Jacqueline Waide

The Job of the Planning Commissioner, Third Edition by Albert Solnit

Workbook

AN INVITATION TO FLY

Basics for the Private Pilot

George B. Semb
University of Kansas

Wadsworth Publishing Company / Continuing Education
Belmont, California
A Division of Wadsworth, Inc.

Continuing Education Editor: Nancy Taylor

Designer: McQuiston & Daughter, Inc.

Cover Photograph: Paul Bowen

Composition: Graphic Typesetting Service

Printed in the United States of America

1 2 3 4 5 6 7 8 9 10—86 85 84 83 82

ISBN 0-534-01057-4
    0-534-01193-4

CONTENTS

PREFACE

TO THE STUDENT

This workbook is designed to accompany *An Invitation to Fly: Basics for the Private Pilot* by Sanford Gum and Bruce Walters. It can also be used to review and prepare for the FAA Private Pilot (Airplane) Written Examination. It is based on principles, regulations, and practices that were current at the time it was printed.

The workbook requires the use of the same supplemental materials as the text, including:

1. San Francisco Sectional Chart
2. Navigation plotter
3. Flight computer or flight navigation calculator
4. Calculator (optional)

The workbook is designed primarily to help you learn the basic information necessary to become a private pilot. Each chapter includes: a summary of the main points, vocabulary and technical exercises to make certain you know the "language" of piloting, discussion questions and exercises that emphasize the important concepts, and multiple-choice review questions, many of which are similar to questions you will find on the FAA Private Pilot (Airplane) Written Exam. Answers to the review questions plus analysis of the questions and answers apppear at the end of each chapter.

As a general guide to studying the text and using this workbook, begin by thoroughly reading the chapter in the text. Next, read the main points in the workbook. These summarize and review the material presented in the text. When you are familiar with the material, it is time to become actively engaged in learning it. Try to do all the vocabulary and technical exercises without referring to the text for help. Once you have attempted them all, refer to the text to check your answers and to restudy those items you missed. Next, answer the discussion questions and exercises, again without referring to the text until you have attempted all of them. Finally, consider the review questions as a posttest to see how much you have learned. Try all of the review questions before you look up the answers at the end of the chapter.

If you follow these guidelines you should be able to answer most of the review questions correctly. Further, you should have a good grasp of the material covered in the chapter. One of the most important parts of this process is your attempt to answer the questions before looking up the answers. Learning specialists have contended for a long time that active involvement in workbook exercises promotes effective learning and retention, and research has shown them to be correct. Therefore, this workbook is designed to encourage you to actively participate in the learning process.

PREPARING FOR THE FAA WRITTEN EXAM

The FAA Private Pilot (Airplane) Written Test is not an easy exam. Nor is it a terribly difficult one, if you are well prepared. One purpose of the text and this workbook is to help you prepare for it.

Written tests are administered by Designated Written Test Examiners and by FAA General Aviation District Officers. Not all FAA offices administer the test, so check to make certain the one you select offers this service.

To take the test, Federal Aviation Regulations require that you: (a) have satisfactorily completed a ground instruction or home study course, (b) present an airman certificate, driver's license, or other official document as proof of identification, and (c) present a birth certificate or other official document showing that you meet the age requirement. For complete details, refer to the Federal Aviation Regulations (FARs), Part 61.

The administrator will give you a test booklet containing several hundred multiple-choice questions and a "random selection" assignment sheet listing the 60 particular questions you are to answer. You will have four hours to complete the test. Each question is to be answered by selecting a single alternative. You may take the following equipment with you to the test center: a protractor or plotter and a flight navigation computer or calculator. Textbooks and notes are forbidden, and the test administrator will provide paper, answer forms, and special pencils. You may also use calculators. However, there are several regulations concerning their use. First, the test administrator will instruct you to turn the calculator on and off before and after the test to ensure that any data stored in it are destroyed. If your calculator is one that stores data even when the switch is off, the administrator may ask you to demonstrate that all memory registers are empty. Second, if your calculator produces hard copy, all printouts must be surrendered to the administrator at the end of the test. Third, you will not be allowed to use any written instructions pertaining to the calculator during the test.

The feedback you will receive is in the form of an Airman Written Test Report that includes not only the grade but also the subject areas in which test items were answered incorrectly. The subject areas are identified on the Written Test Subject Matter Code that accompanies the report. However, the number of subject codes listed on the report does not necessarily represent the number of items answered incorrectly, since when more than one question is missed in a single area, the code for the area appears only once.

Besides reading the text and completing the workbook, it is a good idea to simulate examination conditions whenever possible. One way you can do this is to consider the review questions at the end of each chapter as a mini examination. Set a time limit of four minutes per question and answer all of them before looking up the answers. Another way to help you prepare for the FAA exam is to practice on questions in one of the test item banks available at many airport bookstores. Go through the book without reading specific questions and randomly select 60 of them, the way the FAA exam is constructed. There will be samples of how the random selection process works at the end of the study guide. Make certain the questions you select are evenly distributed throughout the book. Next, allow yourself four hours and answer as many as you can using the test-taking hints provided later in this preface. When you have answered all questions or four hours have elapsed, check your answers against those provided in the book. Making the simulated exercises as similar as you can to the actual exam conditions will greatly aid in your preparation for the FAA exam and may also help to reduce your anxiety.

One of the best and most frequently overlooked ways to prepare yourself for the exam is to be well rested. Staying up late the night before "cramming" often leads to fuzzy thinking and careless errors. So get a good night's sleep the day before the exam. Next, make a checklist of the things you will need for the exam (plotter, calculator, and so on). Use the checklist, much as you would before you started a flight, to be certain that you take all the required paraphernalia. It is easy to become flustered when you discover that you have forgotten something important, so use your checklist. Finally, arrive at the test center early to acquaint yourself with that setting. Find the restroom. Ask about the availability of beverages. Remember, too, that you are not usually allowed to bring food, so eat a good meal before your test.

The multiple-choice questions on the FAA Private Pilot (Airplane) Written Test have a single correct answer. Each item is independent of other items. This means that an answer to one item in no way depends upon or influences the answer to another item. However, as you read through a series of questions on the same subject, you will frequently find answers to one question in the stem of another.

The minimum passing grade will be specified by the test administrator on the written test sheet you receive. Before you begin the exam, read the directions carefully. If you have any questions, ask the administrator.

Many of the questions on the exam may appear to be tricky. Some of the questions may in fact be tricky, but careful analysis of most of them reveals that they are not tricky per se but rather that they are asking for subtle discriminations. For example, a question that asks you to discriminate between 3500 MSL (above sea level) and 3500 AGL (above ground level) is attempting to make certain you understand the difference between two ways of referring to altitude. Although subtle discriminations are sometimes difficult to learn, they are extremely important in flying.

Read each question thoroughly and carefully before selecting an alternative. If the statement refers to a general rule, do not look for exceptions unless the question specifically asks you to do so. Once you have read and understood the question, carefully evaluate each of the alternatives. Treat each one as a true-false statement and eliminate those you know to be obviously incorrect. Then concentrate on those (if any) about which you are uncertain. When answering multiple-choice items of the type that appear on FAA exams, I typically keep a tally sheet of questions about which I am uncertain. In addition, I keep a list of the alternatives about which I am uncertain so that when I return to the question later, it is easy to see where ambiguities still exist. Finally, if time remains, I go through the test a second time.

In general, I do not spend a great deal of time on any single question. If, after you have spent one to two minutes on a question, you still do not understand what is being asked, go on to the next question. At some point later in the exam you may discover an item that either has a direct bearing on what you did not comprehend earlier or that jogs your memory. When that happens, answer the question you are working on, then return immediately to the one you did not understand earlier.

Once you have attempted all of the questions, return to the ones about which you are uncertain and count how many there are in that category. Next, subtract ten minutes from the time remaining and divide the number of unanswered questions into the time remaining. That will give you an idea of how much time to spend on each question. Attempt to answer each question, checking occasionally to be sure that you are not spending too much time on any one question.

When you are down to the last ten minutes, or if you are certain all of your answers are correct, stop and cross check the answer sheet with the tally sheet. If there are any discrepancies, check to see which answer is the one you want and make certain the answer key is marked the way you want it. I cannot emphasize the rechecking process enough. Our research has shown that as many as 10 percent of the answers students record on the answer sheets do not correspond with their tally sheet, so cross check your answers. Finally, if you left any answers blank, pick the best answer and record it. There is no penalty for guessing, so choose the alternative that you think best answers the question.

If you do not pass the test the first time you try, it means that you were not adequately prepared. You will have to wait thirty days from the time you last took the test to reapply, unless an authorized instructor certifies in writing that appropriate instruction has been given and he or she finds you competent to pass the test, in which case you can reapply before the thirty days have expired.

One final comment about the written test concerns cheating. If you cheat you are cheating others as well as yourself. It is something that simply cannot be tolerated. Federal Aviation Regulations 61.37 is presented here for you to read.

FAR 61.37   Written tests: cheating or other unauthorized conduct
(a) Except as authorized by the Administrator, no person may
    (1) copy, or intentionally remove, a written test under this part;
    (2) give to another, or receive from another, any part or copy of that test;
    (3) give help on that test to, or receive help on that test from, any person during the period that test is being given;
    (4) take any part of that test in behalf of another person;
    (5) use any material or aid during the period that test is being given; or
    (6) intentionally cause, assist, or participate in any act prohibited by this paragraph.

(b) No person whom the Administrator finds to have committed an act prohibited by paragraph (a) of this section is eligible for any airman or ground instructor certificate or rating, or to take any test thereof, under this chapter for a period of one year after the date of that act. In addition, the commission of that act is a basis for suspending or revoking any airman or ground instructor certificate or rating held by that person.

I hope the information provided here helps you achieve a high score on the exam. If you find other preparation techniques helpful, please send them to me so I can incorporate them into the next edition of this workbook. My address is: George B. Semb, Department of Human Development, University of Kansas, Lawrence, Kansas 66045.

ACKNOWLEDGMENTS

I would like to thank several individuals who helped edit this workbook. I am particularly indebted to Helene (Bobba) Hopkins for her critical analysis of the material and Angela Calef for her superb editorial skills.

George B. Semb

ABOUT THE AUTHOR

George B. Semb is professor of human development at the University of Kansas. He received his private pilot's license in 1966 and has flown actively since that time. He has written study guides and workbooks for textbooks in psychology, biology, child development, and marriage and family relations. His primary area of research is instructional systems, where he has published or presented over one hundred papers in the last decade.

1/ON BECOMING A PILOT

MAIN POINTS

1. This chapter explains how to obtain Student and Private Pilot (airplane) Certificates as detailed in Part 61 of the Federal Aviation Regulations (FARs).

2. There are no minimum or maximum ages for taking flight lessons. However, you must be at least 16 to fly solo and at least 17 to receive the Private Pilot Certificate.

3. To receive a Student Pilot Certificate, you must be at least 16, be able to read, speak, and understand English, and hold at least a **Third Class Medical Certificate.** This certificate is required to solo an airplane and must be carried when flying solo. It expires on the last day of the month two years following its issue. In addition, to use the aircraft communications radio, you must have a Federal Communications Commission Restricted Radiotelephone Operator Permit.

4. To fly solo as a student pilot (by yourself—no passengers allowed), a Certified Flight Instructor (CFI) must determine that you are familiar with visual flight rules (VFR)—Part 91 of the FARs—and must enter an endorsement in your logbook and on your Student Pilot Certificate. The solo endorsement does not entitle you to fly cross-country; each cross-country flight must be separately endorsed.

5. To apply for the Private Pilot (airplane) Certificate, you must be at least 17; be able to read, speak, and understand English; hold at least a Third Class Medical Certificate; pass the Private Pilot Written Examination; have completed at least twenty hours of dual flight instruction, including three hours of cross-country, three hours in preparation for the flight test within sixty days of the test, and three hours of night flight; and complete twenty hours of solo time, including ten hours in airplanes and ten hours of cross-country flight.

6. Once you have satisfied the above requirements, you are ready for your flight test. It consists of three parts: an oral test, basic flying techniques, and a cross-country flight.

KEY TERMS AND CONCEPTS

Match each term or concept (1–14) with the appropriate description (a–n) below. Each item has only one match.

— 1. Federal Communications Commission   — 2. twenty

— 3. 16   — 4. Third Class

— 5. VFR   — 6. basic flying techniques

— 7. CFI   — 8. 17

— 9. Designated Flight Examiner   —10. meteorology

—11. FARs   —12. aviation physiology

—13. FAA   —14. commercial pilot

a.   person who must endorse logbook for solo flight
b.   agency that issues Restricted Radiotelephone Operator Permit
c.   one part of the private pilot flight test
d.   minimum age for solo flight
e.   flight rules with which you must be familiar in order to solo
f.   type of medical certificate required of student and private pilots
g.   minimum number of hours of solo time required for private pilot certification
h.   minimum age to receive the Private Pilot Certificate
i.   branch of the Department of Transportation responsible for civil aeronautics
j.   branch of medicine dealing with the effects of flight on the body
k.   science of the atmosphere
l.   civilian flight instructor authorized by the FAA to give flight tests
m.   regulations governing civil aviation
n.   airman certified to carry passengers for hire

DISCUSSION QUESTIONS AND EXERCISES

1.   What are three basic requirements you must meet before you can receive a Student Pilot Certificate?

2.   What are six basic requirements you must meet before you can apply for the Private Pilot Certificate?

3.   To apply for the Private Pilot Certificate, you must have received at least twenty hours of instruction. Briefly describe the three categories and time required within each to satisfy this requirement.

4.   To apply for the Private Pilot Certificate, you must have at least twenty hours of solo flight. Briefly describe the three categories and time required within each to satisfy this requirement.

5.   Briefly describe the three parts of the private pilot flight test.

REVIEW QUESTIONS

1.   Assume that your Third Class Medical Certificate was issued on April 1, 1981. This medical certificate is valid for a student or private pilot certificate through
      a. March 31, 1983
      b. April 1, 1982
      c. April 1, 1983
      d. April 30, 1983

2.   Your current and appropriate pilot and medical certificates must be in your personal possession
      a. any time you are flying, regardless of your status (student pilot with or without an instructor, pilot-in-command, or passenger in a plane)

   b. any time you are flying solo as a student pilot
   c. only when flying with an instructor of Designated Flight Examiner
   d. only when still a student pilot

3.   To carry passengers on a solo cross-country flight as a student pilot, you must
   a. have made at least three takeoffs and three landings in an aircraft of the same
      category and class within the preceding ninety days
   b. have made at least three takeoffs and three landings in an aircraft of the same
      category and class within the preceding twenty-four months
   c. carry your current Student Pilot Certificate, your current Third Class Medical
      Certificate, and your logbook appropriately endorsed for the cross-country
      flight by your Certified Flight Instructor
   d. none of the above—student pilots cannot carry passengers!

4.   To receive flight instruction from a Certified Flight Instructor you must be at
least
   a. 15 years of age
   b. 16 years of age
   c. 17 years of age
   d. no minimum age for taking flying lessons

5.   Of the following items, which are you *required* to carry on your person when
flying solo as a student pilot in an airplane with an operating two-way radio?

      1 medical certificate and student certificate
      2 Federal Communications Commission Restricted Radiotelephone Oper-
         ator Permit
      3 Social Security card
      4 driver's license

   a. 1, 2
   b. 1, 2, 3
   c. 1, 2, 3, 4
   d. 2, 3, 4

6.   How many total hours are required (under FAR Part 141), both with a flight
instructor and solo, before you can take the private pilot flight test?
   a. twenty
   b. thirty
   c. forty
   d. fifty

7.   Student pilots are required to accumulate a minimum of twenty hours of dual
flight instruction prior to being able to take the private pilot flight test. Which of the
following is *not* included in the twenty-hour requirement?

    a. three hours of cross-country
    b. three hours within sixty days of the flight test
    c. three hours of night flying
    d. three takeoffs and three landings to a full stop within the past fourteen days

ANSWERS

Key Terms and Concepts

1.	b	2.	g	3.	d	4.	f
5.	e	6.	c	7.	a	8.	h
9.	l	10.	k	11.	m	12.	j
13.	i	14.	n					

Review Questions

1.   d; it expires at the *end* of the month in which it was issued two years hence.
2.   b; solo is pilot-in-command; private pilots must also carry the certificates any time they operate as pilot-in-command.
3.   d; sorry, no passengers while you are flying solo as a student pilot.
4.   d; age restrictions apply only to certificates such as student or private pilot.
5.   a; only FAA and FCC certificates are required.
6.   c; twenty hours with a Certified Flight Instructor and twenty hours solo.
7.   d; there is no requirement on the number of takeoffs and landings within the previous two weeks.

2/THE PRACTICAL SCIENCE OF FLIGHT

MAIN POINTS

1. There are four categories of aircraft: rotorcraft, which generate lift by a "wing" that rotates above the body of the craft; lighter-than-air (LTA) aircraft, which include balloons and blimps; gliders, which are powerless aircraft used primarily for soaring; and airplanes, which use engines and wings to move through the air. Airplanes are classified by the number of engines and how they take off (by sea or by land).

2. You should be able to label an airplane, including the following common structures: the wing group, including **flaps** and **ailerons;** the propulsion group, including the **spinner, propeller,** and engine **cowl;** the empennage group, including the **vertical stabilizer, horizontal stabilizer, elevator** (or **stabilator**), **rudder,** and **trim tab;** the fuselage group; and the undercarriage group, including the nose wheel and landing gear.

3. Bernoulli's principle states that air pressure decreases where the speed of an airflow increases. This principle helps explain one component of **lift.** For example, as air travels over the curved surface of a wing, it must move farther (thus faster) than the air that travels under the wing, which produces upward lift. The forward edge of the wing is called the *leading edge,* and the back edge is called the *trailing edge.* As the wing changes position relative to the movement of the air, the **angle of attack** changes.

4. A second source of lift is produced when the airfoil is slanted such that the relative wind strikes the lower surface of the wing and produces a lifting effect. Newton's law of action and reaction thus applies. The action occurs when the airflow meets the lower surface of the wing; the reaction is the production of lift. Lift produced in this way accounts for a portion of an airplane's total lift compared to that induced by differential movement of air over and under the wing.

5. During flight, conditions are referred to as *static* if no changes are occurring in speed or attitude and as *dynamic* if either of these variables is changing. The four forces acting on the airplane in flight include *gravity,* or weight (the earth's pull), *lift* (produced by air flowing over the wing), **thrust** (generated by the propeller), and **drag** (air resistance to the structure of the airplane). **Induced drag** refers to the drag that exists when lift is being produced. Other sources of drag (generally categorized as **parasite drag**) include that created by the front of the plane (frontal drag) and other protruding structures such as landing gear (interference drag). Lift opposes gravity, and thrust opposes drag.

6. An airplane has three axes of rotation: **lateral, longitudinal,** and **vertical.** Rotation about the lateral axis is referred to as **pitch**, as when the nose of the airplane goes up or down; it is controlled by the *elevator*. For example, when you push the control column or yoke forward, the trailing edge of the elevator (another airfoil) moves down, which in turn produces lift (both dynamic and induced) on the elevator surface. The result is that the tail goes up and the nose goes down. Rotation about the vertical axis is called **yaw,** as when you turn right or left; it is controlled by the *rudder*. For example, when you push the right rudder pedal, the rudder moves to the right. Once again, the forces of lift operate, this time to move the tail of the airplane to the *left* and the nose of the airplane to the *right*. Rotation about the longitudinal axis is referred to as **roll,** as when the control wheel is turned left or right (banking); it is controlled by the *ailerons*. For example, when you turn the control wheel to the left, the left aileron goes *up* and the right aileron goes *down;* this produces lift on the right wing (it goes up) and the plane banks to the left. Go through this several times in your head until you can *see* it happening.

7. Two more control surfaces are *flaps* and *trim tabs*. When flaps are lowered they increase the camber of the wing, thus leading to more lift and more drag. Trim tabs are fine-tuning control surfaces located on the elevators that influence the lateral axis of the plane (pitch). By adjusting the trim tab control, the pilot reduces control wheel (yoke) pressure.

8. A **stall** in an airplane is not engine failure, as it is sometimes referred to in an automobile. Rather, it refers to the movement of air over the control surfaces, particularly the wings, that leads to a loss of lift. As the *angle of attack* (the angle of the airfoil relative to the airflow) increases, induced drag increases, and power must be increased to fly slower (called **slow flight**). The wing of the plane "stalls" when air moving over the top of the wing cannot keep up with air traveling under the wing. This destroys lift, and the result is that the plane begins to descend. An **accelerated stall** can occur at any airspeed provided the pilot commands a sufficient angle of attack to induce it.

9. For each plane you fly, you need to know the maximum permissible load factor, because the greater the angle of bank, the more the wings have to support and the higher the stalling speed. The greatest effect on load factor comes from the elevator,

as forces in the pitch plane are aligned with gravitational forces. Turns can also increase the load factor somewhat.

10. Recovering from a stall necessitates reducing the angle of attack. When approaching a stall, you may be able to do this by lowering the nose. In a full stall you have to use a *positive* stall recovery technique consisting of forward movement of the control column *and* application of full power, while leveling the wings if in a bank.

11. Understanding slow flight and the region of a stall are important during landing because as you slow and turn the plane, you may encounter conditions conducive to a stall or spin (a spin occurs when yaw is induced in a stalled airplane).

12. Ice can significantly affect an airplane's performance by altering its flying characteristics and increasing its weight. You should always avoid known icing conditions.

KEY TERMS AND CONCEPTS, PART 1

Match each term or concept (1–18) with the appropriate description (a–r) below. Each item has only one match.

— 1. 6   — 2. angle of attack
— 3. flaps   — 4. gravity
— 5. airfoil   — 6. lift
— 7. pitch   — 8. roll
— 9. right   —10. trim tabs
—11. up   —12. left
—13. down   —14. Bernoulli's principle
—15. Newton's Third Law of Motion   —16. load factor
—17. yaw   —18. thrust

a.   force of attraction between the earth and the airplane
b.   rotation about the airplane's longitudinal axis
c.   direction the left aileron moves when the control wheel is turned left
d.   force that opposes gravity
e.   direction the elevator moves when the control column is pushed in
f.   principle that explains the area of reduced pressure created above the surface of an airplane wing
g.   rotation about the airplane's vertical axis
h.   weight (in pounds) of a gallon of aviation fuel
i.   direction the airplane rolls when the right aileron goes up and the left aileron goes down
j.   shape designed to obtain lift from the air it passes through
k.   direction the rudder moves when making a left turn
l.   force created by a power plant that gives the airplane forward motion
m.   lowering these produces a steeper glide angle or path
n.   centrifugal force produced by a curved flight path increases this

o.   principle that explains the force obtained when relative wind strikes the lower surface of an airfoil
p.   rotation about the airplane's lateral axis
q.   part of the airplane used to make major adjustments in control wheel pressure
r.   angle between the airfoil's chord and the direction of the relative wind

KEY TERMS AND CONCEPTS, PART 2

Match each term or concept (1–19) with the appropriate description (a–s) below. Each item has only one match.

— 1. parasitic drag   — 2. critical angle of attack
— 3. tricycle   — 4. spin
— 5. induced drag   — 6. static flight conditions
— 7. relative wind   — 8. biplane
— 9. positive stall recovery   —10. ground effect
—11. glider   —12. rotorcraft
—13. stall   —14. camber
—15. adverse yaw   —16. tailwheel (used to be conventional)
—17. empennage
—19. dihedral   —18. accelerated stall

a.   movement of air with reference to an airfoil
b.   this speed decreases as the angle of bank decreases
c.   type of landing gear with a nose wheel and two main gears on the wing or fuselage
d.   angle at which the wing root leaves the fuselage
e.   cushion created by downwash from the wing
f.   force that pushes the nose of the plane away from the direction of a turn
g.   helicopters and gyroplanes are examples
h.   flight in which the airplane's speed and attitude are held constant
i.   simultaneously applying forward pressure to the control wheel and adding full engine power
j.   tail assembly of an airplane
k.   force that slows the forward movement of an airplane through the air due to frontal area and undercarriage resistance
l.   stall that can occur at any speed if the angle of attack is great enough
m.   airplane with two wings
n.   type of landing gear with a tail wheel and two main gears on the wing or fuselage
o.   curvature of an airfoil
p.   occurs when yaw is induced in a stalled airplane
q.   aircraft without an engine; used primarily for soaring
r.   retardant force produced when lift is being produced
s.   a stall occurs when this is exceeded

DISCUSSION QUESTIONS AND EXERCISES

1.   Name the various categories of aircraft and give an example of each.

2.   Figure 2.1 shows a general aviation training airplane. Label each part.

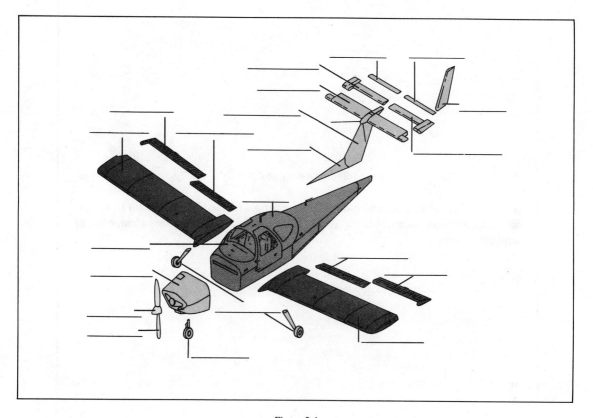

Figure 2.1

3.   What is the difference between the lift produced by the differential pressure of the air moving over the wing and the lift described by Newton's Third Law of Motion? Which accounts for the greater proportion of the airplane's total lift? Explain how both forces work when you turn the control wheel of the airplane to the *right*.

4.   Define each of the following terms: *thrust, lift, drag,* and *gravity.* State which forces oppose each other and explain what happens to each when an airplane lands.

5.   T F Drag opposes lift and thrust opposes gravity.

6.   Define *pitch, yaw,* and *roll.* Give an example of each, being certain to explain how each relevant control surface moves and to describe the resultant change in the airplane's attitude.

7.   T F When you push the left rudder pedal, the rudder moves to the right and the airplane moves to the left.

8.   T F When you push the control column forward, the elevator moves down and the tail of the airplane goes up.

9.   T F When you turn the control column to the right, the right rudder moves up and the left rudder moves down, resulting in rolling the airplane to the right.

10.   How does lowering flaps affect each of the following: takeoff distance, glide path, landing distance, and lift?

11.   What are trim tabs? For what are they used?

12.   Define and explain the relationship among the following terms: *relative wind, flight path, angle of attack,* and *stall.*

13.   T F The relative wind is in the same direction as the flight path of the airplane.

14.   T F *Lift* is the term used to express the relationship between the airfoil's chord and its encounter with the relative wind.

15.   The point along the upper surface at which smooth airflow breaks away is called the _____ point.
      a. dew
      b. pin
      c. separation
      d. stalling

16.   Define *load factor* and explain how it is related to the stalling speed of the airplane.

17.   T F The greater the angle of bank is, the lower the stalling speed will be.

18.   T F Ground effect often causes an airplane to settle to the surface immediately after becoming airborne.

19.   To answer questions a–d, refer to the chart in Figure 2.2.

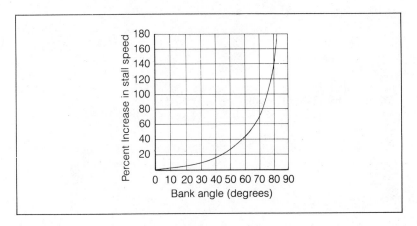

Figure 2.2

a. If your airplane normally (0 degrees of bank) stalls at 40 knots, at what speed will it stall in a 70-degree bank?

b. If your airplane normally (0 degrees of bank) stalls at 50 knots, but you encounter a stall at 60 knots, what is your angle of bank?

c. If your airplane is traveling at 100 knots and stalls when your angle of bank reaches 80 degrees, at what speed would it stall in level flight (0 degrees of bank)?

d. If your airplane normally (0 degrees of bank) stalls at 40 knots but you encounter a stall at 30 knots, what is your angle of bank?

20. Suppose that your plane weighs 2540 pounds, its maximum takeoff weight. How many pounds are the wings supporting if you roll it into a 60-degree bank? At what speed will the airplane stall if it normally (0 degrees of bank) stalls at 35 knots? At what speed will it stall in a 60-degree bank if it weighs only 2000 pounds at takeoff?

21. What is slow flight?

22. What is an accelerated stall?

23. Name and explain the two procedures involved in the FAA positive stall recovery technique.

24. T F An airplane will enter a spin when the elevators lose their effectiveness due to a decrease in the velocity of the relative wind.

REVIEW QUESTIONS

1.   Which of the following statements is accurate?
      a. Air pressure increases as the velocity of the air over the surface of an airfoil increases.
      b. Relative wind increases as the angle of attack decreases.
      c. Rotation of an airplane about its lateral axis is called yawing.
      d. The greater the angle of bank is, the higher the stalling speed will be.

2.   The term *angle of attack* is defined as the
      a. angle between the airplane's climb angle and the horizon
      b. angle between the longitudinal axis of the airplane and the chord line of the wing
      c. angle between the wing chord line and the relative wind
      d. specific angle at which the ratio between lift and drag is the highest

3.   The use of flaps during a landing
      a. decreases the relative wind
      b. increases the airplane's stability
      c. permits an increased approach angle
      d. permits a longer landing distance

To answer questions 4–6, refer to the chart in Figure 2.3.

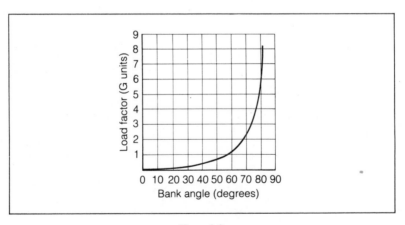

Figure 2.3

4.   If an airplane has a maximum load factor of 4.4 Gs, what is the maximum bank you could make without exceeding this load limit?
      a. roughly 42 decrees
      b. roughly 73 degrees
      c. roughly 77 degrees
      d. impossible to determine from this chart

5.   If your airplane weighs 1640 pounds (maximum takeoff weight), what weight would the wings be supporting during a 60-degree turn?
    a. 820 pounds
    b. 1640 pounds
    c. 2460 pounds
    d. 3280 pounds

6.   If your plane weighs 2800 pounds and has a maximum load factor of 3.7 G units, at what speed will the airplane stall in a 60-degree bank?
    a. 37 knots
    b. 68 knots
    c. 74 knots
    d. impossible to determine from this chart

7.   A hot air balloon is classified as a/an
    a. airplane
    b. glider
    c. lighter-than-air aircraft
    d. rotorcraft

8.   Ice on the wings will have what effect on an airplane's ability to take off?
    a. A shorter takeoff distance may be achieved due to the cold air.
    b. It may prevent the airplane from becoming airborne.
    c. None, as long as the pilot's vision is not obscured.
    d. The engine may overheat due to the increased load.

9.   At what height above the ground is an airplane typically affected by ground effect?
    a. between 0 and 10 feet, assuming calm wind conditions
    b. between 100 and 200 feet, assuming calm wind conditions
    c. less than half of the airplane's wingspan above the surface
    d. twice the length of the airplane's wingspan above the surface

10.   If your airplane is 120 pounds over maximum certified gross weight (3200 pounds) and you decide to drain fuel rather than leave your husband behind, how many gallons of fuel would you have to drain?
    a. 0 gallons (All airplanes are capable of carrying 10 percent above their gross weight on takeoff, provided that before landing they burn any excess over gross.)
    b. 0 gallons (It would be far safer to repack the airplane and leave 120 pounds behind, since fuel is more evenly distributed over the airplane than items in the fuselage.)
    c. 12 gallons
    d. 20 gallons
    e. 32 gallons

11.   An airplane can be stalled
      a. at any airspeed and in any flight attitude
      b. only when the airspeed falls below the published stalling speed
      c. only when the angle of attack exceeds 14 degrees or the angle of bank exceeds
         75 degrees
      d. only when the angle of attack exceeds 14 degrees and the airspeed falls below
         the published stalling speed

12.   To enter a spin, the first thing that must happen is
      a. a nose-high attitude greater than that required to produce separation of air
         flowing over the wings
      b. a partial stall with one wing high and the throttle closed
      c. a stall
      d. an accelerated stall with full power and at least 75 degrees of bank

13.   The back edge of the wing is called the _____ edge.
      a. elevated
      b. horizontal
      c. leading
      d. trailing

14.   During flight, conditions are referred to as _____ if changes are occurring in
speed or attitude.
      a. dynamic
      b. induced
      c. stable
      d. static

15.   When lift is created or when the angle of attack increases, this leads to an
increase in
      a. induced drag
      b. induced lift
      c. induced thrust
      d. parasitic drag

16.   What airplane control surface(s) is (are) responsible for movement about the
longitudinal axis of rotation?
      a. aileron
      b. elevator
      c. flap
      d. rudder

17.   What direction does the right aileron move when the control wheel is turned
right?
      a. down
      b. left

c. right
d. up

18. Movement about the airplane's vertical axis is called
   a. camber
   b. pitch
   c. roll
   d. yaw

19. When flaps are lowered, they _____ drag and _____ lift.
   a. decrease; decrease
   b. decrease; increase
   c. increase; decrease
   d. increase; increase

20. Trim tabs influence movement about the airplane's _____ axis.
   a. elevated
   b. lateral
   c. longitudinal
   d. vertical

21. As the angle of attack increases, induced drag _____ and power must be _____ to continue to fly, even at a slower airspeed.
   a. decreases; decreased
   b. decreases; increased
   c. increases; decreased
   d. increases; increased

22. When an airplane stalls
   a. it descends
   b. it first descends, then ascends
   c. it first ascends, then descends rapidly
   d. it first ascends, then descends slowly

23. The greater the angle of bank, the _____ the wings have to support and the _____ the stalling speed.
   a. less; higher
   b. less; lower
   c. more; higher
   d. more; lower

24. Recovering from a stall necessitates
   a. increasing drag
   b. increasing lift
   c. reducing the angle of attack
   d. all of the above

ANSWERS

Key Terms and Concepts, Part 1

1.	h	2.	r	3.	m	4.	a
5.	j	6.	d	7.	p	8.	b
9.	i	10.	q	11.	c	12.	k
13.	e	14.	f	15.	0	16.	n
17.	g	18.	l				

Key Terms and Concepts, Part 2

1.	k	2.	s	3.	c	4.	p
5.	r	6.	h	7.	a	8.	m
9.	i	10.	e	11.	q	12.	g
13.	b	14.	o	15.	f	16.	n
17.	j	18.	l	19.	d		

Discussion Questions and Exercises (objective questions only)

5.   F; drag opposes thrust and gravity opposes lift.

7.   F; the rudder moves to the left.

8.   T; the nose also goes down.

9.   F; if you substitute *aileron* for *rudder,* the answer is true.

13.   F; it is opposite to the flight path.

14.   F; this defines the angle of attack.

15.   c. Air begins to "burble" at this point, about a 14-degree angle of attack.

17.   F; stalling speed increases as the angle of bank increases.

18.   F; ground effect often causes an airplane to become airborne before sufficient airspeed is obtained to maintain flight above the ground effect level.

19.a.   66 knots; 40 knots $\times$ .65 = 26 knots additional; 40 + 26 = 66. Or 40 knots $\times$ 1.65 = 66 knots.

    b.   About 47 degrees. To calculate this one you need to compute the percentage increase in speed above normal (0 degrees of bank) stalling speed. Since you are traveling 10 knots faster, you divide 10 by 50 to obtain the proportion increase, .20. Multiply by 100 to get the percentage, 20 percent, and refer to the chart to obtain 47 degrees of bank.

    c.   41.67 knots. This one is a bit more difficult: 80 degrees is equal to a 140-degree increase; 100 knots = 240 percent (x); x = 100/2.4; x = 41.67.

    d.   Agh! This one is impossible since angle of bank increases stall speed. You might have speculated that the flaps were lowered, which does decrease the stalling speed, but we will cover that in a later chapter.

20.   5080 pounds. A 60-degree bank increases the load factor by 2 (you should remember that). Referring to the previous chart, a 60-degree bank produces a 40 percent increase in stalling speed, so the airplane will stall at 49 knots.

24.   F; a spin occurs when yaw is induced in a stalled airplane.

Review Questions

1.   d; a is incorrect because increased velocity produces reduced pressure; b is incorrect because relative wind is independent of the angle of attack; c is incorrect because rotation about the lateral axis is called pitching.
2.   c; this is the only acceptable definition.
3.   c; flaps have little effect on stability, no effect on the relative wind, and they permit a shorter landing distance, in addition to the correct alternative, permitting an increased approach angle.
4.   c; use the chart to read across from 4.4 and down to 77 degrees.
5.   d; since a 60-degree angle produces twice the load factor, multiply the weight by 2.
6.   d; this graph does not refer to stalling speed; rather, it refers to the maximum bank the wings will support. You would need to know at what speed your plane stalls and a graph relating percent increase in stalling speed to angle of bank to answer this question.
7.   c; as are blimps.
8.   b; ice or frost destroys the laminar flow of air over the airfoil and may prevent the wings from developing sufficient lift for takeoff.
9.   c; ground effect operates up to about one wingspan above the surface by reducing induced drag. This may cause the airplane to "float" a short distance before touching down.
10.   d; since aviation fuel weighs 6 pounds per gallon, you should drain 20 gallons.
11.   a; remember our discussion of accelerated stalls! Stalls can occur in any attitude and at any airspeed. This is particularly critical to remember when making an approach to a landing when airspeed is typically slow and turns may become unknowingly steep (especially in crosswind conditions).
12.   c; the airplane must first stall, then yaw must be induced.
13.   d; this defines the trailing edge.
14.   a; dynamic as opposed to static (when no changes in speed or attitude are occurring).
15.   a; an increased angle of attack produces induced drag due to the greater air resistance of the surface.
16.   a; ailerons control bank or the amount of roll.
17.   d; the right wing goes down when the airplane rolls right; the aileron goes up to help produce this movement, while the left aileron goes down.
18.   d; this defines yaw, which is controlled by the rudder.
19.   d; both drag and lift increase due to increased camber in the wing.
20.   b; trim tabs are located on the elevator and are fine-tuning control surfaces that influence the airplane's pitch (movement about the lateral axis, although in larger planes trim tabs may be found on either rudder, ailerons, or both in addition to the elevator).
21.   d; induced drag increases, and to maintain slow flight with an increased angle of attack, more thrust (power) must be added.
22.   a; a stall destroys lift and the plane begins to lose altitude.

23.   c; the wings have to support more as the bank increases; this increases stalling speed.

24.   c; the main thing is to decrease the angle of attack, which in turn will reduce drag and restore lift.

3/FLIGHT INSTRUMENTS

MAIN POINTS

1. Basic flight instruments can be classified by what they do and by how they work.

2. The *pitot-static instruments* measure the differential pressure between moving (pitot) air and still (static) air. The **pitot tube** captures air that impacts the airplane head-on and transmits that pressure to the **airspeed indicator.** The **static ports,** mounted at 90-degree angles from the direction of flight, receive air at outside atmospheric pressure. Static pressure is used as a reference for determining airplane speed. It is also routed to the **altimeter** and the **vertical speed indicator.**

3. The difference between pitot pressure and static pressure measures **dynamic pressure** and is represented as **indicated airspeed** (speed through the air, not over the ground). **Calibrated airspeed** is indicated airspeed corrected for minor errors in the instrument itself.

4. The altimeter measures the height of the airplane above some constant reference point (for example, sea level). It does *not* measure the height above the ground, but by knowing the height of the terrain and obstacles upon it, you can calculate the distance between you and the terrain. Central to the operation of the altimeter is a barometer, which measures changes in atmospheric pressure. As altitude increases, pressure decreases. Pressure also changes as the weather changes.

5. There are several different types of altitude: **pressure**—indicated by the altimeter when the altimeter is set to standard pressure; **indicated**—altitude indicated on the altimeter when it is set to local barometric pressure; **true**—an object's actual height above mean sea level (MSL); **absolute**—an airplane's altitude above ground level

(AGL). The altimeter translates changes in pressure to changes in altitude: The conversion is 1 inch of mercury for each 1000 feet in elevation. Translation is not always perfect, however, due to inherent limitations. Finally, remember that as atmospheric conditions change, so does the barometric reading, which in turn affects altitude readings. The saying "From high to low, look out below" refers to the condition in which you fly from a high-pressure area to a low-pressure area. Unless you adjust your altimeter, it will indicate that you are higher than you in fact are, a condition that can have disastrous consequences when you get closer to an obstruction or the ground.

6. Closely allied to the altimeter is the *vertical speed indicator* (*VSI*), which measures the rate of descent or climb, typically in feet per minute. Due to their construction, most VSIs lag behind the airplane's pitch changes and should not be relied upon during rapid pitch changes.

7. Gyroscopic flight instruments include the **attitude indicator, turn coordinator,** and **heading indicator.** A gyroscope operates according to two principles: rigidity in space and precession.

8. The *attitude indicator,* or *artificial horizon,* is a graphic display of airplane, sky, and ground. It represents the airplane with reference to the horizon and indicates changes exactly when they occur, as when the airplane banks or pitches up or down. Most are powered by suction or vacuum rotors. The *turn coordinator* indicates the rate of turn and provides information about yaw (inclinometer). The ball in the inclinometer indicates whether the airplane is slipping or skidding in a turn. Corrections can be effected by "stepping on the ball" with the appropriate rudder pedal. The *heading indicator,* or *directional gyro,* displays the airplane's heading. It must be set by reference to an established heading such as a runway centerline or magnetic compass (in straight and level flight).

9. Airplane gyro instruments are typically powered by either electrical power or suction power. Instruments with similar functions (for example, the turn coordinator and the attitude indicator) are usually powered independently so that if one system fails, the pilot still has a backup source of information (referred to as the concept of redundancy).

10. Two important self-contained instruments are the **magnetic compass** and **outside air temperature gauge.** The magnetic compass indicates direction relative to magnetic north. Its primary practical value is as a reference source for the heading indicator. There are several limitations to its use. First, it points to magnetic north rather than true north (referred to as variation). Second, it can be affected by other instruments (deviation). Third, the compass will dip when the airplane accelerates or decelerates—ANDS (Accelerate—*N*orth; *D*ecelerate—*S*outh). Fourth, there are northerly-southerly turning errors (also a function of magnetic dip); when flying north, the compass will initially indicate a turn in the opposite direction; when flying south, it

will register a turn in the right direction but at an accelerated rate. Finally, in turbulent air, the magnetic compass may be subject to oscillation error.

11. Most instrument panels have a T *arrangement* with the attitude indicator in the middle, flanked on either side by the airspeed indicator and altimeter. The heading indicator completes the leg of the T. It is typically flanked by two less important instruments, the turn coordinator on one side and the vertical speed indicator on the other. The process of checking and rechecking instruments is called **cross check.** It is important to safe flight but is not a substitute for constantly referring to what is going on outside the airplane. Checking back and forth between the outside world and flight instruments is called **composite flying**.

KEY TERMS AND CONCEPTS, PART 1
Match each term or concept (1–17) with the appropriate description (a–q) below. Each item has only one match.

___ 1. 3 degrees per second   ___ 2. static ports
___ 3. magnetic compass   ___ 4. indicated altitude
___ 5. altimeter   ___ 6. precession
___ 7. oscillation errors   ___ 8. cross check
___ 9. variation   ___10. ram air
___11. composite flying   ___12. absolute altitude
___13. 1000   ___14. electrical system
___15. gyroscope   ___16. vertical speed indicator
___17. pitot-static system

a.   receptacles where air at outside atmospheric pressure enters
b.   altitude of an airplane above ground level (AGL)
c.   movement of a gyro's spin axis due to some external force
d.   errors in magnetic compass readings during turbulent flight
e.   altitude read on the altimeter when it is set to local barometric pressure
f.   air that impacts the airplane head-on
g.   power system that relies on alternating current
·h.   instrument that measures the altitude above a given reference point (for example, sea level)
i.   instrument that measures rate of climb and descent
j.   standard turn rate
k.   process of checking and rechecking flight instruments
l.   system that measures and displays information about differential air pressure
m.   1 inch of mercury equals a change in altitude of _____ feet
n.   angle between magnetic north and true north
o.   a mass spinning about an axis
p.   cross-referencing the world outside the cockpit with the flight instruments
q.   instrument that measures the airplane's heading with respect to magnetic north

KEY TERMS AND CONCEPTS, PART 2

Match each term or concept (1–18) with the appropriate description (a–r) below. Each item has only one match.

— 1. acceleration-deceleration errors   — 2. heading indicator
— 3. barometer   — 4. airspeed indicator
— 5. turn coordinator   — 6. indicated airspeed
— 7. gimbals   — 8. calibrated airspeed
— 9. redundancy   —10. attitude indicator
—11. inclinometer   —12. pressure altitude
—13. true altitude   —14. pitot tube
—15. 75   —16. integrated flight
—17. vacuum system   —18. northerly turning error

a. the difference between ram air pressure and static pressure yields this reading
b. altitude read from the altimeter when it is set at standard conditions
c. another name for an artificial horizon
d. instrument that gyroscopically displays the airplane's heading
e. the magnetic compass indicates a turn in the *opposite* direction
f. airspeed corrected for minor installation and mechanical errors
g. concept that no *single* instrument tells it all
h. instrument at the heart of most altimeters
i. number of feet of tolerance suggested by the FAA in altitude difference between the altimeter and field elevation
j. device that tells how fast you are moving through the air
k. object's actual height above mean sea level (MSL)
l. power system that converts engine's rotary motion to air pressure
m. interconnected frames used to suspend a rotating mass
n. device that captures ram air
o. concept that two independent systems perform the same function
p. instrument that provides the pilot with yaw information
q. ball in the turn coordinator that indicates skips or skids
r. errors that occur in the magnetic compass during changes in airspeed

DISCUSSION QUESTIONS AND EXCERCISES

1. What flight instruments require pitot air pressure to operate? Which ones require static pressure?

2.   T F Airspeed changes as a function of wind velocity but not as a function of wind direction.

3.   What happens to air pressure as measured by the static ports as altitude increases? Why?

4.   What is the difference between pitot pressure and static pressure? How is this related to calibrated airspeed?

5.   Name and define the four types of altitude necessary for the safe operation of an airplane.

6.   Suppose that you depart Denver (elevation 5280 feet MSL) and fly to Vinland, Kansas (elevation 880 feet MSL). Suppose further that the altimeter shows a barometric reading of 29.96 when you depart Denver and 29.96 when you land at Vinland. How many feet have you gained or lost in indicated altitude during your trip due to changes in atmospheric conditions?

7.   Suppose that in question 6 Vinland had a barometric reading of 28.74 when you landed. Had you not changed your altimeter to reflect this change, something that is *required* by the FAA, what would your altimeter have read when you landed at Vinland?

8.   Suppose that in question 6 the temperature in Denver was 95 degrees Fahrenheit when you left and 67 degrees when you landed at Vinland. Would your altimeter have registered higher or lower when you landed?

9.   What does the vertical speed indicator measure? What is its major limitation?

10.   What are the two fundamental properties of a gyroscope?

11.   Name the three major gyroscopic instruments and their functions.

12.   State two reasons why most general aviation airplanes have both a vacuum power system and an AC electrical system.

13.   What are two major functions of the magnetic compass?

14.   Name five operating limitations of the magnetic compass and explain what the pilot can do to overcome each of them.

15.   What is the concept of the cross check? How is it related to the basic **T** formation of airplane instrumentation? Be sure to state what instruments are included in the basic **T** and why they are aligned the way they are. Drawing a picture might help you visualize the answer.

16.   What is the concept of composite flying?

REVIEW QUESTIONS

1. Which of the following is *not* related to the pitot-static system?
   a. calibrated airspeed
   b. static ports
   c. turn coordinator
   d. VSI

2. The pitot system provides impact (ram air) pressure for only the
   a. airspeed indicator
   b. airspeed indicator, altimeter, and vertical speed indicator
   c. altimeter and vertical speed indicator
   d. vertical speed indicator

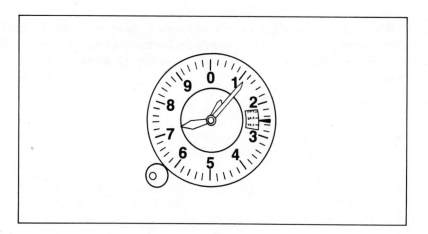

Figure 3.1

3. Refer to the altimeter in Figure 3.1. What is the indicated altitude?
   a. 710 feet
   b. 1720 feet
   c. 7120 feet
   d. 17,120 feet

4. Refer to the altimeter in Figure 3.2. What is the indicated altitude?
   a. 190 feet
   b. 880 feet
   c. 1900 feet
   d. 10,820 feet

Figure 3.2

5. When flying from air that is warm to air that is cold, the airplane will be _____ the altitude indicated on the altimeter.
   a. higher than
   b. lower than
   c. equal to
   d. impossible to predict since air pressure does not change consistently with changes in temperature

6. A magnetic compass will initially indicate a turn toward the *west* if
   a. a left turn is entered while flying north
   b. a right turn is entered while flying north
   c. the aircraft decelerates while on a southerly heading
   d. the aircraft accelerates while on a northerly heading

7. When are indications of a magnetic compass accurate?
   a. as long as airspeed is held constant
   b. during all conditions of flight, as long as the cycle of bank does not exceed 21 degrees
   c. in all conditions of flight
   d. only in straight and level, unaccelerated flight

8. Suppose the pitot tube and static ports became clogged. What instrument or instruments would be affected?

   1 altimeter
   2 airspeed indicator
   3 vertical speed indicator

a. 1, 2
b. 1, 3
c. 2, 3
d. 1, 2, 3

9.   What type of altitude is indicated when the altimeter is set to 29.92 inches of mercury?
    a. density-altitude
    b. indicated altitude
    c. pressure altitude
    d. true altitude

10.   When making a turn away from a northerly heading, your magnetic compass will normally
    a. be inversely proportional to the magnetic variation of the area over which you are flying
    b. indicate correctly, provided the turn is properly coordinated
    c. precede the turn and indicate a greater amount of turn than has actually been made
    d. lag or indicate a turn in the opposite direction

11.   Atmospheric pressure _____ as altitude _____.
    a. decreases; decreases
    b. increases; decreases
    c. remains constant; increases
    d. increases; increases

12.   Static ports are always aligned _____ the line of flight.
    a. at a 45-degree angle away from
    b. directly away from
    c. directly into
    d. perpendicular to

13.   Pitot pressure (from the pitot head or tube) less static pressure (from the static ports), when corrected for minor installation and mechanical errors, yields a measure of the airplane's forward speed called
    a. calibrated airspeed
    b. dynamic airspeed
    c. indicated airspeed
    d. true airspeed

14.   What instrument or device is at the heart of the heading indicator?
    a. gyroscope
    b. inclinometer

c. magnet
d. venturi

15.   Suppose that you are flying over Chagrin Falls, Ohio (field elevation 1850 feet), and that you have just set your altimeter to 29.04 based on radio contact with nearby Cleveland Flight Service Station. Your altimeter reads 4500 feet. This would be defined as

a. absolute altitude
b. indicated altitude
c. pressure altitude
d. true altitude

16.   Suppose that you are flying over Chagrin Falls, Ohio (field elevation 1850 feet), and that you have just set your altimeter to 29.04 based on radio contact with nearby Cleveland Flight Service Station. Your altimeter reads 4500 feet. Next, suppose that you had a second altimeter and set it to standard conditions. What would the second altimeter show?

a. 3620 feet
b. 4500 feet
c. 5380 feet
d. impossible to determine since we do not know the true altitude of Chagrin Falls

17.   Suppose that you are flying over Chagrin Falls, Ohio (field elevation 1850 feet), and that you have just set your altimeter to 29.04 based on radio contact with nearby Cleveland Flight Service Station. Your altimeter reads 4500 feet. Upon landing at Chagrin Falls, you notice that your altimeter reads 1975 feet. You check with Cleveland Flight Service again and find that the current altimeter is still 29.04. What should you do?

a. Change your altimeter to 1850 feet since that is the true altitude and does not change with changes in atmospheric conditions.
b. Have your altimeter checked since the discrepancy is outside the tolerance limits suggested by the FAA.
c. Ignore the discrepancy since it is well within tolerance limits set by the FAA.
d. Leave your altimeter at 1975 feet and report the discrepancy to the nearest Flight Service Station so they can issue a *Notice to Airmen*.

18.   Which of the following conditions, if any, will lead to an indicated altitude greater than the airplane's true altitude?

a. flying from an area of high ground elevation to an area of low ground elevation
b. decreasing air temperature
c. both a and b
d. neither a nor b

19.   Suppose that you depart from Superior, Wisconsin (barometer 29.34), and fly direct to Minot, North Dakota (field elevation 1800 feet). As you approach Minot at an indicated altitude of 6500 feet you receive a new altimeter setting of 29.62. When you change your altimeter to the new setting, approximately what indicated altitude will your altimeter read?
        a. 4420 feet
        b. 4700 feet
        c. 4980 feet
        d. 6220 feet
        e. 6500 feet
        f. 6780 feet

20.   Vertical speed indicators found in most general aviation airplanes tend to
        a. accelerate during an altitude change
        b. accelerate during climbs and lag behind during descents
        c. lag behind an altitude change
        d. lag behind during climbs and accelerate during descents

21.   The movement of a gyroscope's spin axis from its original position due to some external force is called
        a. gimballing
        b. inclination
        c. precession
        d. rigidity in space

22.   Which of the following instruments is used to indicate changes in an airplane's pitch?

        1 attitude indicator
        2 turn coordinator
        3 heading indicator
        4 magnetic compass

        a. 1
        b. 1, 2
        c. 3, 4
        d. 2, 3, 4

23.   The difference between magnetic north and true north is called
        a. acceleration-deceleration error
        b. deviation
        c. oscillation error
        d. variation

24.   Which of the following instruments constitute the basic T arrangement?

    1 attitude indicator
    2 vertical speed indicator
    3 altimeter
    4 heading indicator
    5 magnetic compass
    6 airspeed indicator
    7 turn coordinator

a. 1, 3, 4, 6
b. 1, 4, 6, 7
c. 1, 2, 3, 4, 6
d. 3, 4, 6, 7
e. 1, 2, 3, 4, 5, 6, 7

25. The process of checking and rechecking flight instruments is called
a. composite flying
b. cross check
c. oscillation
d. redundancy

ANSWERS

Key Terms and Concepts, Part 1
1. j   2. a   3. q   4. e
5. h   6. c   7. d   8. k
9. n   10. f   11. p   12. b
13. m   14. g   15. o   16. i
17. l

Key Terms and Concepts, Part 2
1. r   2. d   3. h   4. j
5. p   6. a   7. m   8. f
9. o   10. c   11. q   12. b
13. k   14. n   15. i   16. g
17. l   18. e

Discussion Questions and Exercises
2. F; airspeed is independent of the wind.
6. None; since the barometric conditions are the same in both places, there would be no change in altitude.
7. 2100. Since you are flying from high pressure to low pressure without changing the altimeter setting, actual MSL altitude would be much lower than the altimeter reading. $29.96 - 28.74 = 1.22$ inches of mercury. Since 1 inch = 1000 feet, the altimeter would be off by 1220 feet, and it would have registered 2100 feet

when you landed! Further, had you used your altimeter to enter the pattern (1880 feet MSL), you would have come in contact with the ground *before* you ever reached the pattern.

8. Higher; moving from high to low temperature results in your being lower than your altimeter indicates.

Review Questions

1. c; this is a gyroscopic instrument.
2. a; only the airspeed indicator uses both static and pitot inputs.
3. c; the large hand indicates 100s of feet, the smaller hand 1000s of feet, and the smallest hand 10,000s of feet.
4. b; see the answer to question 3.
5. b; the altimeter reads erroneously high when you fly from warm to cold air or from high to low pressure.
6. b; remember ANDS (*A*ccelerate—*N*orth; *D*ecelerate—*S*outh). In this case, while flying north, you turn right (east) and the compass indicates a turn toward the west.
7. d; changes in acceleration and deceleration and turns may cause distorted readings in the magnetic compass.
8. d; all of these instruments rely on the pitot-static system; only the airspeed indicator, however, uses information from the pitot tube (ram air).
9. c; this is the definition of pressure altitude.
10. d; remember ANDS (see the answer to question 6). In this case, while flying north, a turn *from* north will indicate a turn in the opposite direction.
11. b; the lower you go, the greater is the pressure exerted from the air above.
12. d; they are aligned 90 degrees from the line of flight to allow them to measure "side" pressure.
13. a; pitot pressure less static pressure yields dynamic pressure, which is converted to indicated airspeed. Indicated airspeed, when corrected for minor discrepancies in the system, becomes calibrated airspeed.
14. a; this is one of the gyroscopic instruments. Others are the altitude indicator (artificial horizon) and the turn coordinator (formerly called the turn and slip coordinator).
15. b; this is indicated altitude. If you landed at Cleveland, your altimeter would read the airport's approximate survey height above mean sea level.
16. c; it would indicate higher than you are by about 880 feet (29.92 − 29.04 = .88 inches of mercury). Since 1 inch of mercury equals 1000 feet, .88 inches equals 880 feet.
17. b; the tolerance suggested by the FAA is plus or minus 75 feet between the surveyed altitude and the height indicated on your altimeter when corrected for current ground level atmospheric conditions. Your altimeter is off by 125 feet, which is outside the suggested tolerance limits.
18. b; ground elevation has nothing to do with indicated altitude. However, as air temperature decreases, all things remaining equal, indicated altitude increases.

19.   f; your altimeter would indicate that you are lower than you actually are by $(29.62 - 29.34 = .28) \times 100 = 280$ feet. So while the altimeter indicates 6500 feet, your airplane is actually 6780 feet above sea level.

20.   c; VSIs have a tendency to lag, which means they are most helpful once a flight attitude has been established.

21.   c; this defines precession, one of the two fundamental properties of a gyroscope.

22.   a; pitch, movement about the airplane's lateral axis, is indicated on the attitude indicator, as is the degree of bank (roll).

23.   d; this defines variation, which changes from place to place.

24.   a; these are the four instruments in the basic T, with the altitude indicator at the center. These are the instruments that are used in primary cross check.

25.   b; cross check involves checking and rechecking the instruments in the basic T arrangement.

4/THE POWER PLANT AND ITS SYSTEMS

MAIN POINTS

1. *Reciprocating engines*, the power plant of most general aviation airplanes, produce rotary motion, or **torque**, to do work (measured in horsepower). Fuel and air mixed in the **carburetor** flow into the engine's cylinders through intake valves (the *intake stroke*). Once inside the cylinder the mixture is compressed by the piston (the *compression stroke*) and ignited by an electrical spark that comes from a separate ignition system. The resulting force (the *power stroke*) forces the piston downward, producing torque. As the piston continues to move, this time upward (the *exhaust stroke*), another valve opens (the *exhaust valve*), and exhaust fumes are expelled through the exhaust **manifold**. The four strokes of the piston give the engine its name: the **four-stroke cycle**. Piston movement is translated into torque by a series of **connecting rods** that attach to the **crankshaft**. A crankcase encloses the crankshaft and connecting rods. The **propeller** is at the end of the crankshaft. At the other end of the crankshaft is the **accessory drive pad**, which provides rotary motion for a variety of pumps and other engine systems. Although some aviation engines are liquid cooled, most are air cooled.

2. **Aviation gasoline** must have several properties to prevent **vapor lock**, **detonation**, and **preignition**. **Octane numbers** refer to the ability of avgas to suppress detonation. **Performance numbers** indicate how much beyond a 100-percent octane number a fuel protects against detonation. You can use a higher grade of fuel if you are in a pinch but never a lower grade than that specified by the manufacturer since this may lead to engine malfunctioning (for example, loss of power, detonation, overheating). Automobile gasoline should *never* be used in an airplane engine. During *refueling* be sure that the airplane is properly grounded to avoid a fire and that the fuel vents are clear.

3. There are two general types of fuel systems: *gravity*, common in high-wing aircraft, and *pump*, common in low-wing aircraft. In either system, a **fuel strainer** is located at the lowest point upstream from the carburetor to collect sediment and water. This should be drained before each flight, as should the wing tank drains. Filling the tanks with avgas at the end of the day minimizes water by displacing warm air, from which condensation forms. Fuel passes to the carburetor through a **fuel selector valve** (used to select which tank the fuel comes from).

4. The key to carburetion is the *mixture:* the balance between fuel and air. Mixtures with high air-fuel ratios are called *rich,* and those with low air-fuel ratios are called *lean*. The essential parts of the carburetor are: the *float mechanism,* which controls the amount of fuel in the carburetor; the *fuel strainer,* which filters impurities; the *main metering system,* which controls the amount of fuel in high power settings; the *idling system,* which controls the amount of fuel in low power settings; the *economizer system,* which has some control over the air-fuel ratio; the *accelerating system,* which controls for sudden throttle movements; and the *mixture control system,* which has manual control over the air-fuel ratio. An alternative to carburetor systems is **fuel injection,** which delivers fuel directly to the cylinders. It provides a more uniform flow of fuel and better acceleration and is not subject to carburetor ring.

5. *Ignition* occurs between the compression and power strokes. The ignition system includes a source of high voltage, a timing device, a distribution system among the cylinders, spark plugs, and control switches and shielded wiring. Central to aircraft ignition systems is the **magneto,** which typically runs off the engine accessory pad and produces a high-voltage electrical pulse. Aircraft have *two* magnetos, just as each cylinder has two spark plugs (the concept of redundancy). Further, the entire ignition system is independent of other aircraft systems and can be stopped only by turning off the magneto or stopping engine rotation. The chances of losing power are remote since each magneto has independent spark plugs.

6. The engine lubricating system helps alleviate problems produced by friction (heat and engine inefficiency). The oil system includes a **sump** (attached to the lower side of the engine), a *dipstick,* a *pump,* a *filter,* a *temperature sensing plug* (located at the *outlet* of the oil cooler), and a *pressure sensor*. The latter sensors are routed directly to cockpit indicators. The most important oil used in general aviation today is called **ashless-dispersant oil,** abbreviated AD.

7. The airplane's electrical system operates on both direct current (DC) and alternating current (AC). **Voltage** (a source of electrons) is initially provided by a DC *battery* (to start things off) and then by the AC generator, called an **alternator** (driven by the accessory drive pad).

8. The electrical system has a **master switch** that must be on to activate any of the electrical components. Further, each piece of equipment has an independent **circuit**

breaker, which turns the equipment off in the event of a malfunction. Circuit breakers can be reset in flight (unlike **fuses,** which must be replaced with a fuse of the *same* amperage), but they should not be forced. Finally, there is a **voltage regulator** that controls the variable output of the alternator.

9. *Propellers* convert engine torque to forward thrust. Each propeller blade consists of airfoils, or blade elements, with decreasing angles of attack from hub (where the propeller attaches to the crankshaft) to tip. One effect of the rotating propeller is torque, which tends to revolve the airplane to the left (in the direction opposite to the propeller's rotation). Another effect of the rotating propeller that occurs when the airplane is not in level flight is asymmetric thrust, or P-factor. This effect is exaggerated at higher power settings and high angles of attack. It can be compensated for by adding right rudder pressure during the takeoff roll and when climbing with full throttle and by adding left rudder during descents. There are two types of propellers, **fixed-pitch propellers,** whose blade angles cannot be changed, and **constant-speed propellers,** whose blade angles can be changed by the pilot during flight.

10. Engine controls are generally grouped together on the instrument panel. The *throttle* controls the amount of air-fuel mixture in the carburetor (throttle valve). The **tachometer** displays the number of crankshaft *revolutions per minute* (rpm) of fixed-pitch props. (Like most instruments, green is normal, yellow spells caution, and red indicates maximum.) With constant-speed props, the tach indicates propeller rpms; engine power is registered on the **manifold pressure gauge.** Prop speed should be increased before increasing power; when decreasing power, power must be reduced before reducing propeller speed.

11. Carburetor ice can be a serious problem since as the pressure of the air-fuel mixture decreases and its volume expands, it cools rapidly and may freeze the moisture in the air. The butterfly (throttle) valve area of the carburetor is most susceptible to ice. The easiest way to prevent ice is to use the carburetor heat system, which directs warm air to the carburetor.

12. The *mixture control* limits the amount of fuel to be mixed with air in the venturi. It ranges from full-rich (used during most takeoffs) to lean (when cruising altitude is reached). The **engine primer** is used to direct fuel to the cylinders on cold days. **Fuel quantity gauges** indicate fuel remaining. **Fuel pressure gauges** are common on airplanes with fuel boost pumps.

13. Oil system gauges are present to measure *oil pressure* and *oil temperature*. Pressure should register in the green arc within 30 seconds of starting the engine and should remain there in flight.

14. *Ignition controls* are operated by a single rotary switch labeled Off, R (right magneto), L (left magneto), Both, and Start. Before all flights, the pilot should check

each magneto to make certain it is operating within limits set by the manufacturer. When shutting down the engine, use the mixture control (fuel-lean), not the ignition switch, since the latter leaves fuel deposits in the cylinders.

15. The *ammeter* measures electrical current flowing into the battery when the alternator is operating. The *master switch* must be on for other electrical equipment to operate. This is important in case of fire since it allows you to test each piece of equipment individually. Some aircraft have **cylinder head temperature gauges** for use in adjusting cowl flaps and mixture settings.

KEY TERMS AND CONCEPTS, PART 1

Match each term or concept (1–20) with the appropriate description (a–t) below. Each item has only one match.

— 1. cowl flaps   — 2. oil
— 3. fuel selector valve   — 4. power stroke
— 5. throw   — 6. voltage regulator
— 7. master switch   — 8. exhaust valve
— 9. alternator   —10. throttle valve
—11. magnetos   —12. pitch
—13. amps   —14. carburetor heat system
—15. carburetor   —16. mixture control
—17. manifold pressure gauge   —18. camshaft
—19. horsepower   —20. AC

a.   movable doors that open and close to control air flowing over the engine
b.   part of the carburetor most susceptible to icing
c.   displacement of the crankshaft where connecting rods connect
d.   system that counteracts carburetor icing conditions
e.   device that controls power to all of an airplane's electrical components
f.   unit of measure of an engine's power output
g.   device that allows the pilot to control the air-fuel mixture
h.   valve used to select fuel from one tank or another
i.   device that controls timing of intake and exhaust valves
j.   air-fuel mixture is ignited during this stroke
k.   this measures the flow of electrons
l.   electron current that flows in cycles
m.   an engine-driven alternating current generator
n.   device that displays air-fuel mixture pressure as it enters the cylinder
o.   safety device that controls electrical output of the alternator or generator
p.   terminology describing propeller blade angle
q.   residual gases leave the cylinder through this
r.   device that actually mixes air and fuel together
s.   heart of most aircraft ignition systems
t.   product that lubricates the internal parts of an engine

KEY TERMS AND CONCEPTS, PART 2

Match each term or concept (1–20) with the appropriate description (a–t) below. Each item has only one match.

___ 1. atomization
___ 2. grounding
___ 3. circuit breaker
___ 4. exhaust manifold
___ 5. go-around
___ 6. connecting rods
___ 7. octane number
___ 8. horsepower
___ 9. performance number
___10. accessory drive pad
___11. DC
___12. vapor lock
___13. distributor
___14. counterclockwise
___15. fixed-pitch
___16. primer
___17. ashless-dispersant
___18. fuel boost pump
___19. rpm
___20. intake stroke

a.   capability of suppressing detonation (antiknock value)
b.   cluster of interlocking gears where the crankshaft terminates
c.   device through which residual gases exit from the engine
d.   propellers that cannot change their blade angle
e.   bubbles of gas that block the fuel line
f.   provides fuel pressure for starting some airplane engines
g.   procedure that connects the "return" portion of an electrical circuit to the airframe
h.   rotating device that sends voltage to the appropriate cylinder at the appropriate time
i.   vaporization of fuel into a combustible mixture
j.   speed of the crankshaft's rotation is measured in _____
k.   type of oil used in most general aviation aircraft
l.   connects pistons to the crankshaft
m.   air-fuel mixture is drawn into the cylinder during this stroke
n.   capacity for doing work
o.   electron current that comes in a constant flow
p.   device that controls power to a particular airplane instrument
q.   direction the airplane rotates when power is added as you view it from the rear
r.   aborted landing
s.   device that directs raw fuel directly to the cylinder
t.   rating that indicates how much *beyond* a 100-percent octane number a fuel protects against detonation

KEY TERMS AND CONCEPTS, PART 3

Match each term or concept (1–21) with the appropriate description (a–u) below. Each item has only one match.

___ 1. fuel strainer
___ 2. fuel injection
___ 3. exhaust stroke
___ 4. baffles
___ 5. hub
___ 6. clockwise

___ 7. volts   ___ 8. preignition
___ 9. crankshaft   ___10. cylinder head temperature gauge
___11. ammeter   ___12. float chamber
___13. torque   ___14. connecting rod
___15. constant-speed   ___16. accelerating system
___17. intake valve   ___18. detonation
___19. oil pressure gauge   ___20. tachometer
___21. piston

a.   measures the amount of electrical potential stored in a material
b.   device that measures the alternator's electrical output
c.   propellers whose blade angles can change
d.   system in which fuel goes directly to the combustion chamber
e.   air-fuel mixture enters the cylinder through this
f.   air-fuel mixture is expelled from the cylinder during this stroke
g.   the propeller is attached directly to this part of the engine
h.   gas burns too rapidly in the combustion chamber
i.   you will find one of these at the lowest point upstream of fuel system
j.   fuel enters the carburetor and is deposited here first
k.   device that displays crankshaft revolutions per minute
l.   direction propellers rotate as you view them from the rear
m.   free-swinging device attached to the bottom of a piston
n.   movable plunger that fits inside the cylinder
o.   hot carbon particles cause the spark plugs to fire early
p.   carburetor system that compensates for sudden throttle movement
q.   displays pressure of oil being sent to lubricate the engine
r.   plates installed over an engine designed to direct airflow
s.   rolling force imposed on an airplane by the engine turning the propeller
t.   displays the temperature of the "hottest" cylinder
u.   point at which the propeller attaches to the craftshaft

DISCUSSION QUESTIONS AND EXERCISES

1.   What is meant by a four-stroke engine? What is its ultimate purpose? Briefly describe the four strokes.

2.   How is piston movement translated into propeller movement?

3.   What is the accessory drive pad and what does it do?

4.   Distinguish among vapor lock, detonation, and preignition. What is the difference between performance number and octane number?

5.   Suppose that your airplane takes 100-octane aviation fuel. Should you use 80-octane fuel in a pinch? Why or why not? If 100-octane is not available, should you use automobile gas? Why or why not?

6.   What are the two general types of fuel systems? Why is it important to check the fuel strainer and wing tank drains before each flight?

7.   What are the two main functions of the carburetor? Briefly describe how a fuel injection system is different from a carburetor system.

8.   How does a dual ignition system work and what are its main components? In what two ways can the ignition system be stopped?

9.   Describe the mag check preflight procedures. What are the indications of a malfunctioning magneto?

10.   Briefly describe the components and functions of the engine's lubricating system.

11.   Briefly describe the components and functions of the engine's electrical system. Include a discussion of the master switch, voltage regulator, circuit breakers, and alternator.

12.   What do propellers do? How are they like airplane wings? What is torque and how does it affect the airplane?

13.   Distinguish between fixed-pitch and constant-speed propellers. How does each operate? Name two advantages of each type of propeller.

14.   Briefly describe the functions of the tachometer and the manifold pressure gauge.

15.   What is carburetor icing and where does it normally strike? How does it affect rpm and manifold pressure? What can you do about it?

16.   What does the mixture control do? Explain how you would use it to climb from sea level to 8000 feet MSL and back to sea level again.

17.   Briefly describe the importance and proper use of the oil pressure and oil temperature gauges.

18.   Briefly describe the ignition switch and its proper use for starting and stopping the engine.

19.   What is the ammeter and how should you use it?

20.   T F If the specified grade of fuel is not available, it is best to use automobile gasoline with a slightly higher (but *never* lower) octane rating.

21.   T F Detonation occurs in a reciprocating aircraft engine when the unburned air-fuel mixture in the cylinder explodes rather than burning evenly.

22.   T F It is generally considered good operating practice to check for water in the fuel system only when the aircraft is fueled, since this is the only time the system can collect moisture.

23.   T F Float-type carburetor systems provide more even fuel distribution and faster throttle response than fuel injection systems, but they are less efficient.

24.   T F The carburetor's float mechanism seals the chamber and prevents further fuel from entering.

25.   T F The engine ignition system of most general aviation airplanes is called dual because it is independent of other aircraft systems.

26.   T F Central to the aircraft ignition system is the alternator, which typically runs off the accessory drive pad and which produces a high-voltage electrical pulse for the spark plugs.

27.   T F The most important oil used in general aviation today is called antidetergent.

28.   T F The effect of torque is at a maximum during gliding flight with a reduced throttle setting.

29.   T F With a fixed-pitch propeller airplane, engine power is registered on the tachometer.

30.   T F The red line on a tachometer indicates a maximum rpm reading that may be exceeded only in straight and level flight.

31.   T F Carburetor icing almost always occurs simultaneously at the needle valve and in the float chamber.

32.   T F On a warm, sunny day, if the oil pressure does not reach the green arc within 30 seconds after starting the engine, the engine should be shut down.

33.   T F One result of permitting an airplane engine to idle for a long period of time while on the ground is that the spark plugs may become fouled.

34.   T F If an airplane engine continues to run after the ignition switch is turned to the Off position, the probable cause is a broken magneto ground wire.

35.   T F Applying carburetor heat results in more air going through the throttle valve.

36.   T F In case of an electrical fire, one first turns off the master switch.

37.   T F Engine run-ups for magneto and carburetor heat checks should be kept at a minimum to help avoid excessive vibration caused by air moving over the control surfaces.

38.   T F During long descents one should gradually increase the air-fuel mixture.

39.   T F To compensate for the effect of torque produced by the rotating propeller on takeoff, one should push the control column (yoke) forward.

REVIEW QUESTIONS

To answer questions 1 and 2, refer to Figure 4.1.

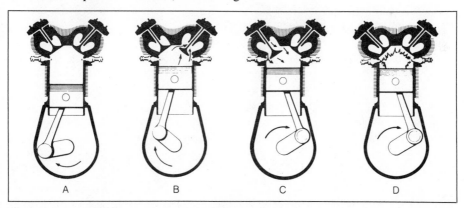

Figure 4.1

1.   Which illustration depicts the power stroke?
      a. A   c. C
      b. B   d. D

2.   What is the proper sequence of the four strokes of the piston of a gasoline
engine?
      a. A, C, B, D
      b. B, A, C, D
      c. C, A, D, B
      d. D, C, A, B

3.   In most general aviation airplanes, the crankshaft is connected directly to the
      a. carburetor
      b. exhaust manifold
      c. intake valve
      d. propeller

4.   Which of the following statements about the use of aviation gasoline is correct?
      a. Using a higher than specified octane usually produces lower than normal
         cylinder head temperatures and thus less power.
      b. Using a higher than specified grade of fuel is permissible if the recommended
         grade is not available.
      c. Using a lower than specified grade of fuel is permissible if the recommended
         grade is not available.
      d. Using a lower than specified grade of fuel may result in reduced power
         output, but it is generally less harmful to the engine than higher than specified
         grades.

5.   Using a lower than specified grade of fuel in an aircraft engine will most likely
cause
      a. an uneven mixture of air and fuel
      b. an increase in power that may overstress the engine
      c. detonation
      d. lower cylinder head temperatures

6.   Preignition occurs in a reciprocating aircraft engine when
      a. hot spots in the combustion chamber ignite the air-fuel mixture prematurely
      b. the air-fuel mixture is too rich
      c. the spark plugs are disconnected
      d. the unburned air-fuel mixture in the cylinder explodes rather than burning
         evenly

7.   The primary reason for filling the fuel tanks to capacity after the last flight of
the day is to reduce airspace in the tanks so that
      a. air cannot enter the fuel lines and cause vapor lock

    b. fuel will not evaporate and create residues that might lead to detonation or
       preignition
    c. fuel will not vaporize and create a fire hazard
    d. moisture will not condense and create water in the fuel system

8.   In comparison with fuel injection systems, float-type carburetor systems are
generally considered to be
    a. equally susceptible to icing
    b. less susceptible to icing
    c. more susceptible to icing
    d. susceptible to icing only when visible moisture is present

9.   What precaution should you take to avoid the danger of fire when refueling an
airplane?
    a. Attach a ground wire to the airplane.
    b. Open the fuel vents.
    c. Put the mixture control at full-rich.
    d. Turn off the carburetor heat.

10.   What part of the carburetor opens or closes as you adjust the power setting?
    a. float mechanism
    b. fuel strainer
    c. mixture control valve
    d. throttle valve

11.   The typical general aviation aircraft has _____ magneto system(s).
    a. one
    b. two
    c. four
    d. an unlimited number of

12.   The engine ignition system
    a. can be stopped by turning off the magnetos from inside the cockpit
    b. cannot be stopped by stopping engine rotation
    c. depends on other aircraft systems for power
    d. all of the above

13.   Which of the following is not part of the airplane engine's lubricating system?
    a. dipstick
    b. pressure sensor
    c. temperature sensing device
    d. throttle valve

14.   What part of the airplane's electrical system controls the variable output of the
generator or alternator?

    a. ammeter
    b. circuit breaker
    c. master switch
    d. voltage regulator

15.   To counteract the effects of torque in a single-engine propeller-driven airplane, a pilot would normally add
    a. left rudder pressure when entering a climb from level cruising flight
    b. left rudder pressure during the takeoff roll and while climbing with full power
    c. right rudder pressure when entering a glide from level cruising flight
    d. right rudder pressure during the takeoff roll and while climbing with full power.

16.   With a constant-speed propeller, what instruments register engine power?
    a. ammeter and tachometer
    b. manifold pressure gauge and tachometer
    c. suction gauge and ammeter
    d. suction gauge and manifold pressure gauge

17.   With a constant speed propeller airplane
    a. propeller speed should be increased before power is added
    b. propeller speed should be increased before power is reduced
    c. propeller speed should be reduced before power is added
    d. propeller speed should be reduced before power is reduced

18.   What area of the carburetor is most susceptible to ice?
    a. accelerating pump
    b. float chamber
    c. mixture control
    d. throttle valve

19.   In an airplane equipped with a fixed-pitch propeller and a float-type carburetor, the first indication of carburetor ice would most likely be
    a. a drop in oil temperature and cylinder head temperature
    b. a drop in manifold pressure
    c. engine roughness
    d. loss of rpm

20.   The carburetor heat system directs
    a. cold air away from the carburetor
    b. moisture away from the carburetor
    c. warm air to the carburetor
    d. all of the above

21.   What is the result of permitting an airplane engine to idle for a long period of time while on the ground?
    a. A hydraulic lock may develop in one or more of the cylinders.
    b. It may cause excessively high oil pressure.
    c. The spark plugs may become fouled.
    d. All of the above are correct.

22.   To properly shut down an airplane engine, one first
    a. pulls the mixture control to full-lean
    b. switches the ignition switch to Off
    c. turns off the fuel valve
    d. turns off the master switch

23.   If the engine oil temperature and cylinder head temperature have exceeded their normal operating range, you may have been
    a. operating with higher than normal oil pressure
    b. operating with the mixture set too rich
    c. operating with too much power and with the mixture set too lean
    d. using fuel that has a higher than specified fuel rating

24.   Which of the following would most likely cause the cylinder head temperature and engine oil temperature gauges to exceed their normal operating range?
    a. climbing too steeply, particularly in hot weather
    b. operating with too much power and with the mixture set too lean
    c. using fuel that has a lower than specified fuel rating
    d. all of the above

25.   What change occurs in the air-fuel mixture when carburetor heat is applied?
    a. It becomes leaner.
    b. It becomes richer.
    c. No change occurs.
    d. Rpm decreases.

26.   In what position should the ignition switch be during takeoff?
    a. Both
    b. L
    c. R
    d. Start

27.   An abnormally high engine oil temperature indication may be caused by
    a. a defective bearing
    b. operating with an excessively rich mixture
    c. the oil level being too high
    d. the oil level being too low

28.   Which of the following statements about carburetor icing is correct?
       a. Carburetor icing would be most likely to form at low power settings when
          the air temperature is between 40 and 60 degrees Fahrenheit with visible
          moisture or high humidity.
       b. The carburetor heater is a deicing device that heats the air after it enters the
          carburetor.
       c. The first indication of carburetor icing in a fixed-pitch propeller airplane is
          an increase in rpm, followed by a rapid decrease in rpm.
       d. All of the above are correct.

29.   The basic purpose of adjusting the air-fuel mixture at altitude is to
       a. decrease the amount of fuel in the mixture to compensate for increased air
          density
       b. decrease the fuel flow to compensate for decreased air density
       c. increase the amount of fuel in the mixture to compensate for the decrease in
          pressure and density of the air
       d. increase the fuel flow to be compatible with the increased air density

30.   Which of the following statements regarding fouling of the spark plugs is
correct?
       a. Carbon fouling of the plugs is caused primarily by operating the engine at
          excessively high cylinder head temperatures.
       b. Excessive heat in the combustion chamber of a cylinder causes oil to form
          on the center electrode of the plug, which causes it to preignite.
       c. Permitting the engine to idle for a long period of time on the ground is the
          best way to clean fouled spark plugs.
       d. Spark plug fouling results from operating with an excessively rich mixture.

31.   As you view it from inside the cockpit, the propeller turns _____, which
produces torque, which turns the airplane _____.
       a. counterclockwise; counterclockwise
       b. counterclockwise; clockwise
       c. clockwise; counterclockwise
       d. clockwise; clockwise

ANSWERS

Key Terms and Concepts, Part 1

1.	a	2.	t	3.	h	4.	j
5.	c	6.	o	7.	e	8.	q
9.	m	10.	b	11.	s	12.	p
13.	k	14.	d	15.	r	16.	g
17.	n	18.	i	19.	f	20.	l

Key Terms and Concepts, Part 2

1.	i	2.	g	3.	p	4.	c
5.	r	6.	l	7.	a	8.	n
9.	t	10.	b	11.	o	12.	e
13.	h	14.	q	15.	d	16.	s
17.	k	18.	f	19.	j	20.	m

Key Terms and Concepts, Part 3

1.	i	2.	d	3.	f	4.	r
5.	u	6.	l	7.	a	8.	o
9.	g	10.	t	11.	b	12.	j
13.	s	14.	m	15.	c	16.	p
17.	e	18.	h	19.	q	20.	k
21.	n						

Discussion Questions and Exercises

20.   F; one should *never* put automobile gasoline in an airplane.

21.   T; self-explanatory.

22.   F; it should be checked before *every* flight.

23.   F; fuel injection systems distribute fuel more evenly and are faster in response to throttle changes.

24.   T; self-explanatory.

25.   F; it is considered dual because it has two separate and independent magneto systems.

26.   F; this defines the magneto, not the alternator.

27.   F; ashless-dispersant is the correct AD.

28.   F; this is when it would be at a minimum.

29.   T; self-explanatory.

30.   F; this is a value that should *not* be exceeded.

31.   F; it almost always occurs near the throttle valve.

32.   T; self-explanatory.

33.   T; fouling may occur due to the rich mixture used for most ground operations.

34.   T; one reason for the run-up is to make sure the magnetos are properly grounded; if they do *not* decrease in rpm when checked, they may be improperly grounded.

35.   F; it causes the mixture to become richer. Since warm air is less dense than cold air, the mixture runs richer.

36.   T; this causes all electrical systems to stop (except the ignition system), after which you can test them individually using the various circuit breakers.

37.   F; one reason is to keep the engine from overheating; it also helps to prevent plug fouling.

38.   T; as altitude decreases, air density increases, so one has to increase the amount of fuel in the mixture to compensate.

39.   F; torque is counteracted by applying right rudder, which moves the nose of the airplane to the left.

Review Questions

1.   d; the piston is forced down by the ignition of the fuel.
2.   c; intake (down), compression (up), power (down), exhaust (up).
3.   d; produces torque.
4.   b; higher grades do not improve performance and may even be harmful, but lower grades are definitely harmful: Loss of power, excessive heat, burned spark plugs, burned valves, high oil consumption, and deterioration may result.
5.   c; detonation is one common result of using a lower than specified grade of fuel.
6.   a; preignition is just that—firing prematurely.
7.   d; this procedure helps prevent condensation of the moisture in the air.
8.   c; they are more susceptible to icing, particularly in the area of the throttle valve.
9.   a; grounding the airplane is a must!
10. d; this mechanism is also most susceptible to carburetor icing.
11. b; it is a dual system, thus providing redundancy.
12. a; or it can be stopped by stopping engine rotation (as when you pull the mixture control to full-lean). It is independent of other aircraft systems for power.
13. d; the throttle valve is part of the carburetor.
14. d; this is the job of the voltage regulator.
15. d; torque moves the airplane to the left and is exaggerated at high power settings and low airspeeds.
16. b; self-explanatory.
17. a; this avoids unnecessary loads on the engine.
18. d; this is where ice is most likely to form.
19. d; rpm decreases due to less air-fuel mixture. In constant-speed propeller airplanes it would be indicated by a drop in manifold pressure.
20. c; this helps melt ice when it is present and helps prevent ice when conditions are right, as at low power settings in high humidity conditions when the temperature is between 40 and 60 degrees Fahrenheit.
21. c; fouling may occur due to the rich mixture used during most ground operations.
22. a; leaning the mixture removes fuel residues from the cylinders.
23. c; high engine temperature can result from insufficient cooling caused by too lean a mixture, too low a grade of fuel, low oil, or insufficient airflow over the engine.
24. d; the answer to question 23.
25. b; the mixture runs richer. Since warm air is less dense than cold air, the mixture gets richer.
26. a; *both* provide the redundancy of the ignition system.
27. d; low oil level means that not much lubricant is available to cool the engine.
28. a; the carburetor is particularly susceptible to icing during these conditions when the throttle is at a low setting.
29. b; decreasing the fuel flow makes the mixture leaner, thus compensating for decreased air density.
30. d; rich mixtures may not burn completely, thus leaving carbon deposits.
31. c; as the propeller turns clockwise (to the right), it produces torque, which in turn moves the airplane to the left (counterclockwise).

5/AIRPLANE WEIGHT AND BALANCE

MAIN POINTS

1. A teeter-totter is a lever on either side of a *fulcrum*. The length of the lever is called the *arm*. The force of a weight acting at the end of the arm is called a **moment.** Arm, moment, and weight are related such that Weight × Arm = Moment, Arm = Moment/Weight, or Weight = Moment/Arm.

2. Airplanes must balance through a single point called the **center of gravity (CG),** around which all moments are equal. The CG must be kept within certain limits to maintain control surface stability. The reference point from which moment arms are measured is called the **datum** or **datum line.**

3. The datum in most planes is located near the nose. The CG and all other components that might go in the plane are measured in inches from the datum. Weight times distance from the datum yields a moment. The sum of the airplane's empty weight plus everything you put in it is called **gross weight.** If you sum the moments and divide by the gross weight, you have the new CG location relative to the datum.

4. *Empty weight* is the airplane's weight with all listed equipment, hydraulic fluid, undrainable engine oil, and unusuable fuel (not available to the engine due to aircraft design). **Basic empty weight** is empty weight plus full oil. Gas weighs 6 pounds per gallon, and oil weighs 7.5 pounds per gallon. **Useful load** includes *usable fuel* and the *payload* (occupants, cargo, and baggage). **Maximum ramp weight** is the manufacturer's maximum ground maneuvering weight. **Maximum takeoff weight** is the maximum for the start of the takeoff run. **Maximum landing weight** is the maximum weight approved for touchdown.

5. The two basic questions are: Is gross weight within allowable limits? Is the CG within allowable limits? After determining how much useful load you have and where

it will go, you use the Pilot's Operating Handbook to determine the fuselage station number (arm) for each item, which is listed conveniently in inches from the datum. Multiply weight by its arm and you have the moment; add all moments and divide by the gross weight to get the new CG. (Most modern Pilot's Operating Handbooks give moments for empty airplanes, passengers, fuel, and baggage or cargo weights to save your time.)

6. Changing the weight and/or the CG frequently changes the airplane's performance characteristics. For example, high gross weights require a greater angle of attack to maintain level flight. Thus, the airplane will stall at higher airspeeds, climb at lower climb angles, and burn more fuel. Forward CGs make the plane more stable but require extra elevator pressure to raise the nose. Also, the airplane will stall at a slightly higher airspeed since the tail is trimmed down, reducing lift from the wings. An aft CG makes the plane less stable and increases the chances of serious stalls or spins. Since the tail is trimmed up, the elevator produces some additional lift, which in turn reduces stalling speed and increases fuel efficiency. These changes are minor and acceptable when the airplane is loaded within the limits defined in the Pilot's Operating Handbook, but they become extremely dangerous when those limits are exceeded.

7. There are two common formats for solving weight and balance problems: tabular and graphical. Both methods require that you first figure *zero fuel condition,* then the *fuel loading,* which together yield the *ramp condition.* The *takeoff condition* compensates for fuel burned during taxi and run-up. The *landing condition* takes into account fuel burned during flight. The tabular format refers you to a table of moment limits versus weight to determine if you are within an acceptable range of CG values, using proportional interpolation if necessary. The graphical method presents moment values as index units for each compartment of the plane. The sum of the moments and weight is used to determine if you fall within the CG envelope.

8. Good pilots make weight and balance planning a *habit!* Although it may be a chore to rearrange the payload or embarrassing to ask someone for their actual weight (if you remember that most people, particularly those who are overweight, *underestimate* their weight, you can frequently compensate for this "error"), remember that your safety and the safety of your passengers is at stake. Finally, be sure to check during your flight to make certain that trim changes are in the predicted direction. Anything out of the ordinary could mean that your weight and balance computations were in error.

KEY TERMS AND CONCEPTS

Match each term or concept (1–16) with the appropriate description (a–p) below. Each item has only one match.

___ 1. ramp weight   ___ 2. fuselage station (FS) number
___ 3. empty weight   ___ 4. moment
___ 5. payload   ___ 6. takeoff condition
___ 7. CG envelope   ___ 8. landing condition

___ 9. useful load   ___10. arm
___11. maximum gross weight   ___12. usable fuel
___13. datum   ___14. fulcrum
___15. zero fuel condition   ___16. center of gravity (CG)

a.   reference point from which all moments are measured
b.   ramp condition less weight and moment of fuel used for taxi and run-up
c.   number of inches an item is from its datum
d.   weight of fuel aboard that is available to the engine
e.   airplane's weight with all equipment and unusable fuel
f.   weight of cargo, occupants, and baggage
g.   weight of an item times its distance from the datum (arm)
h.   takeoff condition less weight and moment of fuel burned in flight
i.   weight and moment of an airplane with payload but no fuel load
j.   point in an aircraft about which all moments are equal
k.   distance of a station or item from the datum
l.   everything that can be loaded into an airplane until its maximum ramp weight is reached
m.   maximum weight to which an aircraft is certified by the FAA
n.   support point of a level
o.   weight and moment of an airplane with payload and fuel included
p.   range of weight and balance operating limits

DISCUSSION QUESTIONS AND EXERCISES

1.   What is the relationship among arm, moment, and weight? How does this apply to general aviation aircraft?

2.   What are the two major factors about the airplane's weight and balance a pilot must attend to before the airplane flies?

3.   What is basic empty weight? How is it different from empty weight?

4.   Name three effects of each of the following on the airplane's flight characteristics:

    a. high gross weight

    b. operations with a forward CG

    c. operations with an aft CG

5.   How are fuselage stations and moment related?

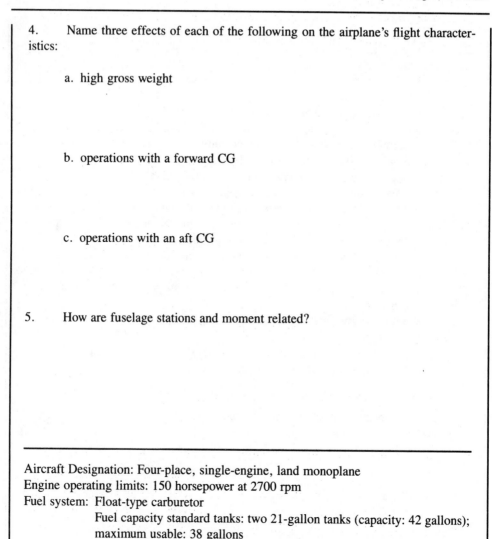

Aircraft Designation: Four-place, single-engine, land monoplane
Engine operating limits: 150 horsepower at 2700 rpm
Fuel system: Float-type carburetor
    Fuel capacity standard tanks: two 21-gallon tanks (capacity: 42 gallons);
    maximum usable: 38 gallons
    Optional long-range tanks: total capacity: 52 gallons; maximum usable:
    48 gallons
Oil capacity: 8 quarts (not included in empty weight)
Propeller: Fixed-pitch
Landing gear: Fixed tricycle gear
Wing flaps: Electrically operated, 0 to 40 degrees
Empty weight: 1364 pounds
Maximum gross weight: 2300 pounds
Maximum weight in baggage compartment: 120 pounds

Figure 5.1 Excerpt from a Pilot's Operating Handbook.

6.   To answer questions a–e, refer to Figure 5.1 and assume that the airplane is loaded as follows:

Pilot	160 pounds
Front seat passenger	148 pounds
Rear seat passenger	122 pounds
Rear seat passenger	176 pounds
Baggage	80 pounds
Oil	Full
Fuel (standard tanks)	Full

a. How is the airplane loaded?

b. Assume that you plan to load the airplane with 120 pounds of baggage, 8 quarts of oil, and four persons whose total weight is 698 pounds. What is the total amount of usable fuel (standard tanks) that can be aboard without exceeding the maximum certified gross weight?

c. What is the combined maximum weight of four persons and baggage that can be loaded without exceeding the maximum certified gross weight if the airplane is serviced to capacity with oil and fuel (long-range tanks)?

d. Suppose that you have filled the airplane's long-range fuel tanks to capacity and there are 8 quarts of oil in the engine. You wish to carry four persons aboard, whose total weight is 680 pounds. There will be no baggage aboard. How close would this airplane be to maximum certified gross weight limits?

e. During the preflight, you note that there are 8 quarts of oil in the engine and the standard fuel tanks are filled to capacity. The total weight of the pilot and passengers is 670 pounds. What is the total weight of the baggage, if any, that can be loaded aboard without exceeding the maximum certified gross weight of the airplane?

7.   If a copy of the textbook is available, refer to the sample tabular weight and balance problem (text Figures 5.6 to 5.10). Assume that you are the pilot and that you have a fuel load of 15 gallons. Compute a new landing condition for the airplane, assuming that you use 10 gallons. Is the airplane's CG at landing within its operating envelope? What is the new CG (in inches aft of the datum)?

REVIEW QUESTIONS

1.   Which of the following items are included in the licensed empty weight of an airplane?
    a. full fuel tanks and engine oil to capacity, but excluding crew and baggage
    b. hydraulic fluid and usable fuel
    c. only the airplane, power plant, and equipment installed by the manufacturer
    d. unusable fuel, optional equipment, and undrainable oil

2.   If a camera bag originally in the front of the plane is moved to the baggage compartment (located aft of the cabin), how will this affect the airplane's center of gravity?
    a. The CG would change unpredictably as flight altitude changed.
    b. The CG would move aft.
    c. The CG would move forward.
    d. The CG would remain the same.

3.   If you have a 40-pound weight and an 80-inch arm, what is the moment?
    a. 2 inch-pounds
    b. 32 inch-pounds
    c. 120 inch-pounds
    d. 3200 inch-pounds

4.   The point in the aircraft around which all moments are equal is called the
    a. ballast
    b. center of gravity
    c. datum
    d. equilibrium point

5.   The set of weight and balance operational restrictions assigned to your airplane is called the
    a. CG envelope
    b. fuselage station number
    c. load limit
    d. moment limit

6.   Which of the following conditions would probably lead to an increase in stalling speed?
    a. an increased angle of bank
    b. operations at high gross weight
    c. operation with a forward CG
    d. all of the above

7.   Of the following items, which should be considered *first* in completing a weight and balance form?
    a. baggage
    b. fuel loading
    c. fuel to destination
    d. ramp condition

Aircraft designation: Single-engine, land monoplane (seating arrangement: pilot and passenger side-by-side plus a child's seat in the baggage area)

Engine operating limits: 100 horsepower

Fuel system: Float-type carburetor
    Fuel capacity standard tanks: two 13-gallon tanks (capacity: 26 gallons); maximum usable: 22.5 gallons
    Optional long-range tanks: total capacity: 38 gallons; maximum usable: 35 gallons

Oil capacity: 6 quarts, *included* in empty weight

Propeller: Fixed-pitch

Landing gear: Fixed tricycle gear

Wing Flaps: Electrically operated, 0 to 40 degrees

Empty weight: 1104 pounds

Maximum gross weight: 1600 pounds

Maximum weight in baggage compartment: 120 pounds

Figure 5.2
Excerpt from a Pilot's Operating Handbook.

To answer questions 8–11, refer to Figure 5.2.

8.   What is the combined maximum weight of two persons and baggage that can be loaded without exceeding the maximum certified gross weight if the airplane is serviced with 6 quarts of oil and the standard fuel tanks are full?
    a. 340 pounds
    b. 350 pounds
    c. 355 pounds
    d. 361 pounds

9.   Assume that the total weight of the pilot and passenger is 285 pounds and the airplane's standard fuel tanks are full. Under these conditions, how much baggage could be loaded without exceeding the maximum certified gross weight?
   a. 1 pound
   b. 44 pounds
   c. 56 pounds
   d. 76 pounds

10.   Assume that the airplane is loaded as follows:

Pilot	170 pounds
Passenger	125 pounds
Baggage	65 pounds
Oil	Full
Fuel (standard tanks)	Full

This airplane is loaded
   a. 1 pound less than the maximum allowable gross weight
   b. 10 pounds more than the maximum allowable gross weight
   c. 10 pounds less than the maximum allowable gross weight
   d. 74 pounds more than the maximum allowable gross weight

11.   What is the combined maximum weight of two persons (with no baggage) that can be loaded without exceeding the maximum certified gross weight if the airplane is serviced to oil capacity and the long-range fuel tanks are full?
   a. 275 pounds
   b. 286 pounds
   c. 331 pounds
   d. 361 pounds

   To answer questions 12–17, refer to Figure 5.3a and b and use the following information:

Empty weight	1225
Pilot and passenger	275
Wild rice in sack on rear seat	200
Baggage	80

Fuel capacity: 42 gallons, 40.5 usable
Moment in index units for basic empty weight: 48.6

12.   What is the airplane's maximum certified gross weight?
   a. 1485 pounds
   b. 1674 pounds
   c. 2200 pounds
   d. impossible to determine from the data given

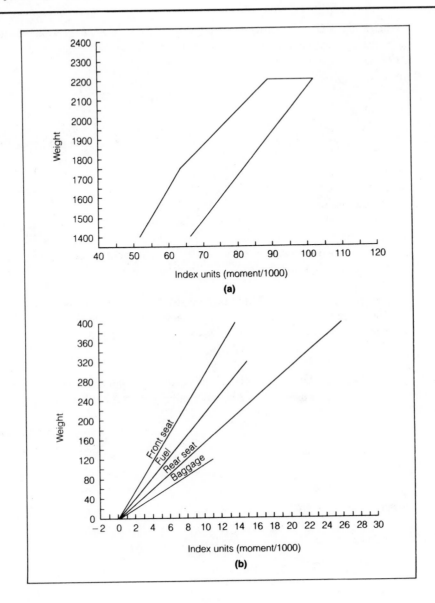

Figure 5.3

13.   What will the airplane's ramp weight be if the pilot uses the maximum allowable fuel without exceeding maximum certified gross limits?

    a. 1780

    b. 2023

    c. 2032

    d. 2200

14.   What is the CG in index units if the pilot uses the maximum allowable fuel without exceeding maximum certified gross limits?

    a. 85.2
    b. 87.6
    c. 90.1
    d. 93.6

15.   If the pilot were to move the baggage to the rear seat, what would happen to the CG?

    a. Its movement cannot be predicted given these data.
    b. It would move backward.
    c. It would move forward.
    d. It would not move at all.

16.   If the pilot filled the tanks to maximum capacity without exceeding maximum certified gross weight and then flew for 5.1 hours burning 8 gallons per hour, what would happen?

    a. Gross weight limits would not be exceeded, but CG limits would.
    b. The airplane would exceed both gross weight and CG limits.
    c. The airplane would not exceed gross weight or CG limits.
    d. The airplane would run out of fuel.

17.   If the pilot filled the tanks to maximum capacity without exceeding maximum certified gross weight and then flew 4.2 hours burning 8 gallons per hour, what would the CG (in index units) be upon landing?

    a. 74.1
    b. 76.3
    c. 78.4
    d. 80.6

ANSWERS

Key Terms and Concepts

1.	o	2.	c	3.	e	4.	g
5.	f	6.	b	7.	p	8.	h
9.	l	10.	k	11.	m	12.	d
13.	a.	14.	n	15.	i	16.	j

Discussion Questions and Exercises

6.a.   2293, or 7 pounds under gross weight. Empty weight (1364), pilot and front seat passengers (308), rear passengers (298), baggage (80), oil (8 quarts × 7.5 pounds per gallon = 15), and fuel (38 × 6 = 228) = 2293, which is 7 pounds under maximum certified gross weight.

   b.   17.1 gallons. Use the data in 6a. The total left for fuel is 103 pounds, or 17.1 gallons (6 pounds per gallon).

c.   633 pounds. Use the total in 6a. Fuel: $48 \times 6 = 288$; 2300 less fuel (288), less oil (15), less empty weight (1364) equals 633 pounds.

d.   47 pounds over allowable gross weight. Use the data in 6a and make the appropriate substitutions.

e.   23 pounds are left for baggage. Again, use the data in 6a and make the appropriate substitutions.

7.
Basic empty condition	1190 pounds	1023 inch-pounds
Pilot	170 pounds	158 inch-pounds
Subtotal: zero fuel condition	1360 pounds	1181 inch-pounds
Fuel loading (15 gallons)	90 pounds	73 inch-pounds
Subtotal: ramp condition	1450 pounds	1254 inch-pounds
Less fuel for run-up	− 5 pounds	− 4 inch-pounds
Subtotal: takeoff condition	1145 pounds	1250 inch-pounds
Less fuel to landing condition	− 60 pounds	− 49 inch-pounds
	1385 pounds	1201 inch-pounds

Referring to text Figure 5.9, we see that for a gross weight of 1385 the amount can be between 1178 and 1232, using interpolation to figure out the exact values, and we are well within that range. Using text Figure 5.10, the CG is approximately 86.75, again well within the CG envelope.

Review Questions

1.   d; empty weight includes the airframe, fixed equipment, unusable fuel, undrainable oil, and hydraulic fluid.

2.   b; CG changes anytime weight is shifted. If weight moves back, the CG moves back.

3.   d; moment = arm × weight. In this case, moment = $80 \times 40 = 3200$ inch-pounds.

4.   b; this defines the CG.

5.   a; this defines the CG envelope, a range of values for relating weights and balances.

6.   d; as you recall from Chapter 2, increasing the angle of bank increases stalling speed. Operation with a high gross weight or a forward CG destroys lift, which in turn increases stalling speed.

7.   a; the first thing to figure is payload and empty condition.

Beware: Most of these questions refer to oil. Make sure you know that oil is not included in empty weight and that it weighs *7.5 pounds per gallon*, not 7.5 pounds per quart.

8.   d; empty weight (1104) plus usable fuel ($22.5 \times 6 = 135$) equals 1239 pounds. Since oil is included in the empty weight, it is not relevant to this computation. Subtract 1239 from the maximum gross weight to arrive at 361 pounds (two medium-size adults).

9.   d; empty weight (1104) plus usable fuel ($22.5 \times 6 = 135$) plus 285 equals 1524 pounds, which is 76 pounds less than the maximum gross weight.

10. a; payload (360 pounds) plus empty weight (1104) plus fuel (22.5 × 6 = 135) equals 1599 pounds, 1 pound less than the maximum gross weight.

11. b; fuel (35 × 6 = 210) plus empty weight (1104) equals 1314, which leaves 286 pounds when subtracted from the maximum gross weight.

12. c; looking at Figure 5.3a, one can see from the top of the CG envelope that the maximum gross weight is 2200 pounds.

13. b; all of the weights are given in the data except the allowance for fuel. Since the pilot can fill the tanks to capacity, usable fuel will weigh 243 pounds (40.5 × 6); 1225 + 275 + 200 + 80 + 243 = 2023 pounds.

14. c; refer to Figure 5.3b to determine index units for pilot and passenger (9.5), rice (13.0), baggage (7.5), and fuel (11.5). This total, 41.5, plus the moment for basic empty weight, 48.6, equals 90.1 index units, which for a gross weight of 2023 pounds is well within the CG envelope.

15. c; by refiguring the data you can determine how much it would move forward.

16. d; since this requires 40.8 gallons (5.1 × 8), the pilot would run out of fuel, as only 40.5 gallons are available for use.

17. d; see the answer to question 14. Fuel is what needs to be recalculated. The pilot used 4.2 × 9 = 37.8 gallons, which when subtracted from usable fuel leaves 6.9 gallons, or 41.4 pounds, which has a moment of about 2.0 index units. So 9.5 + 13.0 + 7.5 + 2.0 + 48.6 = 80.6.

6/PERFORMANCE: MEASURING AN AIRPLANE'S CAPABILITIES

MAIN POINTS

1. Airplane design depends a great deal upon what the designer intended. For example, some airplanes are aerodynamically sleek so they can go fast. Others have pontoons so they can land on water. Others have large fuselages so they can carry a large payload.

2. Atmospheric conditions influence both flight instruments and flight characteristics. *Atmospheric pressure* decreases as altitude increases due to less gravitational force. A 1000-foot change of altitude corresponds to 1 inch of mercury. Air temperature also decreases as altitude increases. The reference point for measuring air pressure (*International Standard Atmosphere*) is 59 degrees Fahrenheit (15 degrees Celsius) and 29.92 inches of mercury at sea level. When you set your altimeter to 29.92 and read the height from the altimeter, you have a measure of *pressure altitude*—that is, the altitude above a pressure level of 29.92. The higher the barometric pressure is, the lower the pressure altitude.

3. **Density-altitude** reflects three variables: pressure, temperature, and humidity. Warm temperatures make air expand and thus produce a higher density-altitude, as do actual increases in altitude. Water vapor tends to displace air molecules, which also makes air less dense. A cold, dry day at sea level would have a low density-altitude, while a warm, humid day in Mexico City (elevation over 5000 feet MSL) would have a high density-altitude. Pressure altitude is necessary to compute exact density altitude. Figure 6.1 shows a chart relating outside air temperature (OAT) and pressure altitude to density-altitude. The solid diagonal line from upper left to lower right represents ISA values.

4. Atmospheric factors affect takeoff performance. Less air pressure means longer takeoff runs and slower climb rates since there is less thrust and less lift. The pilot must calculate the effects of density-altitude on the takeoff run. Another atmospheric variable is the wind. Headwinds decrease takeoff distances and tailwinds increase it. Airplane and runway characteristics also affect takeoff performance. As mentioned in an earlier chapter, more lift is required as weight is increased and when the plane is loaded toward the forward CG limit; thus, both increase takeoff distance. Flaps, when partially extended, can have the opposite effect and may be recommended for some airplanes for soft field departures. The slope of the runway will also affect takeoff distance. A downhill slope decreases it and an uphill slope increases it. Rain, snow, and ice may not impede mail carriers, but they can and do impede airplanes. A third and final category of variables affecting takeoffs is your technique as a pilot.

5. For the purpose of calculating takeoff performance, we will use indicated airspeed (uncorrected for errors in the instrument itself). First, determine pressure altitude either by setting the altimeter at 29.92 and reading it directly from the altimeter or by computing it from the pressure and altitude data available. For example, in Lawrence, Kansas (field elevation 852 feet), an atmospheric condition of 30.06 would have a pressure altitude of $852 + ([29.92 - 30.06] \times 1000) = 852 - 140$, or 712 feet. Next, you need to calculate the effect of the wind. The direction of surface wind is always given as *coming from* a magnetic heading. Using a wind components chart (see Figure 6.2), one finds the angle between the wind direction and flight path and the wind velocity to determine headwind and crosswind components. Next, using a takeoff distance chart (see Figure 6.3), one integrates the effects of density-altitude, gross weight, wind components, and obstacle heights.

6. There are two airspeeds you must know: the **best angle of climb,** which yields the greatest altitude per distance traveled; and the **best rate of climb,** which gives you the greatest increase in altitude per unit of time. There are a number of tables to help calculate climb performance, such as rate of climb tables and time, fuel, and distance to climb tables (see Figure 6.4). Once obstacles are cleared, use the recommended cruise climb speed to help prevent engine overheating.

7. Cruise speed depends upon your objective: maximum speed, maximum range, or maximum endurance (best ratio of fuel per unit of time). Fuel mixture should be leaned as recommended in the Pilot's Operating Handbook, to enhance engine performance and to realize published fuel consumption values. Once aloft, winds remain a factor whether headwind, tailwind, or crosswind. Actual speed through the air is called **true airspeed** (TAS;) it is near indicated airspeed at low altitude but higher than IAS at high altitudes. Once again, there are graphs such as the one shown in Figure 6.5 and tables such as the one shown in Figure 6.6 to determine true airspeed given various power settings and density-altitudes. There are also graphs such as those in Figures 6.7 and 6.8 to help calculate range and endurance given various pressure altitudes and power settings.

8. Fuel efficiency can be improved by keeping your airplane clean, loading it lightly, keeping ground operations to a minimum, climbing directly on course, leaning the engine as recommended, and using shallow glide paths.

9. One key to effective landings is to establish the proper final approach airspeed and attitude early. The use of flaps, for example, requires even more planning as the airplane responds more sluggishly. A typical landing chart is shown in Figure 6.9.

10. For reference purposes, you should know that the vertical axis on a graph is called the *ordinate* and that the horizontal axis is called the *abscissa*.

KEY TERMS AND CONCEPTS

Match each term or concept (1–21) with the appropriate description (a–u) below. Each item has only one match.

___ 1. humidity
___ 2. short field
___ 3. best rate of climb
___ 4. atmospheric pressure
___ 5. tailwind
___ 6. true
___ 7. chocks
___ 8. crosswind
___ 9. pressure altitude
___10. indicated
___11. holding
___12. maximum endurance
___13. International Standard Atmosphere (ISA)
___14. soft field
___15. magnetic
___16. density-altitude
___17. maximum range
___18. best angle of climb
___19. crabbing
___20. abscissa
___21. ordinate

a.   runway with dirt or grass surface
b.   "actual" speed through the air
c.   best ratio of fuel consumed per unit of time
d.   heading used as a reference for wind direction
e.   wind condition that will increase landing distance
f.   amount of water vapor the air contains
g.   pressure exerted by the air due to gravitational force
h.   flying a fixed pattern for traffic control purposes
i.   airspeed that gives you the greatest altitude gain per unit of time
j.   wind from any other direction but the nose or tail
k.   flying an airplane with its nose at an angle to the ground track
l.   altitude corrected for air temperature and pressure
m.   dry air, 59 degrees Fahrenheit at a barometer setting of 29.92
n.   airspeed that gives you the greatest altitude gain for the distance traveled
o.   airspeed uncorrected for density-altitude or instrument error
p.   best ratio of nautical miles per gallon of fuel consumed
q.   runway with an obstacle at the departure end

r.   altitude read by setting the altimeter at 29.92
s.   wedges that keep an airplane from rolling when parked
t.   vertical axis on a graph
u.   horizontal axis on a graph

DISCUSSION QUESTIONS AND EXERCISES

1.   Give two examples illustrating how a designer's intent can influence an airplane's performance characteristics.

2.   Define each of the following terms:

        a. atmospheric pressure

        b. International Standard Atmosphere (ISA)

        c. pressure altitude

        d. density-altitude

3.   State how each of the following affects density-altitude:

        a. air pressure

        b. temperature

        c. humidity

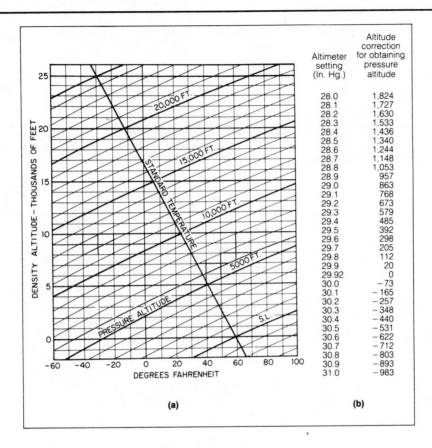

Altimeter setting (In. Hg.)	Altitude correction for obtaining pressure altitude
28.0	1,824
28.1	1,727
28.2	1,630
28.3	1,533
28.4	1,436
28.5	1,340
28.6	1,244
28.7	1,148
28.8	1,053
28.9	957
29.0	863
29.1	768
29.2	673
29.3	579
29.4	485
29.5	392
29.6	298
29.7	205
29.8	112
29.9	20
29.92	0
30.0	−73
30.1	−165
30.2	−257
30.3	−348
30.4	−440
30.5	−531
30.6	−622
30.7	−712
30.8	−803
30.9	−893
31.0	−983

(a) (b)

Figure 6.1

4. To answer questions a–c, refer to Figure 6.1.

a. If the outside air temperature is 98 degrees Fahrenheit in Denver, Colorado (elevation 5330 feet), what is the density-altitude?

b. If the density-altitude is 10,000 feet and the pressure altitude is 12,000 feet, what is the outside air temperature?

c. Given an outside air temperature of −20 degrees Celsius and a pressure altitude of 3000 feet, what is the density-altitude?

5.   How and why does density-altitude affect the takeoff run?

6.   Briefly describe how and why each of the following affects the takeoff run:

a. headwind

b. tailwind

c. gross weight

d. runway gradient

e. snow-covered runway

7.   Define indicated airspeed.

8.   When an airport traffic controller reports that "the wind is 120 at 15," exactly what is the controller saying?

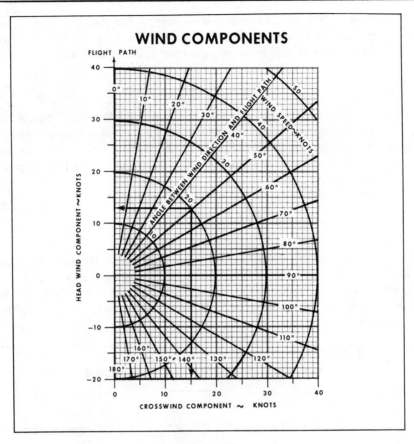

Figure 6.2

9. Suppose that the barometer is 30.18 at Ashland (field elevation 980 feet). What is the pressure altitude at Ashland?

10. To answer questions a and b, refer to Figure 6.2.

a. Suppose that you are about to land on runway 36 at Ashland and the wind is reported as "290 at 30." What is the headwind component in this example? What is the crosswind component?

b. Suppose that you are taking off on runway 7 at Ashland. The crosswind component is 20 knots and the headwind component is 20 knots. What is the wind speed (in knots)? From what direction is the wind blowing?

11.   Assume that runway 7 at Ashland (field elevation 980 feet, barometer 29.92) has just been regraded and is currently covered with gravel. Given an outside air temperature of 20 degrees Celsius, a gross weight of 1620 pounds, and a headwind component of 10 knots, what will your takeoff roll be to clear a 35-foot hedgerow at the end of the runway?

12.   Refer to Figures 6.2 and 6.3a and b. Suppose that your 1500-pound gross weight airplane is about to depart runway 31 at South Lake Tahoe (field elevation 4870 feet, hard-surface runway). Winds are reported as 340° at 18 knots, the temperature is 22 degrees Celsius, and the barometer is 29.32. How much runway will you need to get off the ground?

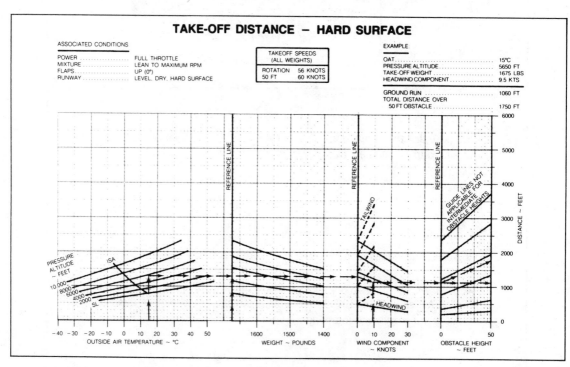

Figure 6.3a

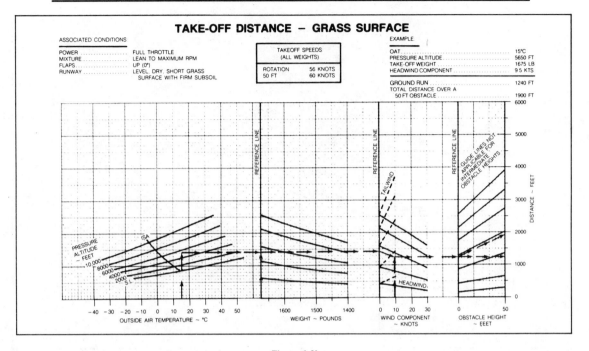

Figure 6.3b

13.   What is the difference between the best angle of climb speed and the best rate of climb speed?

14.   To answer questions a–d, refer to Figure 6.4a and b and question 12. Suppose that you plan to climb to 9500 feet, where the outside air temperature is 2 degrees Celsius. Assume that the average pressure altitude is 8000 feet and the average OAT is 6 degrees Celsius.

    a. What is your rate of climb going to be?

    b. How long will it take you to get to altitude?

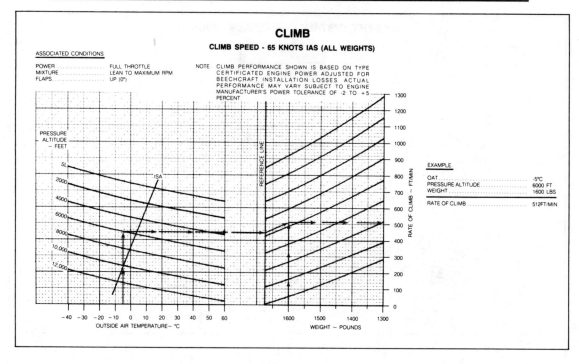

Figure 6.4a

c. How much fuel will you burn during the climb?

d. How far will you be from the airport when you reach altitude?

15.   What is the difference between maximum endurance and maximum range?

16.   Differentiate among indicated airspeed, calibrated airspeed, and true airspeed.

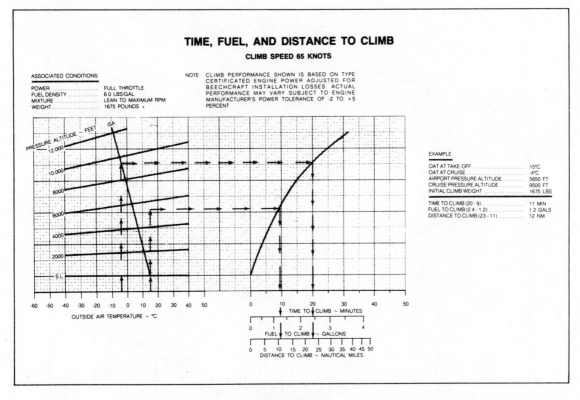

TIME, FUEL, AND DISTANCE TO CLIMB

CLIMB SPEED 65 KNOTS

Figure 6.4b

17.   Refer to question 14 and Figure 6.5. Suppose that you cruise at 2400 rpm. What will your true airspeed be?

18.   Refer to question 17 and Figure 6.6. What will your fuel flow at cruise be? Your indicated airspeed? Your true airspeed?

19.   Refer to question 18 and Figures 6.7 and 6.8. What is your maximum range at 2400 rpm? What is your maximum endurance at 2400 rpm?

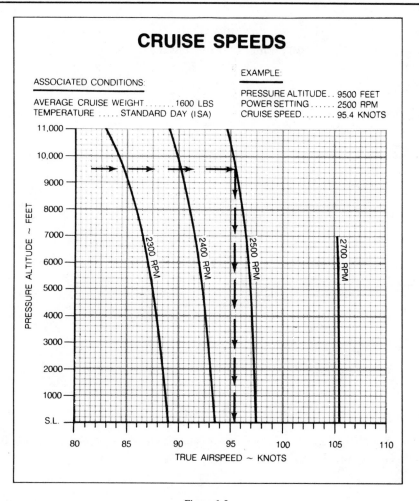

Figure 6.5

20.   Name five things you can do as a pilot to conserve fuel.

21.   What is one of the most important factors that contributes to a safe and efficient landing?

CRUISE PERFORMANCE
STANDARD DAY
AVERAGE CRUISE WEIGHT = 1600 POUNDS

ALTITUDE FEET	THROTTLE SETTING RPM	FUEL FLOW GPH	IAS KNOTS	TAS KNOTS
2500	2700	8.0	101	105
	2500	6.4	94	97
	2400	5.7	90	93
	2300	5.2	85	88
3500	2700	7.8	100	105
	2500	6.3	92	97
	2400	5.7	88	93
	2300	5.2	84	88
4500	2700	7.7	99	105
	2500	6.3	91	97
	2400	5.6	87	93
	2300	5.1	82	88
5500	2700	7.6	97	105
	2500	6.2	89	97
	2400	5.5	85	92
	2300	5.0	81	87
6500	2700	7.4	96	105
	2500	6.1	88	97
	2400	5.4	84	92
	2300	5.0	79	87
7500	2500	6.0	86	96
	2400	5.3	82	91
	2300	4.9	77	86
8500	2500	5.8	85	96
	2400	5.3	80	91
	2300	4.9	76	85
9500	2500	5.7	83	95
	2400	5.2	79	90
	2300	4.8	74	85
10500	2500	5.6	81	95
	2400	5.1	77	90
	2300	4.7	72	84
11500	2500	5.5	80	94
	2400	5.0	75	89
	2300	4.7	70	82

Figure 6.6

22. To answer questions a–d, refer to question 12 and Figures 6.1, 6.2, and 6.9. Suppose that you have nearly completed your flight from South Lake Tahoe and are approaching Monterey Peninsula Airport (hard surface; field elevation: 232 feet; barometer: 30.04; temperature: 20 degrees Celsius; winds from 180° at 10 knots). During the flight you burned 18 gallons of fuel, and you have been cleared to land on runway 23.

a. What is your gross landing weight?

b. What is the pressure altitude? What is the density-altitude?

c. What is the headwind component at Monterey? What is the crosswind component?

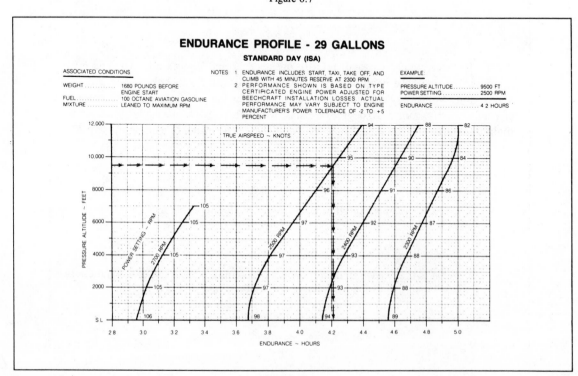

RANGE PROFILE - 29 GALLONS

STANDARD DAY (ISA)

ASSOCIATED CONDITIONS

WEIGHT .....1680 POUNDS BEFORE ENGINE START
FUEL........100 OCTANE AVIATION GASOLINE
MIXTURE ....LEANED TO MAXIMUM RPM

NOTES 1 RANGE INCLUDES START, TAXI, TAKE-OFF, AND CLIMB WITH 45 MINUTES RESERVE FUEL AT 2300 RPM
2 PERFORMANCE SHOWN IS BASED ON THE TYPE CERTIFICATED ENGINE POWER ADJUSTED FOR BEECHCRAFT INSTALLATION LOSSES. ACTUAL PERFORMANCE MAY VARY SUBJECT TO ENGINE MANUFACTURER'S POWER TOLERANCE OF -2 TO +5 PERCENT

EXAMPLE:

PRESSURE ALTITUDE.....**9600**FEET
POWER SETTING.........2500 RPM

RANGE....................392 NM

Figure 6.7

ENDURANCE PROFILE - 29 GALLONS

STANDARD DAY (ISA)

ASSOCIATED CONDITIONS

WEIGHT..........1680 POUNDS BEFORE ENGINE START
FUEL...........100 OCTANE AVIATION GASOLINE
MIXTURE.........LEANED TO MAXIMUM RPM

NOTES 1 ENDURANCE INCLUDES START, TAXI, TAKE OFF, AND CLIMB WITH 45 MINUTES RESERVE AT 2300 RPM
2 PERFORMANCE SHOWN IS BASED ON TYPE CERTIFICATED ENGINE POWER ADJUSTED FOR BEECHCRAFT INSTALLATION LOSSES ACTUAL PERFORMANCE MAY VARY SUBJECT TO ENGINE MANUFACTURER'S POWER TOLERNACE OF -2 TO +5 PERCENT

EXAMPLE:

PRESSURE ALTITUDE..........9500 FT
POWER SETTING ....2500 RPM

ENDURANCE ....4 2 HOURS

Figure 6.8

LANDING DISTANCE - HARD SURFACE - FLAPS DOWN (30°)

APPROACH SPEED: 63 KNOTS (ALL WEIGHTS)

ASSOCIATED CONDITIONS:

POWER	RETARD TO MAINTAIN 550 FT/MIN ON FINAL APPROACH
FLAPS	DOWN (30°)
RUNWAY	PAVED, LEVEL, DRY SURFACE
BRAKING	MAXIMUM
WEIGHT	1521 LBS

EXAMPLE:

OAT	25°C
PRESSURE ALTITUDE	1332 FT
HEADWIND COMPONENT	9.5 KTS
GROUND ROLL	640 FT
TOTAL OVER 50 FT OBSTACLE	1220 FT

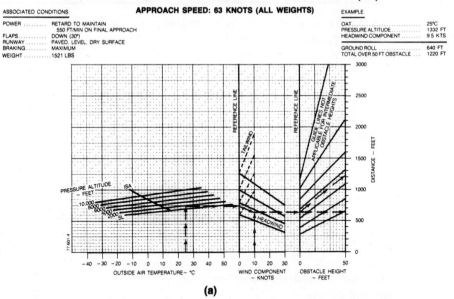

(a)

LANDING DISTANCE - GRASS SURFACE - FLAPS DOWN (30°)

APPROACH SPEED: 63 KNOTS (ALL WEIGHTS)

ASSOCIATED CONDITIONS:

POWER	RETARD TO MAINTAIN 550 FT/MIN ON FINAL APPROACH
FLAPS	DOWN (30°)
RUNWAY	LEVEL, DRY, SHORT GRASS WITH FIRM SUBSOIL
BRAKING	MAXIMUM
WEIGHT	1521 LBS

EXAMPLE:

OAT	25°C
PRESSURE ALTITUDE	1332 FT
HEADWIND COMPONENT	9.5 KTS
GROUND ROLL	400 FT
TOTAL OVER 50 FT OBSTACLE	900 FT

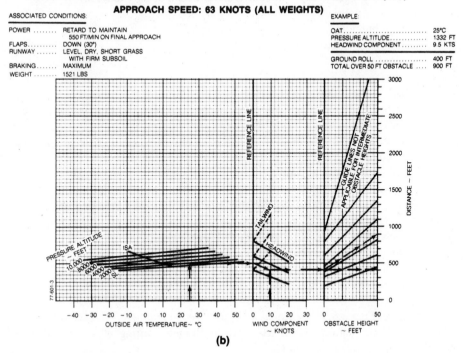

(b)

Figure 6.9

d. How much distance will be required to land given a 50-foot power line near the approach end of runway 23?

REVIEW QUESTIONS

1.   Your altimeter reading when the Kollsman window is set to 29.92 inches of mercury is a measure of
     a. atmospheric pressure
     b. density-altitude
     c. International Standard Atmosphere (ISA)
     d. pressure altitude

2.   Which of the following will contribute to a high density-altitude?
     a. high air pressure
     b. high humidity
     c. low temperature
     d. all of the above

3.   Which of the following statements is correct?
     a. Density-altitude affects takeoff performance but not landing performance.
     b. Density-altitude increases as altitude increases.
     c. Extra speed should be used to land at an airport with a high density-altitude to compensate for the thinner air.
     d. All of the above are correct.

4.   Which of the following combinations of atmospheric conditions will reduce airplane takeoff performance?
     a. high altitude, high temperature, and high humidity
     b. high altitude, high humidity, and low temperature
     c. high altitude, low temperature, and low humidity
     d. low altitude, low temperature, and low humidity

5.   Refer to Figure 6.1. Assuming an airport elevation of 3165 feet, an outside air temperature of 93 degrees Fahrenheit, and an altimeter setting of 30.10 inches of mercury, what is the density-altitude?
     a. 3000 feet
     b. 3850 feet
     c. 5800 feet
     d. 6800 feet

6.   Suppose that the elevation of an airport is 3165 feet, the outside air temperature is 70 degrees Fahrenheit, and the altimeter setting is 30.10 inches of mercury. Using Figure 6.1, the density-altitude is determined to be approximately
    a. 3000 feet
    b. 3350 feet
    c. 4350 feet
    d. 6200 feet

7.   Which of the following conditions will increase the takeoff roll?
    a. a downhill gradient
    b. a headwind
    c. a soft field
    d. decreasing gross weight

8.   Given:

    Landing runway   29
    Wind   240° at 25 knots

    Refer to Figure 6.2. What is the crosswind component?
    a. 19 knots
    b. 21 knots
    c. 25 knots
    d. 30 knots

9.   Refer to Figure 6.2. The wind is reported to be from 360° at 15 knots and you plan to land on runway 4. What will be the headwind component?
    a. 8 knots
    b. 10 knots
    c. 12 knots
    d. 14 knots

10.   If the barometer is 30.32 and you are at 120 feet MSL, what is the pressure altitude?
    a. −280 feet
    b. 80 feet
    c. 100 feet
    d. 520 feet

11.   Given:

    Gross weight   1500 pounds
    Pressure altitude   2500 feet
    Outside temperature   100 degrees Fahrenheit (38 degrees Celsius)
    Wind (headwind)   10 knots
    Runway surface   Grass

Refer to Figure 6.3. What is the total takeoff distance required to clear a 50-foot obstacle?

    a. 1300 feet
    b. 1500 feet
    c. 1700 feet
    d. 1900 feet

12.   Given:

Pressure altitude	4000 feet
Outside temperature	41 degrees Fahrenheit (5 degrees Celsius)
Gross weight	1600 pounds
Tailwind	5 knots
Runway surface	Hard

Refer to Figure 6.3. What is the total takeoff distance?

    a.   900 feet
    b. 1100 feet
    c. 1300 feet
    d. 1500 feet

To answer questions 13 and 14, refer to Figure 6.10.

13.   Given:

Pressure altitude	5000 feet
Gross weight	1700 pounds
Outside temperature	91 degrees Fahrenheit
Wind (headwind)	10 knots

The total takeoff distance required to clear a 50-foot obstacle is

    a. 984 feet
    b. 1000 feet
    c. 1250 feet
    d. 1500 feet

14.   Given:

Gross weight	2300 pounds
Outside temperature	109 degrees Fahrenheit
Pressure altitude	Sea level
Wind (headwind)	10 knots

TAKE-OFF DATA

TAKE-OFF DISTANCE FROM HARD SURFACE RUNWAY WITH FLAPS UP

GROSS WEIGHT POUNDS	IAS AT 50' MPH	HEAD WIND KNOTS	AT SEA LEVEL & 59°		AT 2500 FT. & 50°F		AT 5000 FT. & 41°F		AT 7500 FT. & 32°F	
			GROUND RUN	TOTAL TO CLEAR 50 FT OBS	GROUND RUN	TOTAL TO CLEAR 50 FT OBS	GROUND RUN	TOTAL TO CLEAR 50 FT OBS	GROUND RUN	TOTAL TO CLEAR 50 FT OBS
2300	68	0	865	1525	1040	1910	1255	2480	1565	3855
		10	615	1170	750	1485	920	1955	1160	3110
		20	405	850	505	1100	630	1480	810	2425
2000	63	0	630	1095	755	1325	905	1625	1120	2155
		10	435	820	530	1005	645	1250	810	1685
		20	275	580	340	720	425	910	595	1255
1700	58	0	435	780	520	920	625	1095	765	1370
		10	290	570	355	680	430	820	535	1040
		20	175	385	215	470	270	575	345	745

NOTES: 1. Increase distance 10% for each 25°F above standard temperature for particular altitude.
2. For operation on a dry, grass runway, increase distances (both "ground run" and "total to clear 50 ft. obstacle") by 7% of the "total to clear 50 ft. obstacle" figure.

Figure 6.10

The total takeoff distance required to clear a 50-foot obstacle is
a. 936 feet
b. 1404 feet
c. 1170 feet
d. 2042 feet

15. Refer to Figure 6.4a. Assume that it is 30 degrees Celsius, that the pressure altitude is 2000 feet, and that you are at 1550 pounds gross weight. What will your rate of climb be?
a. 550 feet per minute
b. 600 feet per minute
c. 650 feet per minute
d. 700 feet per minute

16. Refer to Figure 6.4b. Assume that you depart Lubbock (pressure altitude: 2000), where it is 18 degrees Celsius, and climb to a pressure altitude of 9500, where it is −2 degrees Celsius. What is your time to reach cruising altitude?
a. 13 minutes
b. 15 minutes
c. 17 minutes
d. 20 minutes

To answer questions 17 and 18, refer to Figure 6.11.

MAXIMUM RATE-OF-CLIMB DATA

GROSS WEIGHT POUNDS	AT SEA LEVEL & 59°F			AT 5000 FT. & 41°F			AT 10,000 FT. & 23°F			AT 15,000 FT. & 5°F		
	IAS MPH	RATE OF CLIMB FT MIN	GAL. OF FUEL USED	IAS MPH	RATE OF CLIMB FT MIN	FROM S.L. FUEL USED	IAS MPH	RATE OF CLIMB FT MIN	FROM S.L. FUEL USED	IAS MPH	RATE OF CLIMB FT MIN	FROM S.L. FUEL USED
2300	82	645	1.0	81	435	2.6	79	230	4.8	78	22	11.5
2000	79	840	1.0	79	610	2.2	76	380	3.6	75	155	6.3
1700	77	1085	1.0	76	825	1.9	73	570	2.9	72	315	4.4

NOTES: 1. Flaps up, full throttle, mixture leaned for smooth operation above 3000 ft.
2. Fuel used includes warm up and take-off allowance.
3. For hot weather, decrease rate of climb 20 ft. min. for each 10°F above standard day temperature for particular altitude.

Figure 6.11

17.   Given:

   Pressure altitude   Sea level
   Temperature   89 degrees Fahrenheit
   Gross weight   2000 pounds
   Indicated airspeed   79 miles per hour

Obtain the altimeter indication after a 5-minute climb following takeoff.
a. 3900 feet
b. 4000 feet
c. 4100 feet
d. 4260 feet

18.   Given:

   Pressure altitude   5000 feet
   Temperature   51 degrees Fahrenheit
   Gross weight   2000 pounds
   Indicated airspeed   79 miles per hour

   How much altitude would you expect to gain after takeoff and climb for 3 minutes?
   a. 1770 feet
   b. 1810 feet
   c. 1830 feet
   d. 1850 feet

19. Refer to Figures 6.5 and 6.6. Given a barometric setting of 30.36 and an indicated altitude of 5500 feet, what is your true airspeed and your fuel flow per hour?
    a. 87 miles per hour; 5.0 gallons per hour
    b. 93 miles per hour; 5.6 gallons per hour
    c. 97 miles per hour; 6.3 gallons per hour
    d. impossible to determine given these data

20. Refer to Figures 6.5 and 6.6. Given a barometric setting of 29.22 and an indicated altitude of 5500 feet, what is your true airspeed and your fuel flow per hour if you maintain 2500 rpm?
    a. 92 miles per hour; 5.4 gallons per hour
    b. 92 miles per hour; 6.1 gallons per hour
    c. 97 miles per hour; 6.1 gallons per hour
    d. 97 miles per hour; 5.4 gallons per hour

21. Refer to Figures 6.7 and 6.8. Assume a pressure altitude of 8000 feet and 2400 rpm. What is your maximum range and maximum endurance?
    a. 385 miles; 4.1 hours
    b. 405 miles; 4.5 hours
    c. 425 miles; 4.7 hours
    d. 450 miles; 4.1 hours

22. Refer to Figure 6.7. How much could you extend your range at a pressure altitude of 6400 feet if you were to reduce the throttle from 2400 rpm to 2300 rpm?
    a. 6 miles
    b. 8 miles
    c. 10 miles
    d. 12 miles

To answer questions 23 and 24, refer to Figure 6.12.

23. Given:

Gross weight	2750 pounds
Outside air temperature	52 degrees Fahrenheit
Pressure altitude	2000 feet
Wind (down runway)	8 knots

The total landing distance over a 50-foot obstacle would be
    a. 1397 feet
    b. 1560 feet
    c. 1622 feet
    d. 1856 feet

NORMAL LANDING DISTANCES

ASSOCIATED CONDITIONS

POWER	OFF
FLAPS	35
GEAR	DOWN
RUNWAY	PAVED, LEVEL, DRY SURFACE
WEIGHT	2750 POUNDS
APPROACH SPEED	85 MPH/74 KTS IAS

NOTES:

1. GROUND ROLL IS APPROXIMATELY 45% OF TOTAL DISTANCE OVER 50 FT. OBSTACLE
2. FOR EACH 100 LBS. BELOW 2750 LBS. REDUCE TABULATED DISTANCE BY 3% AND APPROACH SPEED BY 1 MPH.

WIND COMPONENT DOWN RUNWAY KNOTS	SEA LEVEL		2000 FT		4000 FT		6000 FT		8000 FT	
	OAT °F	TOTAL OVER 50 FT OBSTACLE FEET	OAT °F	TOTAL OVER 50 FT OBSTACLE FEET	OAT °F	TOTAL OVER 50 FT OBSTACLE FEET	OAT °F	TOTAL OVER 50 FT OBSTACLE FEET	OAT °F	TOTAL OVER 50 FT OBSTACLE FEET
0	23	1578	16	1651	9	1732	2	1820	6	1916
	41	1624	34	1701	27	1787	20	1880	13	1983
	59	1670	52	1752	45	1842	38	1942	31	2050
	77	1717	70	1804	63	1899	56	2004	49	2118
	95	1764	88	1856	81	1956	74	2066	66	2187
15	23	1329	16	1397	9	1472	2	1555	6	1644
	41	1372	34	1444	27	1524	20	1611	13	1707
	59	1414	52	1491	45	1575	38	1668	31	1770
	77	1458	70	1540	63	1626	56	1727	49	1833
	95	1502	88	1588	81	1682	74	1784	66	1898
30	23	1079	16	1142	9	1212	2	1289	6	1372
	41	1119	34	1186	27	1260	20	1341	13	1430
	59	1158	52	1230	45	1308	38	1395	31	1489
	77	1199	70	1275	63	1357	56	1449	49	1548
	95	1240	88	1320	81	1407	74	1502	66	1608

Figure 6.12

24.   Given:

Gross weight	2750 pounds
Outside air temperature	36 degrees Fahrenheit
Pressure altitude	4000 feet
Wind	Calm

The total landing distance over a 50-foot obstacle would be

a. 1787 feet
b. 1797 feet
c. 1815 feet
d. 1842 feet

To answer questions 25–27, refer to Figure 6.13.

GROSS WEIGHT LBS.	APPROACH SPEED, IAS, MPH	AT SEA LEVEL & 59° F.		AT 2500 FT. & 50° F.		AT 5000 FT. & 41° F.		AT 7500 FT. & 32° F.	
		GROUND ROLL	TOTAL TO CLEAR 50 FT. OBS	GROUND ROLL	TOTAL TO CLEAR 50 FT. OBS	GROUND ROLL	TOTAL TO CLEAR 50 FT. OBS	GROUND ROLL	TOTAL TO CLEAR 50 FT. OBS
1600	60	445	1075	470	1135	495	1195	520	1255

—LANDING DISTANCE— FLAPS LOWERED TO 40° - POWER OFF HARD SURFACE RUNWAY - ZERO WIND

NOTES: 1. Decrease the distances shown by 10% for each 4 knots of headwind.
2. Increase the distance by 10% for each 60°F. temperature increase above standard.
3. For operation on a dry, grass runway, increase distances (both "ground roll" and "total to clear 50 ft. obstacle") by 20% of the "total to clear 50 ft. obstacle" figure.

Figure 6.13

25. Given:

Gross weight	1600 pounds
Pressure altitude	3750 feet
Headwind	12 knots
Temperature	46 degrees Fahrenheit

What would be the approximate landing ground roll distance?
a. 338 feet
b. 432 feet
c. 445 feet
d. 470 feet

26. Given:

Gross weight	1600 pounds
Pressure altitude	1250 feet
Wind	4 knots
Temperature	55 degrees Fahrenheit

What would be the approximate landing ground roll distance?
a. 412 feet
b. 445 feet
c. 458 feet
d. 504 feet

27. Given:

Gross weight	1600 pounds
Pressure altitude	3750 feet
Wind	Calm
Temperature	46 degrees Fahrenheit

What would be the approximate total distance required to land over a 50-foot obstacle?
- a. 1105 feet
- b. 1135 feet
- c. 1165 feet
- d. 1195 feet

28.   After takeoff, which of the following airspeeds would permit the pilot to gain the most altitude in a given period of time?
- a. best angle of climb speed
- b. best rate of climb speed
- c. cruising climb speed
- d. minimum control speed

ANSWERS

Key Terms and Concepts

1.	f	2.	q	3.	i	4.	g
5.	e	6.	b	7.	s	8.	j
9.	r	10.	o	11.	h	12.	c
13.	m	14.	a	15.	d	16.	l
17.	p	18.	n	19.	k	20.	t
21.	u						

Discussion Questions and Exercises

4.a. About 8400 feet. Read up the chart from 98 degrees Fahrenheit (use interpolation) until you intersect the 5000-foot line (plus a little). Now read over to the ordinate (density-altitude).

b. About −25 degrees Celsius or −13 degrees Fahrenheit. Read across from density-altitude (on the ordinate) until the horizontal 10,000-foot line intersects the diagonal 12,000-foot pressure altitude line. Next, read *down* to the abscissa (temperature) from this intersection.

c. The exact answer is impossible to determine from this graph because the two lines do not intersect.

8. He or she is saying that, with respect to the *magnetic* compass, the wind is out of the southeast (120°) at 15 knots.

9. 720 feet. To figure this, subtract 30.18 from 29.92 = −0.26 inches of mercury, which times 1000 (1 inch mercury = 1000 feet in altitude) yields −260 feet, which must be subtracted from Ashland's field elevation to yield a pressure altitude of 720 feet.

10.a. Headwind component = 10 knots; crosswind component = 28 knots. Moving along the curved 30-knot line, find the intersection of 30 knots and 70° (360° − 290° = 70°), then read across (to the ordinate) to determine the headwind component (10 knots) and down (to the abscissa) to determine the crosswind component (28 knots).

b. Read up from 20 knots on the abscissa (crosswind component) until you intersect the vertical line that represents 20 knots on the ordinate (headwind component). At this point, you have to construct a curved line that "parallels" or coincides with the curved line that represents a wind speed of 30 knots. Using interpolation, that comes out to be about 28 knots. To figure wind direction, one must again use interpolation, this time between the 40° and 50° Angle between Wind Direction and Flight Path line. The angle is about 45°. You are departing runway 7 (70°), so the wind is coming from either (70° − 45° = 25°) or (70° + 45° = 115°). From these data, it is impossible to determine which direction.

11. At least 1000 feet. Use the grass surface chart. Find 20 degrees Celsius on the OAT axis (abscissa) and read up to the pressure altitude line (980 feet). Read across horizontally to the reference line. Project the sloped line until you intersect 1620 pounds, then read across to the next reference line. Project the headwind line diagonally until you intersect 10 knots, then read across to the last reference line. Now project the obstacle height line diagonally and read the takeoff distance from the right ordinate. Since the guideline is not applicable for intermediate distances, assume that you have to clear a 50-foot obstacle. *Note:* The chart shows distances based on a level dry grass surface with a firm subsoil. A takeoff on a hard-packed gravel surface could require somewhat more distance.

12. About 900 feet. First, you need to figure pressure altitude: (29.92 − 29.32) × 1000 = 600 feet, which must be added to field elevation, so the pressure altitude is 5470. Second, you need to figure the wind component, so refer to Figure 6.2. The angle is 340 − 310 = 30°. 30° intersects the 18-knot curved line, yielding a headwind component of about 15 knots. Now you are ready for Figure 6.3. Read up from 22 degrees Celsius until you intersect 5470 feet. Read across to the reference line and project diagonally until you intersect 1500 pounds. Read across to the next reference line and project down diagonally until you intersect 15 knots of headwind. Then read across to the distance scale, which in this case is about 900 feet.

14.a. Read up Figure 6.4b from 6 degrees Celsius until you intersect the 8000-foot curved line and read across to the reference line. Next, go diagonally up the chart parallel to the nearest line until you intersect 1500 pounds. Then read across to the rate of climb ordinate, which in this case is approximately 470 feet per minute.

b. Refer to Figure 6.4b. For the initial value, read up from 22 degrees Celsius to pressure altitude 5470, across to the curved line, and down to the scales at the bottom (8 minutes to climb, 1 gallon of fuel, and 8 miles). Next, do the same for −2 degrees Celsius and 9500 feet + 600 feet (correction for current atmospheric conditions) = 10,100 feet. This yields 24 minutes, 2.8 gallons of gas, and 27 nautical miles. Subtracting the initial values from the final values yields 16 minutes to climb using 1.8 gallons of fuel to get 19 miles from the airport.

17. The pressure altitude is 9500 feet + 600 feet (correction for current atmospheric conditions) = 10,100 feet. Reading across Figure 6.5 from 10,100 feet to the 2400-rpm line and then down to the abscissa (time airspeed), you obtain a value of about 89.5 knots.

18.   The altitude, corrected for current atmospheric conditions, is 10,100 feet (9500 + 600). Looking at 2400 rpm cruise for 9500 feet yields 5.2 gallons per hour, while at 10,500 feet, it is 5.1 gallons. Interpolating between these two values yields 5.2 gallons per hour. Using the same process for IAS and TAS yields 78 knots and 90 knots, respectively.

19.   On Figure 6.7 read over from a pressure altitude of 10,100 to the 2400-rpm line and then down to the range, which in this example is 409 miles. On Figure 6.8 read over from a pressure altitude of 10,100 feet until you intersect 2400 rpm, then read down to endurance, which in this example is 4.64 hours, or 4 hours and 38 minutes.

22.a.   Your takeoff weight was 1500 pounds and you burned 18 gallons × 6 pounds per gallon, so the gross landing weight is 1500 − 108 = 1392 pounds.

   b.   ([29.92 − 30.04] × 1000) + 232 feet = −120 + 232 = 188 feet MSL. The density-altitude for 20 degrees Celsius at 188 feet is approximately 800 feet.

   c.   The headwind component is approximately 6 knots and the crosswind component is about 8 knots.

   d.   Using Figure 6.9, read up from 20 degrees Celsius to the 188-foot line (close to the SL, or sea level, line) and over to the reference line. Go down parallel to the nearest diagonal line until you intersect 6 knots (the headwind component) and then across to the last reference line. Now go diagonally up to determine the landing distance, which in this example is about 1100 feet.

Review Questions

Note: Since the review questions parallel the discussion questions, detailed explanations of the calculations are not given. Use the corresponding discussion questions as sources if your answers do not agree with these.

1.   d; this is how one measures pressure altitude. Another way to calculate it is to remember the formula ([29.92 − current pressure] × 1000) + field (or true) elevation. Remember, current pressure can be greater than 29.92, in which case you would subtract the resulting number from field or true elevation.

2.   b; low pressure, high humidity, and high temperature all increase density-altitude.

3.   b; as altitude increases, air pressure decreases, which in turn leads to a higher density-altitude. Approach speed should stay the same. You should remember, however, that at high density-altitudes, you will be moving faster relative to the ground at the same indicated airspeed. Finally, density-altitude affects both takeoff *and* landing performance.

4.   a; all of these contribute to high density-altitude, which in turn affects the lift that can be generated and the power that can be developed to effect takeoff. The higher the density-altitude is, the longer the takeoff roll and slower the rate of climb.

5. c; see the answer to discussion question 4 for a detailed explanation of how to use the density-altitude charts.

6. c; see the answer to discussion question 4.

7. c; a soft field provides more resistance for the wheels and thus increases the takeoff roll, as will increasing the gross weight, taking off uphill, tailwinds, moving the CG forward, and increasing the density-altitude.

8. a; $290° - 240° = 50°$ crosswind component. Use interpolation to find the 25-knot line and read down to find the crosswind component. See discussion question 10 for more detail.

9. c; see 8 above and the answer to discussion question 10.

10. a; use the formula outlined in review question 1: $([29.92 - 30.33] \times 1000)$ + true altitude = $(-0.4 \times 1000) + 120 = -400 + 120 = -280$ feet.

11. a; see the answer to discussion question 11 for details on how to solve this problem.

12. b; see the answer to discussion question 11.

13. a; read across from a gross weight of 1700 pounds to the 5000-foot column. The headwind component is 10 knots, so the value is 820 feet since you are going to have to clear a 50-foot obstacle. The outside temperature is 91 degrees − 41 degrees Fahrenheit = 50 degrees above standard temperatures for that altitude, so you have to increase 820 by 2×10 percent, or 20 percent, which is 164 feet. Total takeoff distance is thus 984 feet.

14. b; use the same procedure as in 13 above.

15. d; see the answer to discussion question 14.

16. c; see the answer to discussion question 14.

17. a; the final gross weight is 2000 pounds and IAS is 79 miles per hour. Read across to sea level. Your rate of climb is 840 feet per minute, so after 5 minutes you should be at $840 \times 5 = 4200$ feet. No, not quite. What have I forgotten? Air temperature, right? We need to subtract 20 feet per minute for every 10 degrees above 59 degrees Fahrenheit, so we subtract $3 \times 20 = 60$ feet per minute. Multiplying 780 feet per minute by 5, we arrive at 3900 feet.

18. a; see 17 above.

19. d; no rpm data are given, so it is impossible to calculate any results.

20. c; first figure the pressure altitude $(29.92 - 29.22 = .7 \times 1000 = 700$ feet + 5500 = 6200 feet. Read across Figure 6.5 on the 6200-foot line and when you intersect 2500 rpm, read down to TAS, in this case about 97 knots. Or read the value by interpolating from Figure 6.6. Use Figure 6.6 to find, again by interpolation, the fuel usage, 6.1 gallons per hour.

21. b; see the answer to discussion question 19.

22. c; see the answer to discussion question 19 for the use of Figure 6.11.

23. c; this requires interpolating between 0 and 15 knots; 8 knots is about halfway. At 52 degrees and 2000 feet for 0 knots, the landing distance is 1752 feet. At 52 degrees and 2000 feet for 15 knots, it is 1491 feet. Take the difference, 1752 − 1491 = 261, and divide by 2: 130.5. Now add this result to 1491 (or subtract from 1792) to get 1621.5 feet.

24.   c; here one must interpolate again, this time between 27 degrees and 45 degrees; 36 degrees is about halfway between. Applying the logic in 23 above, 1842 − 1787 = 55/2 = 28. Add 28 to 1787 and we get 1815 feet.

25.   a; interpolate midway between 2500 and 5000 feet (495 − 470 = 25/2 = 12.5). Add this to 470 to get 482.5. Correct for headwind by deducting 30 percent (or multiply by 0.7, which achieves the same end) to arrive at 338 feet.

26.   a; again, interpolation and correction for headwind are necessary, as in 25 above.

27.   c; use interpolation again, as in 25 above.

28.   b; this defines the best rate of climb.

7/AIRPORTS, AIRSPACE, AND LOCAL FLYING

MAIN POINTS

1. Airports with towers to supervise ground and air traffic are called **controlled;** those without towers are called **uncontrolled.** The airport and its surrounding territory is called the *terminal area*. Controlled airports have an **airport traffic area (ATA)** where specific procedures exist. The **local flying area** is a zone up to 50 miles from a given airport and typically has training areas set by local FBOs.

2. Planning a flight, even one in which you simply practice landings, requires considerable attention to details, such as the airplane, the weather (required by the FAA), and runway conditions. That is why normal procedures are conducted by reference to checklists. The *preflight inspection* includes an examination of various parts of the airplane. *Ground operations* require coordinating your attention between events outside the cabin and indicators inside the cabin. Once you take off, the *in-flight checklists* become relevant. Next, there is a *landing checklist*. Finally, there is a *postflight checklist* to complete before leaving the aircraft.

3. Specific emergency procedures for your airplane can be found in the Pilot's Operating Handbook. You should be thoroughly familiar with this information. In any emergency, there are three things you should do: maintain airplane control, analyze the situation and take proper action, and land as soon as conditions permit.

4. *Runways* are represented by one- or two-digit numbers corresponding to the magnetic heading divided by 10. For example, a runway with a magnetic heading of 210° is runway 21, and its reciprocal (when used in the opposite direction) is runway 3 (a heading of 030°). L (left), R (right), and C (center) are used to denote parallel runways. A **basic runway** has a white number with a dashed centerline. A nonprecision instrument approved runway displays threshold markings (broad parallel stripes) before

97

the runway number. Precision approach runways have more sophisticated markings (to be discussed in a later chapter). **Displaced thresholds** are marked by a series of chevrons at the end of the runway that create an area for clearance. This area may be used for rollout when landing in the opposite direction. A wide band of chevrons running up the center of the area before the threshold indicates an **overrun** or *stopway* that should not be used for any aircraft operation. An X at either end is used to mark a runway that is closed. **Taxiways** are marked with yellow centerlines. **Holding lines** are solid yellow lines that are perpendicular to the taxiway. They are at least 100 feet from the runway and are not to be crossed at controlled airports until cleared by the tower. Under category II operations, the tower may tell you to stop at special holding lines (two lines connected by bars).

5. Preestablished traffic patterns exist for operating at airports. This information is available from the tower at controlled airports and from an FSS or UNICOM frequency or from the **segmented circle** at uncontrolled airports. The segmented circle may have a tetrahedron and a wind cone or wind tee. The outside of the segmented circle may also have base to final approach indicators. An X in the circle means the field is closed.

6. Unless authorized by the FAA, the standard traffic pattern consists exclusively of left turns (except at entry). The legs of a pattern are: **upwind** or **takeoff,** to about 300 feet AGL; **crosswind,** 90 degrees to the upwind leg and not to be entered until crossing the departure end of the runway; **downwind,** parallel to the runway but in the opposite direction: it is typically flown at 1000 feet AGL, the **pattern altitude; base,** parallel to the crosswind leg but at the opposite end of the field; and **final,** upwind, in line with landing on the runway. The term *long final* refers to that portion just after turning from base; *short final* refers to that segment just prior to the threshold. Pattern entry is usually accomplished at an angle of 45 degrees to the downwind leg, while traffic departure usually involves a 45-degree turn away from the crosswind leg. At controlled airports, the tower will tell you what pattern restrictions apply.

7. The normal **glide path** is about 3 degrees to the horizon. Many airports have **visual approach slope indicators (VASI)** consisting of two or three sets of colored lights (white, pink, and red). A safe, correct approach is one where red is maintained over white. Red/pink and red/red indicate that the pilot is too low, and white/pink and white/white indicate that the pilot is too high.

8. An uncontrolled airport may have a facility designated an **Aeronautical Advisory Station (AAS)** and operate a private radio service called *UNICOM* (frequency shown on chart). Another use of UNICOM is for pilots to advise one another of taxiing, pattern, departure, and arrival intentions. (At controlled airfields, UNICOM operates on 122.95 or 123.0 and provides nontraffic service such as fuel requests.) Finally, when no UNICOM exists, use 122.9 (MULTICOM) for pilot communication. *Flight Service Stations* (FSS)—referred to, for example, as Kansas City Radio—provide weather

information, flight plan filing services, and airport advisory services if they are located at uncontrolled fields. Controlled airports require two-way radio communication authorization for any movement on the ground or in the ATA (5-mile radius and up to, but not including, 3000 feet AGL). The speed limit in an air traffic area (ATA) is 180 mph (156 knots). In the event of radio failure, light signals are used to give the pilot directions. At many busy airports, prerecorded information is available via **Automatic Terminal Information Serivce (ATIS).** Another service available at many airports is radar, whereby the controller can monitor progress and give specific approach and departure instructions. **Terminal Radar Programs** are available in two stages, II and III, depending upon the degree of control over IFR and VFR aircraft. At very busy airports, the control area is expanded to include a larger area of airspace called a **terminal control area (TCA).** It is shaped like an upside-down wedding cake, and positive control is exercised when operating within it. TCAs are of two types, I and II. Group II TCAs require a 4096-code transponder, two-way radio, and navigation radio; you must also operate in accordance with instructions given by the controller. Group I TCAs have even more stringent requirements (student pilots cannot land at group I TCA airports, and an encoding altimeter is required).

9. Controlled airspace also exists outside of airport terminal areas. The **positive control area (PCA)** exists from 18,000 feet MSL to 60,000 feet MSL, or FL 180 to FL 600, where FL means **flight level** and 180 refers to 18,000 feet. It is IFR territory and requires transponder and two-way radio. The **continental control area** (FL 145 up indefinitely) covers the 48 states and parts of Alaska and allows VFR flight (with certain restrictions). *Control areas* also exist for airways and other locations. **Control zones** help separate VFR from IFR traffic and exist around airports with instrument approach capability. They extend from the surface to the base of the continental control area and typically extend outward at least 5 miles from the airport. Flight under a ceiling in a control zone requires 3-mile visibility and a ceiling of at least 1000 feet. **Special VFR** clearance may be obtained in a control zone if you have 1-mile visibility and can stay clear of clouds. A control zone demarked by Ts on the chart means no special VFR is allowed. **Transition areas** around airports are indicated by magenta boundaries on sectional charts (a floor of 700 feet AGL) and around airways by blue boundaries (a 1200-foot floor). They extend up to the base of the continental control areas and are also designed to help separate VFR and IFR aircraft. Special-use areas include *prohibited areas* (no flights permitted), *restricted areas* (marked on charts; may be flown over only with permission), *warning areas*, *military operation areas* (MOAs), and *alert areas*. *Air Route Traffic Control Centers* (called "Center") may provide VFR pilots with radar monitoring if the controller's workload permits it.

10. Radio communication typically occurs on frequencies between 118.000 and 135.975 megahertz (MHz). Most modern radios have the transmitter and receiver combined in one unit (transceiver). Talking on the radio involves natural conversational tone and knowledge of the **phonetic alphabet.** There is no easy way to learn the phonetic alphabet except to memorize it. The quickest I have ever seen anyone learn

it accurately is two minutes. See if you can beat that record. If you do let me know how you did it. Some *numbers* are also pronounced in special ways. For example, nine is pronounced "niner." Multidigit numbers are given by saying each number individually (for example, "heading two zero zero"). When a decimal is present, it is referred to as "point" (for example, UNICOM might be "one two three point zero"). One exception to the decimal rule is barometric pressure, which is read without a decimal (for example, "three zero zero six"). Altitudes below 10,000 are read in thousands and hundreds (for example, "seven thousand two hundred"). From 10,000 to FL 180, the thousand digit is stated separately, followed by the hundreds (for example, "one three thousand four hundred" for 13,400). *Time* is given with reference to the Greenwich meridian (zulu time) and follows military standards (0000–2400 hours). *Airplane call signs* are used to identify each aircraft and are given without the prefix *N* (for example, Beechcraft N3456V would be identified "Beechcraft three four five six victor").

11. The following sequence is customary for initiating a radar communication: (1) ground facility being called, (2) aircraft call number, (3) location and altitude, (4) intentions, (5) other information (for example, ATIS received).

12. Night flying has its own peculiar characteristics and considerations. Night vision is different from daylight vision. Your eyes require a considerable *adaptation period* (20 to 30 minutes) to adjust to night vision, and this adjustment can easily be disrupted by sudden bursts of light. Cockpit illumination, whether red or white, should be kept at a minimum. Since night vision is concentrated in the eye's *peripheral* area, you may need to glance at objects quickly and indirectly several times to identify them correctly. Sometimes oxygen is recommended to maintain the pilot's visual acuity. Finally, you should be aware that illusions are much more prevalent at night than during the day.

13. Airplane lights include an **anticollision light** system (beacons or strobe lights), **position** or *navigation* **lights** (red, left wing; green, right wing; white, tail—required for night flight), and **landing lights.** Landing or position lights can be used to signal the control tower at night in the event of a radio failure. Airports are identified by a rotating beacon featuring alternating green and white lights at night (a double-flashing white light alternating with green indicates a military airfield). If the beacon is rotating during the day, it means the weather is below VFR minimums. If present, green lights indicate the threshold, red lights the departure end, white lights the side boundaries, and blue lights taxiway turnoffs. When flying at night, it is wise to carry a flashlight in the event the lights fail. Finally, when flying at night, rely primarily on your instruments and not your senses for the airplane's attitude, altitude, vertical speed, and airspeed. Instruments seldom lie (except when they malfunction); senses frequently do, especially at night.

14. When flying in the vicinity of large aircraft, pilots need to exercise extreme caution. Wake turbulence, such as that generated by the wing tips (called **wing tip**

vortices), is potentially hazardous, particularly in low-airspeed and high-lift situations, as when aircraft (yours included) take off and land. Since vortices drop at a rate of 400 to 500 feet per minute, do not pass directly below and behind a transport. On takeoff behind a "heavy," which will be delayed by the tower for at least 3 minutes, lift off *before* the heavy's rotation point and climb above its climb path. On landing, stay *above* the heavy's glide path and touch down beyond where it landed. Finally, on parallel runways, beware of vortices that may drift from one runway to the next. Another form of turbulence is **jet blast,** which is particularly prevalent on the ground directly behind transports at high power settings.

KEY TERMS AND CONCEPTS, PART 1

Match each term or concept (1–20) with the appropriate description (a–t) below. Each item has only one match.

___ 1. airport at night   ___ 2. departure
___ 3. words twice   ___ 4. prime meridian
___ 5. ceiling   ___ 6. airport traffic area
___ 7. autokinesis   ___ 8. threshold
___ 9. azimuth   ___ 10. group II TCA
___ 11. crosswind   ___ 12. alert area
___ 13. flashing white   ___ 14. control area
___ 15. ATIS   ___ 16. vector
___ 17. 156   ___ 18. restricted airspace

a.   leg of pattern not to be entered before you cross the departure end of the runway
b.   point beyond which landing aircraft can contact the runway
c.   exists at controlled airports with specific flight procedures—5-mile radius and up to 3000 feet AGL
d.   alternating green and white beacon
e.   red lights mark this end of the runway at night
f.   repeat each key word or phrase twice
g.   located in Greenwich, England
h.   synonymous with *direction*
i.   airspace in which operation must be authorized
j.   airspace that may, for example, contain a high volume of military pilot training
k.   lowest layer of clouds beneath which you are flying
l.   designated airspace such as a VOR federal airway
m.   airspeed (in knots) not to be exceeded in an ATA
n.   illusion that a fixed object moves when you stare at it
o.   two-way radio, 4096-code transponder, and mandatory radar service
p.   being given a heading and altitude to fly
q.   airport information service you are listening to at an airport that might begin "information echo"
r.   light signal used to indicate "return to starting point on airport"

KEY TERMS AND CONCEPTS, PART 2

Match each term or concept (1–20) with the appropriate description (a–t) below.
Each item has only one match.

— 1. glide slope
— 3. call sign
— 5. 19
— 7. FSS
— 9. UNICOM
—11. control zone
—13. prohibited area
—15. jet blast
—17. long final
—19. VHF

— 2. tetrahedron
— 4. taxiway turnoff
— 6. terminal area
— 8. vector
—10. verify
—12. holding line
—14. ARTCC
—16. positive control area
—18. uncontrolled

a.   where you file flight plans and receive weather information
b.   these are typical radio frequencies: 122.8, 123.0, 122.95
c.   angle of descent on final approach
d.   portion of the pattern after base leg
e.   three-dimensional triangle
f.   place on taxiway when you must stop at a controlled airport
g.   reciprocal runway heading indicator for magnetic 010°
h.   airport and its surrounding territory
i.   airport without an operating tower to control ground and air traffic
j.   exhaust gases emitted by heavy transports
k.   blue lights mark this point on the runway at night
l.   double-check the accuracy of the transmission
m.   118.000 to 135.975 MHz fall within these radio frequencies
n.   heading issued to an aircraft to provide navigational guidance by radar
o.   airspace in which aircraft flight is not allowed
p.   provides air traffic control to IFR flight along controlled airways
q.   FL 180 to FL 600
r.   airspace (typically at least a 5-mile radius from the airport) upward from the surface to 14,500 MSL
s.   aircraft identification number—for example, N7017G

KEY TERMS AND CONCEPTS, PART 3

Match each term or concept (1–21) with the appropriate description (a–u) below.
Each item has only one match.

— 1. wing tip vortices
— 3. upwind
— 5. short final
— 7. local flying area
— 9. 45

— 2. Stage III radar service
— 4. squelch
— 6. rock your wings
— 8. steady red
—10. flashing red

___11. read back   ___12. magenta
___13. transponder   ___14. MULTICOM
___15. transmitter   ___16. X
___17. 3   ___18. position lights
___19. nonprecision approach   ___20. segmented circle
___21. clear

a.   positive radar separation of all VFR and IFR traffic, unless the pilot requests otherwise
b.   radio device that sends out a signal when it detects a radar wave
c.   signal you should use when your radio has failed to let a control tower know that you have received a signal
d.   light signal used to indicate "give way to other aircraft; continue to circle"
e.   light signal used to indicate "airport unsafe—do not land"
f.   color used to depict uncontrolled airports and their legends
g.   122.9, the frequency used for radio transmissions during special events
h.   a flight path parallel to the landing runway in the direction of landing
i.   normal glide slope angle (degrees)
j.   portion of the pattern just prior to the threshold
k.   this device typically has approach to final indicators
l.   markings on a runway to indicate that it is closed
m.   angle at which you should enter the downwind leg
n.   runway with only a heading number, dashed centerline, and broad parallel stripes
o.   area up to 50 miles from a given airport
p.   word you should yell before engaging the starter
q.   miniature horizontal cyclones generated by heavy transports
r.   lights on the wing tips and tail
s.   repeat all the transmission that has just been received
t.   portion of a radio that broadcasts
u.   transceiver control that balances volume and static

KEY TERMS AND CONCEPTS, PART 4

Match each term or concept (1–21) with the appropriate description (a–u) below. Each item has only one match.

___ 1. anticollision light   ___ 2. engine starting checklist
___ 3. chevrons   ___ 4. downwind
___ 5. controlled airport   ___ 6. overrun
___ 7. basic runway   ___ 8. base
___ 9. group I TCA   ___10. transceiver
___11. UHF   ___12. transition area
___13. active   ___14. Stage II radar service
___15. MOA   ___16. reciprocal
___17. continental control area   ___18. flashing green
___19. peripheral vision

a.   airspace designated for military operations
b.   field of vision to either side of the eyes when the eyes are focused
c.   controlled airspace extending upward from 700 feet (from an airport with an instrument approach) or 1200 feet (from an airway) upward to the base of the next control area
d.   airspace over the 48 states and parts of Alaska from 14,500 MSL upward
e.   two-way radio, encoding altimeter, mandatory radar service, no student pilots landing at or taking off from the primary airport
f.   radar sequencing of arriving VFR and IFR traffic; advisories for departing VFR traffic
g.   light signal used to indicate "clear to taxi"
h.   a direction 180° from a given direction
i.   airport with an operating tower to control ground and air traffic
j.   beacon or strobe system on fuselage
k.   area of a runway marked by a wide band of chevrons indicating that this area should not be used for any aircraft operation
l.   pattern leg parallel to the runway but in the opposite direction from it
m.   pattern leg parallel to crosswind but at the opposite end of the field
n.   radio transmitter and receiver combined in a single unit
o.   markings on a runway to indicate a displaced threshold
p.   runway with only a heading number and dashed centerline
q.   initial oil pressure check occurs with reference to this checklist
r.   runway being used for takeoffs and landings
s.   radio frequencies used mostly for military communications

DISCUSSION QUESTIONS AND EXERCISES

1.   What is the difference between a controlled and an uncontrolled airport? What is the difference between an airport traffic area and the local flying area?

2.   Name three things typical checklists require pilots to do during each of these phases:

   a. preflight inspection

   b. engine starting

c. before and during takeoff

d. climb, cruise, and descent

e. before landing

f. after landing and shutdown

3.   Although emergency procedures vary from aircraft to aircraft, there are three basic rules that apply to all aircraft and all emergencies. What are they?

4.   Briefly characterize each of the following:

a. basic runway

b. runway heading indicator

c. nonprecision approach runway

d. displaced threshold

e. closed runway

f. taxiway

g. holding line

h. overrun

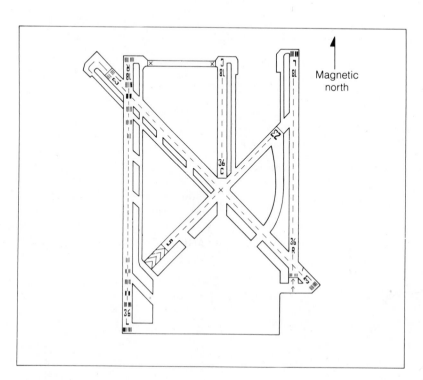

Figure 7.1

5.   Refer to Figure 7.1. Indicate for each approach end what type of runway it is and what specific restrictions, if any, apply.

6.   What is a segmented circle? Draw one for the following airport: runways 2-20 with left traffic for R2 and right traffic for R20; runways 10-28 with left traffic for R10 and right traffic for R28. The wind is from 290°. Put a tetrahedron in the circle. If you were landing here, what runway would you land on and what would be the traffic pattern direction?

7.   Use the data in discussion question 6 and suppose that you have decided to practice some touch and goes. The wind is still 290° at 15 knots. The pattern altitude is 1000 feet, field elevation is 2720 feet, and the barometric pressure is 29.54. Describe how you will fly the pattern, indicating for each leg the direction of flight (you do not need to adjust for the crab angle), altitude AGL, and altitude on the altimeter.

8.   Briefly describe the meanings of the color components of the visual approach slope indicator (VASI).

9.   Briefly characterize each of the following. Include special restrictions, communication functions, and communication frequencies or procedures as appropriate.

    a. UNICOM

    b. MULTICOM

    c. FSS

    d. ATA

e. ATIS

f. Stage I radar service

g. Stage II radar service

h. Stage III radar service

i. group I TCA

j. group II TCA

10.   Briefly indicate what each of the following light signals means for both ground and air operations:

a. steady green

b. flashing green

c. steady red

d. flashing red

e. flashing white

f. alternating red and green

11.   Indicate what you should do if your radio fails in each of the following conditions:

a. The receiver fails in flight.

b. You have no radio capability on the ground.

c. The transmitter and receiver fail in flight.

d. The transmitter fails in flight.

12. What is the difference between controlled and uncontrolled airspace?

13. Briefly describe each of the following control areas. It may help to draw a picture.

a. positive control area

b. continental control area

c. control area

d. control zone

e. transition area

f. prohibited area

g. restricted area

h. military operations area (MOA)

i. Air Route Traffic Control Center (ARTCC)

14.   You need to commit the phonetic alphabet to memory. If you have not learned
it, study the letters and their names right now. Then reproduce as many as you can
from memory in the space below. Once you have done as many as you can, complete
the table, if necessary, by referring to your textbook. This exercise will help you learn
the alphabet and will serve as a handy reference for review.

15.   Describe exactly how you would say each of the following using standard radio
communication language:

    a. Beechcraft N2497C

    b. a heading of 290°

    c. an altitude of 3120 feet

    d. an altitude of 15,800 feet

e. 2240 zulu

f. Kansas City ARTCC

g. Birmingham FSS

h. Repeat the transmission that was just received.

i. Double-check the accuracy of the transmission.

j. The message has been received and understood.

k. 123.6

l. a barometer reading of 30.09

16.   List the five things you should state when initiating radio contact.

17.   Suppose that you are flying in a Beechcraft 77 (N7280Q) equipped with a two-way radio and transponder (squawking 1200) over Marietta, Georgia, at 5500 feet on

a heading of 170°. You intend to land at Dekalb airfield and have carefully listened to the ATIS, information echo. Write out exactly what you would say when contacting Atlanta Approach Control.

18.   Identify four extra precautions you should take when preparing for a night flight.

19.   What is autokinesis? Give an example. What should you do to recover from it?

20.   Briefly describe the function and location of each of the following airplane lights:

        a. anticollision light

        b. position (navigation) lights

        c. landing lights

21.   What lights should you use to signal a control tower if your radio fails in flight?

22.   Briefly describe standard runway lighting, taxi lighting, and beacon configurations at civilian and military airports.

23.   What are wing tip vortices? When and why are they most dangerous? Describe how you should avoid them during each of the following:

    a. flight

    b. takeoff

    c. landing

REVIEW QUESTIONS
1.   The runway being used for takeoffs and landing is referred to as the _____ runway.
    a. active
    b. authorized
    c. current
    d. landing

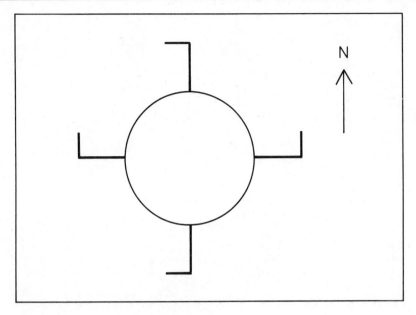

Figure 7.2

2.   The segmented circle shown in Figure 7.2 indicates that the airport traffic is
      a. left-hand for runway 17 and right-hand for runway 35
      b. left-hand for runway 35 and right-hand for runway 17
      c. right-hand for runway 9 and left-hand for runway 27
      d. right-hand for runway 35 and right-hand for runway 9

3.   Which of the following wind indicators has (have) the small end pointing into
the direction of the wind?
      a. tetrahedron
      b. tetrahedron, wind cone
      c. tetrahedron, wind tee
      d. wind cone, wind tee

4.   The numbering of runways 13 and 31 at Topeka indicates that the runway is
oriented approximately
      a. 013° and 031° magnetic
      b. 013° and 031° true
      c. 130° and 310° magnetic
      d. 130° and 310° true

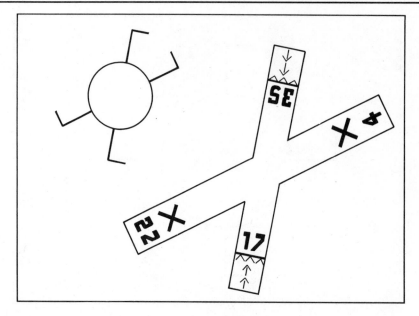

Figure 7.3

5.   Refer to the runway markings and segmented circle in Figure 7.3. Which statement is correct?
     a. Only runways 35 and 17 are authorized for takeoffs and landings.
     b. You should land on runway 22 using left-hand traffic, as it is aligned with
        the prevailing wind direction.
     c. You may land on runways 35 and 17 but must stop prior to crossing runways
        4 and 22.
     d. You should plan your approach to land beyond the X marking on runway 4.

     To answer questions 6–8, refer to Figure 7.4.

6.   Which hand signal means "cut engines"?
     a. B
     b. H
     c. I
     d. K

7.   Suppose that a signaler were to give you the following directions: start engine,
come ahead, turn right, and all clear. What is the correct sequence?
     a. B, H, F, D
     b. B, D, E, A
     c. K, A, F, H
     d. D, K, E, A

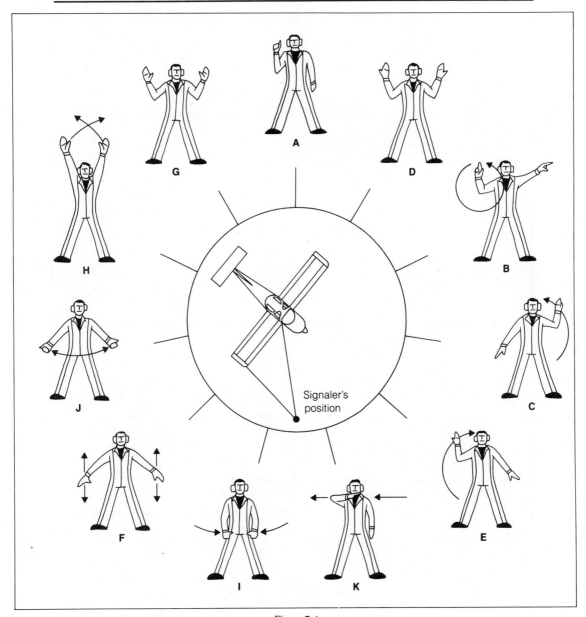

Figure 7.4

8.	The hand signal labeled D means
	a. come ahead
	b. emergency stop
	c. OK
	d. stop

9.   Solid yellow lines that run perpendicular to the taxiway are called
      a. displaced thresholds
      b. holding lines
      c. stopways
      d. thresholds

10.   What leg(s) of a standard traffic pattern is (are) flown perpendicular to the
downwind leg?
      a. base, crosswind
      b. base, final
      c. crosswind, final
      d. final

11.   The normal glide path is about _____ to the horizon.
      a. 3 degrees
      b. 5 degrees
      c. 10 degrees
      d. 15 degrees

12.   White over white on the visual approach slope indicator (VASI) means
      a. above the glide path
      b. below the glide path
      c. on the glide path
      d. system inoperative

13.   Assume that you are approaching an airport that is equipped with a visual
approach slope indicator (VASI). To comply with regulations, an airplane approaching
to land on a runway served by a VASI should
      a. intercept and remain on the glide slope until touchdown only if the aircraft
         is operating on an instrument flight plan
      b. maintain an altitude at or above the glide slope
      c. maintain an altitude that captures the glide slope at least 2 miles downwind
         from the runway threshold
      d. remain below the glide slope

14.   At uncontrolled airports not served by UNICOM, it is a good operating practice
to broadcast position and intentions on the MULTICOM frequency of
      a. 121.5 MHz
      b. 122.9 MHz
      c. 123.0 MHz
      d. 123.6 MHz

15.   Automatic Terminal Information Service (ATIS) is the continuous broadcast of
recorded information

     a. alerting pilots of radar identified aircraft when their aircraft is in unsafe proximity to terrain or obstructions

     b. of a routine, noncontrolling nature in selected high-activity terminal areas

     c. concerning nonessential information to relieve frequency congestion

     d. concerning sky conditions limited to ceilings below 1000 feet and visibilities of less than 3 miles

16. If Air Traffic Control advises that radar service is being terminated when you are departing a terminal radar service area, the transponder should be set to code

     a. 0000

     b. 1200

     c. 4096

     d. 7700

17. Which statement about UNICOM is correct?

     a. UNICOM frequencies are assigned exclusively for communication purposes at private airports.

     b. UNICOM frequencies are used by Flight Service Stations at airports without towers to provide airport advisory service.

     c. UNICOM is not to be used for air traffic control purposes.

     d. UNICOM is used for air traffic control purposes at airports without towers.

18. Where are airport traffic areas in effect?

     a. at all airports

     b. at all airports that have a Flight Service Station on the field

     c. only at airports that have an operating control tower

     d. only at airports within a control zone

19. Stage III service within terminal radar service areas (TRSAs) utilizes radar to provide

     a. radar vectoring if the weather minimums are below VFR conditions

     b. separation between all participating VFR aircraft and IFR aircraft operating within TRSAs

     c. separation between all VFR aircraft operating within TRSAs

     d. separation between IFR aircraft, because VFR aircraft are not permitted in the area

20. A group I terminal control area (TCA)

     a. cannot be used by student pilots who are flying solo for landing or taking off from the primary airport

     b. requires an encoding altimeter and transponder

     c. requires two-way radio communication

     d. all of the above

21.   With regard to operating within a group I terminal control area (TCA), which of the following statements is correct?
   a. Authorization from ATC is required prior to operating in the area.
   b. Private pilots are not permitted to fly within the TCA.
   c. The pilot must be instrument rated and must file an IFR flight plan.
   d. All of the above statements are correct.

22.   A steady red ATC light signal directed to an aircraft on the ground is a signal to the pilot of that aircraft to
   a. exercise extreme caution
   b. return to the starting point on the airport
   c. stop taxiing
   d. taxi clear of the runway in use

23.   If you receive an alternating red and green light from a control tower during final approach for landing, what action should you take?
   a. Exercise extreme caution.
   b. Give way to other aircraft and continue circling.
   c. No action since this light is not applicable to aircraft in flight.
   d. You would not land; the airport is unsafe.

24.   A steady green ATC light signal directed to an aircraft on the ground is a signal that the pilot
   a. is cleared to take off
   b. should exercise extreme caution
   c. should return to the starting point on the airport
   d. should stop taxiing

25.   What flight levels are included in the positive control area?
   a. 3000 to 14,500 feet MSL
   b. 10,000 to 48,000 feet MSL
   c. 14,500 to 60,000 feet MSL
   d. 18,000 to 60,000 feet MSL

26.   Unless otherwise authorized, two-way radio communications with ATC are required for landings or takeoffs
   a. at tower-controlled airports within control zones only when weather conditions are less than VFR
   b. at all tower-controlled airports only when weather conditions are less than VFR
   c. at all tower-controlled airports regardless of the weather conditions
   d. within control zones regardless of the weather conditions

27.   When operating an airplane within a control zone under special VFR
   a. the pilot must remain clear of clouds
   b. visibility must be at least 1 statute mile

c. both a and b

d. neither a nor b

28. _____ extend upward from either 700 feet AGL (near airports) or 1200 feet AGL (near airways) to the base of the continental control area.

a. control areas

b. control zones

c. restricted areas

d. transition areas

29. Unless otherwise indicated, a magenta boundary around a transition area means that it has a floor of _____ feet AGL.

a. 700

b. 1200

c. 3000

d. 14,500

30. What is the correct way to state a barometric reading of 29.32?

a. "two niner three two"

b. "two niner point three two"

c. "twenty nine thirty two"

d. "twenty nine point thirty two"

31. What is the correct way to state an altitude of 11,200 feet?

a. "one one thousand two hundred"

b. "one one thousand two zero zero"

c. "eleven thousand two hundred"

d. "eleven thousand two hundred zero zero"

32. Which of the following terms is used to double-check the accuracy of a transmission?

a. acknowledge

b. affirmative

c. roger

d. verify

33. About how long does it take the eyes to fully adapt to the dark?

a. 20 to 30 seconds

b. 1 to 2 minutes

c. 10 to 12 minutes

d. 20 to 30 minutes

34. When flying at night, you should remember that

a. it takes 20 to 30 minutes to adapt to the lower level of light

b. peripheral vision is relatively better than straight ahead

c. color vision deteriorates

d. all of the above

35.   Lights installed on the wing tips and tail of an airplane are called
        a. anticollision lights
        b. directional lights
        c. position lights
        d. taxiing lights

36.   What color lights mark a taxiway turnoff point on a runway at night?
        a. blue
        b. green
        c. red
        d. white

37.   Which statement about control zones is true?
        a. Designated control zones are located only at those airports that have a control
           tower in operation.
        b. They are not depicted on sectional aeronautical charts.
        c. They extend upward from 700 feet AGL and terminate at the base of the
           continental control area.
        d. Unless they underlie the continental control area, control zones have no upper
           limit.

38.   Wake turbulence behind a jet airliner is generated just after takeoff, because
        a. maximum lift is being produced by the wings
        b. the acceleration to higher speeds amplifies the turbulence
        c. the airliner's gear and flaps are extended
        d. the jet engines are at maximum thrust at slow airspeeds

39.   Suppose you are crossing the flight path of a large jet airplane that is ahead of
you at the same altitude. To avoid wake turbulence you should
        a. descend and adjust speed to maneuvering speed
        b. descend and fly parallel to the jet's flight path
        c. descend below the jet's flight path
        d. fly above the jet's flight path

ANSWERS

Key Terms and Concepts, Part 1

1.	d	2.	e	3.	f	4.	g
5.	k	6.	c	7.	n	8.	b
9.	h	10.	o	11.	a	12.	j
13.	r	14.	l	15.	q	16.	p
17.	m	18.	i				

Key Terms and Concepts, Part 2

1.	c	2.	e	3.	s	4.	k
5.	g	6.	h	7.	a	8.	n
9.	b	10.	l	11.	r	12.	f
13.	o	14.	p	15.	j	16.	q
17.	d	18.	i	19.	m		

Key Terms and Concepts, Part 3

1.	q	2.	a	3.	h	4.	u
5.	j	6.	c	7.	o	8.	d
9.	m	10.	e	11.	s	12.	f
13.	b	14.	g	15.	t	16.	l
17.	i	18.	r	19.	n	20.	k
21.	p						

Key Terms and Concepts, Part 4

1.	j	2.	q	3.	o	4.	l
5.	i	6.	k	7.	p	8.	m
9.	e	10.	n	11.	s	12.	c
13.	r	14.	f	15.	a	16.	h
17.	d	18.	g	19.	b		

Discussion Questions and Exercises

6. See Figure 7.5.

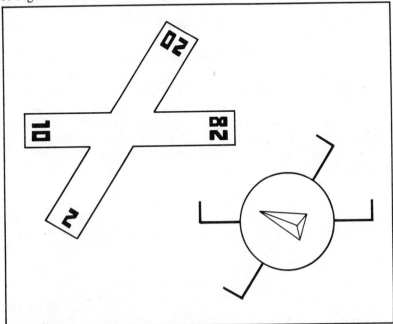

Figure 7.5

7.   Takeoff leg: a heading of 280°, climb to at least 300 feet AGL (3020 feet on the altimeter), and make certain you are past the approach end of the runway. Crosswind: turn right to a heading of 010° and continue your climb. Downwind: turn right to a heading of 100° and continue your climb to 3700 feet MSL (1000 feet AGL). Base leg: turn right to a heading of 190° and continue your descent. Final: continue your descent and turn right to a heading of 280°. If you have set your altimeter (as required by the FAA) to 29.54, your altimeter will correspond with current conditions, and no further altitude corrections will have to be made.

15.a.   "Piper two four niner seven charlie"
  b.   "heading two niner zero"
  c.   "three thousand one hundred twenty feet"
  d.   "one five thousand eight hundred feet"
  e.   "two two four zero zulu"
  f.   "Kansas City Center"
  g.   "Birmingham Radio"
  h.   "say again"
  i.   "verify"
  j.   "acknowledge"
  k.   "one two three point six"
  l.   "three zero zero niner" (no decimal)

Review Questions
1.   a; this is called the active runway.
2.   b; assume that you are on base leg for each runway and determine what direction you would turn onto final: 35—left; 17—right; 27—right; 9—left.
3.   a; the tetrahedron's small end points into the wind; for the wind cone and wind tee, the large end points into the wind.
4.   c; runways are aligned in the approach direction and are rounded to the nearest magnetic heading divided by 10. For example, a runway with a magnetic heading of 26° would be called runway 3 (26° is closest to 30°, which divided by 10 gives 3).
5.   a; runways 4 and 22 are closed as indicated by the X. The tetrahedron indicates that the wind is out of the northeast. If runway 22 were open, you would land on it as it is aligned directly into the wind. Since it is closed, you should use runway 18.
6.   d; you need to memorize these.
7.   b; you need to memorize these.
8.   a; you need to memorize these.
9.   b; these indicate that you should stop and wait for further instructions.
10. a; final and downwind are parallel but in the opposite direction; base and crosswind are perpendicular to downwind.
11. a; normal glides are 3 degrees relative to the horizon.
12. a; white/white means too high, red/red too low, and red/white you are on the glide path.
13. b; the main requirement is that the pilot stay at or above the glide slope.

14. b; this frequency is called MULTICOM and has a variety of uses, such as pilot-to-pilot communications.

15. b; ATIS provides this service continuously to relieve controllers from the tedium of repeating it to all aircraft.

16. b; the normal setting during VFR flight is 1200.

17. c; UNICOM provides airport advisory service at certain airports; no traffic control function is presumed or allowed. UNICOM frequencies are published on sectional charts.

18. c; an ATA extends for 5 statute miles from the center of the airport and up to but not including 3000 feet above the ground. It also must have an operating control tower to be classified as an ATA. When the control tower is not operating, it is not an ATA.

19. b; Stage III radar service separates all IFR traffic and those VFR aircraft that request the service.

20. d; group I TCAs are controlled airspace; they are shaped like upside-down wedding cakes. Group II TCAs have slightly less stringent requirements.

21. a; authorization is required in group I TCAs.

22. c; more signals for you to memorize.

23. a; more signals for you to memorize.

24. a; more signals for you to memorize.

25. d; FL 180 to FL 600.

26. c; all ATAs require two-way radio communications unless other arrangements have been made.

27. c; both of these are requirements before one can get authorization from ATL for special VFR clearance.

28. d; these define transition areas and exist for the separation of VFR and IFR traffic.

29. a; 700 feet for magenta and 1200 feet for blue; the upward boundary is 14,500 feet.

30. a; barometric pressure is stated without the decimal.

31. a; thousands first (stated separately), followed by hundreds.

32. d; more words for you to learn. Do not fret, though. When you use the radio a lot, you will learn these easily by practicing them.

33. d; adapting to the dark takes a very long time—something you should remember when flying at night.

34. d; all of these things happen at night; also, you are more susceptible to illusions.

35. c; these form a directional triangle: red—left wing; green—right wing; white—tail.

36. a; blue lights mark the turnoff points; red is at the departure end of the runway, green is at the approach end; and white lights run along the sides.

37. d; unless under the continental control area (floor 14,500), they have no upper limit.

38. a; the most significant vortices occur at the wing tips as the wings begin to develop maximum lift (at the point of takeoff and on approach). You should try to lift off before the point where a transport lifted off and to land beyond its

point of touchdown. Remember, too, that vortices sink and that they can be blown across other runways. If you ever want to experience vortices, stand under or near the final approach path of a jetliner, as close to the touchdown point as is safe. Vortices will actually fall on you, and you will hear the hissing of the air long after the jet has passed overhead. If you are ever near National Airport in Washington, D.C., there is a park at the approach end of runway 18 that is an ideal place to catch vortices.

39.   d; since vortices sink, you should try to stay above the larger airplane's flight path.

8/METEOROLOGY: A PILOT'S VIEW OF WEATHER

MAIN POINTS

1. Air consists primarily of nitrogen (78 percent), oxygen (21 percent), other gases, and varying amounts of water vapor. The atmosphere contains air and **particulate matter** such as pollen and pollutants that can affect precipitation as well as pilot visibility. The three levels of the atmosphere are the **troposphere** (surface to 29,000 feet near the poles and 54,000 feet near the equator), where most weather occurs; the **stratosphere** (29,000–54,000 feet to 40–60 miles), where the atmosphere is stable; and the **ionosphere** (upward to about 300 miles).

2. Atmospheric pressure can be measured in inches of mercury (the International Standard Atmosphere, ISA, is the pressure at sea level, 29.92), *pounds per square inch* (*psi*; standard is 14.7), and *millibars* (*mb*; the standard is 1013.2). Millibar pressures are commonly used on weather charts. Pressure decreases as altitude increases at a decreasing rate—that is, lower altitudes lose pressure more quickly than higher altitudes.

3. As water vapor increases, **condensation** (for example, clouds) or **precipitation** (discharge of moisture) may occur. Precipitation is affected by temperature (warm air can hold more moisture than cold air) and the presence of particles on which the moisture can condense. **Relative humidity** refers to the percentage of water vapor present compared to the amount it *could* hold at a constant pressure. When this value nears 100 percent, the air is called *saturated*. The temperature at which condensation occurs is called the **dew point**. Because condensation is more likely to occur as the temperature of the air decreases, it is important to monitor both the current temperature and the dew point. When the spread between OAT and dew point is within 4 degrees Fahrenheit and narrowing, condensation (for example, fog) should be expected. Formation of water droplets also depends on particles in the air called **condensation nuclei**.

Two ways by which water changes to gas are **evaporation** (water to gas) and **sublimation** (solid to gas).

4. The surface of the earth absorbs and releases heat, depending upon its color and texture. For example, the land both absorbs and releases heat more quickly than water, which accounts for many weather patterns in coastal areas. The amount of radiation from the sun also depends upon the sun's *angle of incidence*, which is more acute during the winter than it is during the summer.

5. Air loses temperature at an average rate of about 2 degrees Celsius per 1000 feet in the troposphere (called the *lapse rate*), but this can be affected by many variables. It is important to know how the air and the surface below it are heated. *Radiation* heats the air and surface as it strikes them. *Conduction* refers to heating by direct contact, as when molecules strike each other. *Convection* refers to currents set up as hot air rises or cool air falls. Lateral transfer of heat (for example, a moving air mass) is called *advection*.

6. The principles of heat exchange affect the global circulation of the atmosphere, as does the earth's rotation. The apparent motion of the air is called the **Coriolis force**, and it imparts a lateral component to the flow of winds. Generally, in the Northern Hemisphere, polar winds are from the east (**polar easterlies**), middle latitudes have **prevailing westerlies,** and as you approach the equator, northeast winds (**northeast trades**) prevail. As polar easterlies meet prevailing westerlies, *circulation* begins, always in a counterclockwise direction around low-pressure regions and in a clockwise direction around high-pressure regions.

7. Weather charts have points of continuous equal pressure called **isobars**. An elongated high-pressure area is called a *ridge*, and an elogated low-pressure area is called a *trough*. Winds above the friction level tend to flow parallel to the isobars. Rotational winds are called cyclones when associated with lows and anticyclones when associated with highs. How close together the bars are (called the **pressure gradient**) indicates the intensity of the winds. A steep gradient (bars close together) indicates higher winds.

8. The three *weather zones* are: the equator to 30° latitude—a belt of high pressure straddles the 30° line; 30° to 60°—a belt of prevailing westerlies but much mixture of air from north and south; and 60° to the pole—low pressure along 60° latitude. Other forces operating on the atmosphere include *gravity*, *friction* (for example, mountains), and *centrifugal force*.

9. The *ceiling* is defined as the height above the ground of the lowest layer of clouds, provided clouds cover more than half the sky. **Sky cover** varies from *clear* to *scattered* (10 to 50 percent cover) to *broken* (60 to 90 percent) to *overcast* (90 to 100 percent). *Visibility* refers to horizontal distance, normally given in feet (when it is poor) or miles. Several conditions contribute to limited visibility. *Fog* is dangerous because

it cannot always be predicted. It is *most likely* to occur when relative humidity is high, condensation nuclei are present, and the air is cooling (as in the early evening after the sun sets). Four types of fog are: **radiation fog**, or ground fog, which occurs in the early morning under clear skies and calm winds; **advection fog**, which occurs when moist air moves over a cool surface, as in coastal areas; **upslope fog**, which occurs when moist air moves up to a cool region, as against a mountain; and **frontal fog,** which occurs when evaporating rain is lifted. *Precipitation* also affects visibility (snow more than light rain). **Obscurations** (for example, dust, smog) limit visibility and may lead to reports of sky obscured or sky partially obscured since no ceiling can be accurately defined. The terms used to refer to weather conditions are **visual meteorological conditions (VMC)** which means that flight can be maintained by use of outside references, and **instrument meteorological conditions (IMC)**, which means that visual flight is not possible. These terms are not the same as VFR and IFR, both of which are a set of *rules*, not weather conditions. Finally, the most significant measure of visibility aloft is **slant range** ("over the nose") **visibility**.

10. Ice that forms from a sublimation process (water vapor turns directly into a solid) is called *frost*. Frost on the airplane affects drag and lift and may prevent the airplane from becoming airborne. *Icing* is most likely to occur when there is visible moisture, OAT is at or below freezing, and the aircraft skin is at or below freezing. To avoid ice, VFR pilots should stay out of clouds and away from freezing rain. Structural ice comes in two varieties: **clear ice**, which is very dangerous and hard to detect and remove; and **rime ice**, which is also dangerous but brittle and easier to detect.

11. Vertical motion of the air can lead to unstable atmospheric conditions and turbulence. Dry air is more stable than moist air, and the **adiabatic lapse rate** is about 3 degrees per 1000 feet for dry air as compared to 1.1 degrees to 2.8 degrees Celsius for moist air. **Convective currents** (or *thermals*) develop as different shades and densities of the land differentially absorb and reflect heat, leading to vertical air movement. Around large bodies of water, convective currents produce **onshore winds** during the day as cool air over the ocean moves in to replace warm air over the land and **offshore winds** at night. *Surface obstructions* also affect turbulence. Even small buildings, hangars, and trees can affect the flow of the wind (called **land flow turbulence**) and can be particularly disruptive as the wind increases in velocity. Flying near mountains can also be dangerous due to updrafts and downdrafts created by *mountain flow*. These vertical movements are also accentuated by an increase in the wind's velocity and can sometimes be identified by **lenticular** (almond or lens-shaped) **clouds** on the leeward (downwind) side of the mountain. **Wind shear** is a sudden change in the wind's horizontal or vertical movement. It is common when there is a reversal of the lapse rate **(temperature inversion)** or when low-altitude winds are different from surface winds. Finally, there is **clear air turbulence (CAT)**, which is difficult to predict; it typically occurs at higher altitudes.

12. Clouds are visible moisture and come in a variety of different forms and sizes. The three general types of clouds are **cumulus** (piled up), **stratus** (layered), and **cirrus**

(thin, wispy). Additional descriptive words include *alto* (high), *nimbo* (rain), and *fracto* (broken). High clouds (16,500 to 45,000 feet) are referred to as *cirriform*. Middle clouds (6500 to 16,500 feet AGL) are usually referred to as *alto*, and low clouds typically have bases less than 6500 AGL. The basic types of cumulus clouds are *cumulus, altocumulus, stratocumulus*, and *cumulonimbus*. The stratus clouds include *stratus, altostratus*, and *nimbostratus*. The cirrus group includes *cirrus, cirrostratus*, and *cirrocumulus*.

13. Of special note are **cumulonimbus** clouds (Cb clouds), or thunderstorms. Put simply, they are dangerous. They are a product of exaggerated vertical movement and instability, and they come in a variety of types, such as **orographic**—upslope lifting of moist air as it approaches a mountain range—and *frontal*—in which one air mass lifts another. Cbs develop in three stages: *cumulus*, with rapid vertical development; *mature*, marked by updrafts and heavy downdrafts out from the center with rain and sometimes hail; and *dissipating*, identified by the classic anvil-shaped cirriform forms at the apex. Cbs can produce hail, lightning, updrafts and downdrafts, and tornadoes. Navigating around Cbs requires great care: One should give them a berth of at least 20 miles. Due to severe vertical movement, flying under them is dangerous, particularly in mountainous regions. If you are caught in or near a thunderstorm, maintain maneuvering speed and control the airplane's *attitude*. Attempt to keep pitch and bank as level and constant as possible.

14. An **air mass** is an extensive body of air with fairly consistent stability, temperature, and moisture content. As an air mass begins to move along a pressure gradient, it behaves in a predictable way. The line of discontinuity between two differing air masses is called a **front.** The four main air mass sources are: *arctic*, the coldest regions, from the poles; *polar*, cold regions, high-pressure systems; *tropical*, a warm region, low-pressure systems; and *equatorial*, the warmest region, low pressure and calm winds. Masses that form over water are called *maritime* and contain more moisture than those that form over land, called *continental*. Air masses are classified as cold or hot in reference to the ground over which they pass. A cold air mass, designated k on a surface weather map, is a body of air that is colder than the ground over which is passes, while a warm air mass *(w)* is warmer than the surface over which it is moving. Cold air moving over a warm surface produces convective currents (hot air rises) and is unstable, while warm air moving over cold surfaces is stable. *Maritime Polar air masses* are moist, unstable, and conducive to Cb buildups. *Continental Polar air masses* tend to be stable, dry, and characterized by cirrus clouds. *Maritime Tropical air masses* are typically humid, unstable internally, and characterized by stratiform clouds. *Continental Tropical air masses* are dry, unstable, and not likely to produce much precipitation. In the United States, polar and arctic air moves from the northwest and tropical air from the southwest. In general, cold air masses move faster.

15. *Fronts* (lines of discontinuity between two differing air masses) are named for the *advancing* air mass. A **warm front** is a mass of warm air replacing cold air, and

a **cold front** is a mass of cold air supplanting warm air. An **occluded front** is one in which a cold front outraces a slower-moving air mass and moves it aloft. A **stationary front** is one in which the two fronts are balanced and the *zone of discontinuity* remains relatively constant. **Frontogenesis** refers to the creation of a front, as when one air mass overtakes another. When the air masses normalize, the front dissipates (**frontolysis**). Frontal passage is typically characterized by simultaneous changes in temperature, barometric pressure, wind direction, and cloud formation.

16. *Warm air masses* tend to be moist and to climb over retreating cold air masses. As a warm air mass climbs over the cold air its temperature decreases and condensation begins, usually in the form of drizzle or light rain. The frontal zone is usually stable and is preceded by high cirriform clouds. As the front passes, the wind changes from southeast to southwest, the barometer is steady or changes only slightly, the temperature rises, and frontal weather dissipates. Warm fronts typically have extensive cloud cover ahead of the front and low cloud cover near the front, things important for VFR pilots to remember in making flight plans.

17. *Cold air masses* move faster than warm ones and tend to push themselves under warm air masses. This gives rise to cumulus clouds, turbulence, and frequently thunderstorms. **Squall lines**, tightly knit lines of discontinuity, often precede the front and are characterized by highly unstable conditions. As the front passes, visibility improves, the wind shifts from southwest to northwest, the temperature drops, and the barometer dips as the front passes, then rises. Flying the front is not advisable.

18. *Occluded air masses* are ones that have been overtaken from behind by faster-moving cold fronts and forced aloft. There is almost always thunderstorm activity in the stratiform cloud layers, the most severe of which is found in the northernmost 50 to 100 miles.

19. *Stationary air masses* move very slowly if at all. Winds associated with the frontal zone usually run parallel to the line of discontinuity. Such fronts are characterized by low cloud layers, drizzle, and an occasional thunderstorm. Sometimes frontal waves may develop as cold and warm air begins to rotate, creating a miniature low-pressure cell (**cyclogenesis**).

KEY TERMS AND CONCEPTS, PART 1

Match each term or concept (1–19) with the appropriate description (a–s) below. Each item has only one match.

___ 1. adiabatic lapse rate
___ 2. stratosphere
___ 3. VMC
___ 4. troposphere
___ 5. visibility
___ 6. temperature inversion
___ 7. clear
___ 8. radiation
___ 9. ridge
___ 10. onshore
___ 11. maritime
___ 12. ceiling

—13. mature
—15. cirrus
—17. station pressure
—19. condensation nuclei

—14. frontolysis
—16. overcast
—18. polar easterlies

a. extends from 54,000 feet at the equator to about 40 to 60 miles above the earth
b. dissipation of a front
c. Cb stage in which there are heavy downdrafts out of the center
d. reversal of the normal lapse rate
e. wind typically encountered on the beach during the day
f. flight can be maintained by use of outside references
g. horizontal distance one can see
h. lowest layer of clouds covering more than one-half of the sky
i. high-pressure area that takes an elongated form
j. winds flowing from the North Polar regions
k. temperature change of mechanically lifted dry air of about 3 degrees Celsius per 1000 foot change in elevation
l. particles such as pollen suspended in the air
m. pressure to which you set your altimeter before taking off
n. extends from the surface to 29,000 feet over the poles
o. air mass that forms over water
p. clouds that have a wispy, horsehair appearance
q. dangerous form of icing that is difficult to detect
r. condition of the sky when 95 percent covered by clouds
s. heat derived directly from the sun's rays

KEY TERMS AND CONCEPTS, PART 2

Match each term or concept (1–20) with the appropriate description (a–t) below. Each item has only one match.

— 1. advection
— 3. offshore
—5. trough
— 7. scattered
— 9. radiation
—11. IMC
—13. 29.92
—15. squall line
—17. angle of incidence
—19. precipitation

— 2. counterclockwise
— 4. anticyclones
— 6. ionosphere
— 8. atmosphere
—10. 14.7
—12. convection
—14. evaporation
—16. dissipating
—18. wind shear
—20. prevailing westerlies

a. direction wind moves around a low-pressure system
b. circulatory motion of the air caused by heat transfer
c. angle at which the sun's rays strike the earth

d.   discharge of moisture from the atmosphere
e.   IAS inches of mercury at sea level
f.   air, water vapor, and particulate matter
g.   outer layer of the atmosphere
h.   tightly knit line of discontinuity that sometimes precedes a cold front
i.   Cb stage in which anvil-shaped clouds form at the apex
j.   sudden change in wind speed or direction
k.   wind typically encountered on the beach at night
l.   flight cannot be maintained by use of outside references
m.   fog caused by the ground's cooling at night
n.   condition of the sky when 30 percent covered by clouds
o.   low-pressure area that takes an elongated form
p.   winds flowing between 30° and 60° latitude
q.   high-pressure areas and their associated rotational winds
r.   water changes from a liquid to a gas
s.   IAS pounds per square inch (psi) at sea level
t.   fog caused by moist air moving over a cold surface; common in coastal areas

KEY TERMS AND CONCEPTS, PART 3

Match each term or concept (1–20) with the appropriate description (a–t) below.
Each item has only one match.

— 1. standard lapse rate   — 2. rime
— 3. 1013.2   — 4. front
— 5. upslope   — 6. pressure gradient
— 7. continental   — 8. broken
— 9. saturated   —10. cumulus
—11. cold air mass   —12. slant range
—13. stratus   —14. clockwise
—15. occluded front   —16. cyclones
—17. nitrogen   —18. advection
—19. thermals   —20. warm front

a.   body of air that is colder than the surface over which it is traveling
b.   clouds that are formed in layers
c.   dangerous form of ice composed of small, brittle particles
d.   fog caused when a moist air mass is lifted; common in the mountains
e.   condition of the sky when 75 percent covered by clouds
f.   low-pressure areas and their associated rotational winds
g.   direction wind moves around a high-pressure system
h.   lateral transfer of heat within an air mass as it passes over a surface
i.   temperature decreases 2 degrees Celsius per 1000 feet in elevation
j.   air that has a relative humidity of 100 percent
k.   IAS millibars (mb) at sea level
l.   occurs when an advancing mass of warm air supersedes a cold air mass

m.   air mass that forms over land
n.   a rapidly moving cold front forces a slower moving air mass aloft
o.   line of discontinuity between two differing air masses
p.   clouds that appear to be piled up
q.   convective currents caused by differential heat reflection and absorption of the ground
r.   "over-the-nose" visibility
s.   most prevalent gas in the air
t.   pressure changes perpendicular to the isobars

KEY TERMS AND CONCEPTS, PART 4

Match each term or concept (1–11) with the appropriate description (a–k) below. Each item has only one match.

— 1. cumulonimbus   — 2. isobars
— 3. fog   — 4. cirrostratus
— 5. sublimation   — 6. dew point
— 7. northeast trades   — 8. Coriolis force
— 9. conduction   —10. obscuration
—11. relative humidity

a.   continuous equal pressure lines on a weather chart
b.   winds flowing from 30° latitude to the equator
c.   heat transferred directly from one molecule to another
d.   a solid changes directly to a gas (for example, ice to water vapor)
e.   ratio of water vapor in the air to the maximum amount it could hold
f.   layer of cirrus clouds
g.   raining cumulus cloud
h.   apparent motion of the air
i.   temperature at which condensation or precipitation occurs
j.   condition that limits visibility, such as smog
k.   clouds that are lying on or near the ground

DISCUSSION QUESTIONS AND EXERCISES

1.   What is the difference between air and the atmosphere? Why is the distinction important?

2.   State two characteristics of each of the three layers of the atmosphere: stratosphere, ionosphere, and troposphere.

   a. stratosphere

   b. ionosphere

   c. troposphere

3.   What are the three common ways to report air pressure? For each, state the
value associated with standard conditions.

4.   How does the *rate of change* in air pressure change as altitude increases? Give
an example.

5.   What two things control precipitation in addition to the water vapor itself?
Explain how and why each affects precipitation.

6.   Define each of the following:

      a. relative humidity

      b. dew point

      c. condensation nuclei

      d. evaporation

      e. sublimation

7.   Explain how each of the following affects air temperature:

      a. the earth's rotation

      b. unequal heating of land and water

c. the earth's revolution around the sun

8.   Define the following lapse rates:

a. standard lapse rate

b. adiabatic lapse rate—dry air

c. adiabatic lapse rate—moist air

9.   Briefly describe the Coriolis force. How is it important in understanding global circulation patterns?

10.   Briefly describe the three zones or cells that affect global circulation in the Northern Hemisphere and their associated weather conditions.

11.   State in what direction winds circulate around high-pressure and low-pressure systems in the Northern Hemisphere.

12.   Define each of the following terms:

   a. ridge

   b. trough

   c. cyclone

   d. anticyclone

   e. pressure gradient

13.   What is the relationship between the steepness of a pressure gradient and the stability of the air?

14.   Briefly state how each of the following factors affects the wind:

a. gravity

b. friction

c. centrifugal force

15.   Briefly define each of the following sky cover conditions:

a. clear

b. scattered

c. broken

d. overcast

16.   What is fog? What three conditions are necessary for its formation?

17.   Briefly describe each of the following types of fog:

a. radiation

b. advection

c. upslope

d. frontal

18.   What is an obscuration? Give an example. Distinguish between reports of sky obscured and sky partially obscured.

19.   Distinguish among visual meteorological conditions (VMC), VFR, instrument meteorological conditions (IMC), and IFR.

20.   What three conditions are particularly conducive to the formation of ice? Briefly distinguish between rime ice and clear ice. What is the best way for a VFR pilot to avoid icing conditions?

21.   Briefly state how turbulence is related to each of the following:

a. lapse rate

b. convective currents

c. the coastline

d. land flow

e. mountain flow

f. wind shear

g. temperature inversion

22.   What is clear air turbulence? Why is it so difficult to deal with?

23.   Briefly characterize each of the following cloud types, including a description of what each looks like, what weather each is associated with, and the altitudes at which each is likely to be encountered:

a. stratus

b. cumulus

c. cirriform

    d. stratocumulus

    e. nimbostratus

    f. cirrocumulus

24.   Why are cumulonimbus clouds considered particularly dangerous? Briefly characterize the three stages of the Cb life cycle.

25.   Why is it particularly dangerous to fly underneath a line of thunderstorms?

26.   What is the most important thing you should do if you are caught in a thunderstorm cloud? Name at least three other things you should also do.

27.   Briefly characterize the four air mass source regions.

28.   Distinguish between continental and maritime air masses. How do they typically differ in temperature and moisture content?

29.   Distinguish between warm and cold air masses.

30.   Briefly describe each of the following air mass types:

       a. maritime Polar

       b. continental Polar

       c. maritime Tropical

d. continental Tropical

31. Briefly characterize each of the following:

a. warm front

b. cold front

c. occluded front

d. stationary front

e. cyclogenesis

32.   In general, what should the VFR pilot do when weather begins to "close in"?

33.   T F The layer of the atmosphere that gives rise to northern lights is the ionosphere.

34.   T F The atmosphere gains pressure less quickly as altitude increases.

35.   T F Air that has a relative humidity of 100 percent is called sublimated.

36.   T F One factor in the intensity of solar radiation is the sun's rotation around
the earth.

37.   T F The primary process by which the sun heats the air is called radiation.

38.   T F The direction of circulation around a region of low pressure in the Northern Hemisphere is counterclockwise.

39.   T F The steeper the pressure gradient is, the more likely high-velocity winds
are.

40.   T F Wind speed along the isobars decreases as the center of a low-pressure
area approaches and increases as the center of a high approaches.

41.   T F Prevailing visibilities are given in thousands of feet when visibility is
good.

42.   T F Fog is a cloud that is lurking on or near the ground.

43.   T F Fog caused by cooling of the ground at night (common under clear skies
with calm winds) is called advection fog.

44.   T F VMC and VFR refer to identical weather conditions.

45.   T F Clear ice will accumulate rapidly in flight when temperatures are between freezing and −15 degrees Celsius and you are flying in cumuliform clouds.

46.   T F Frost may form in flight when a cold aircraft descends from a zone of subzero temperatures to a zone of above-freezing temperatures and high relative humidity.

47.   T F Moist air is typically less stable than dry air.

48.   T F Onshore winds are common during the day, while offshore winds are common during the night.

49.   T F Convection currents become less intense as the surface temperature increases.

50.   T F An almond or lens-shaped cloud that appears stationary but that may reflect winds of 50 knots or more is referred to as a lenticular cloud.

51.   T F Reversal of the normal lapse rate is called a temperature inversion.

52.   T F A temperature inversion often develops near the ground on clear, cool nights in calm wind conditions.

53.   T F The overhanging anvil of a thunderstorm points in the direction from which the storm has moved.

54.   T F Hail may be found in any level within a thunderstorm but not in the clear air outside the storm cloud.

55.   T F The most important thing a pilot who enters a thunderstorm should do is keep a constant airspeed.

56.   T F A cold air mass is colder than the surface over which it passes.

57.   T F A squall line is typically associated with a fast-moving warm front.

58.   T F Warm fronts are frequently associated with low ceilings and limited visibilities.

REVIEW QUESTIONS
1.   Which of the following atmosphere levels is farthest from the ground?
   a. blastosphere
   b. ionosphere
   b. stratosphere
   d. troposphere

2.   Which of the following numbers represents ISA conditions in pounds per square inch of mercury at sea level?
   a. 14.7
   b. 29.92
   c. 123.6
   d. 1013.2

3.   The percentage of water vapor present in the air in relation to how much water the air could hold under a constant pressure at current conditions is called
   a. condensation level
   b. dew point
   c. relative humidity
   d. saturation level

4.   Water changes from a solid to a gas through a process called
   a. condensation
   b. evaporation
   c. saturation
   d. sublimation

5.   If the temperature–dew point spread is 4 degrees and decreasing and the temperature is 62 degrees Fahrenheit, what type of weather is most likely to develop?
   a. fog or low clouds
   b. freezing precipitation
   c. rain showers
   d. thunderstorms

6.   Hot air rises. This is an example of
   a. advection
   b. conduction
   c. convection
   d. radiation

7.   On a weather map, isobars that are close together represent a steep
   a. anticyclone
   b. pressure gradient
   c. ridge
   d. trough

8.   What causes surface winds to flow across the isobars at an angle rather than parallel to the isobars?
   a. Coriolis force
   b. heat radiation from the surface
   c. surface friction and wind flow toward lower pressure
   d. the difference between air temperature and dew point temperature

9. If 88 percent of the sky is covered by clouds, the sky is classified as
   a. broken
   b. clear
   c. overcast
   d. scattered

10. Which of the following conditions is (are) necessary for fog formation?
   a. a cooling tendency
   b. absence of condensation nuclei
   c. low relative humidity
   d. all of the above

11. Advection fog is formed as a result of
   a. moist air condensing as it moves over a cooler surface
   b. moist, unstable air being cooled as it is forced up a sloping land surface
   c. the addition of moisture to a mass of cold air as it moves over a body of water
   d. the ground cooling adjacent air to the dew point temperature on clear, calm nights

12. Visibility "over the nose" of the airplane refers to the
   a. longitudinal range minus the vertical range
   b. obscuration range
   c. slant range
   d. vertical range minus the longitudinal range

13. Which of the following condition(s) is (are) necessary for structural icing to occur?
   a. aircraft skin below freezing
   b. OAT at or above freezing
   c. relative humidity between 60 and 90 percent
   d. all of the above

14. Select the statement about aircraft structural icing that is true.
   a. It is impossible for weather forecasters to identify regions where icing is possible.
   b. Rime ice is the most common type of ice encountered in cumuliform clouds.
   c. The most rapid accumulations of clear ice are usually at temperatures from 0 degrees to -15 degrees Celsius.
   d. The most common type of icing encountered in lower level stratus clouds is clear ice.

15. The type of ice that forms on an aircraft surface depends upon
   a. an inversion aloft
   b. the increase in flight altitude
   c. the size of the water drops or droplets that strike the aircraft surface
   d. the temperature–dew point spread

16.   What aerodynamic effect will structural icing have on an airplane?
       a. Drag increases; thrust is not affected.
       b. Lift decreases; weight increases.
       c. Stalling speed decreases.
       d. Weight increases; lift is not affected if drag and thrust remain constant.

17.   Dry air tends to be _____ stable and to lose heat _____ rapidly than moist
air.
       a. less; less
       b. less; more
       c. more; less
       d. more; more

18.   Which of the following statements is correct?
       a. Convection currents become more intense as the surface temperature
          increases.
       b. Lenticular clouds on the downwind side of a mountain are evidence that a
          mountain wave has dissipated.
       c. Onshore winds are common at night due in part to the fact that water retains
          its heat.
       d. All of the above are correct.

19.   Which statement describes the normal characteristics of standing lenticular
clouds?
       a. The clouds are almond or lens shaped and show little or no movement, but
          they may contain strong winds and turbulence.
       b. The clouds are gray or dark, contain very little turbulence, and are not a
          hazard to flight.
       c. The clouds have billowing tops and comparatively high bases, producing
          continuous rain.
       d. The clouds have dense boiling tops. They contain violent turbulence and are
          considered the most hazardous of the cloud types.

20.   Suppose that hazardous low-level wind shear is encountered during the initial
climb after takeoff. Select the true statement.
       a. Low-level wind shear may be associated with a thunderstorm's gust front
          that precedes the actual storm.
       b. The pilot should decrease power to compensate for the increase in lift.
       c. The wind direction will always change from a headwind to a tailwind when
          flying through wind shear.
       d. When passing through wind shear the ground speed will usually remain
          constant.

21.   Hail is most likely to be associated with _____clouds.
       a. cirrocumulus
       b. cumulonimbus

    c. cumulus
    d. stratocumulus

22.   Gray, uniform, sheetlike clouds with light drizzle and smooth air lurking at 2000 feet AGL would be classified as
    a. altocumulus
    b. cumulus
    c. nimbostratus
    d. stratus

23.   In regard to flying in the vicinity of thunderstorms, you should be aware that
    a. avoidance of lightning and hail is assured by flying in the clear air outside the confines of a thunderstorm cell
    b. avoidance of severe turbulence is assured by circumnavigating thunderstorms and clearing the edges of the storms by 5 miles
    c. the most severe conditions, such as heavy hail, destructive winds, and tornadoes, are generally associated with squall line thunderstorms
    d. the overhanging anvil of a thunderstorm points in the direction from which the storm has moved

24.   Which statement about hail is true?
    a. Hail is usually produced by cirrocumulus clouds.
    b. Hail is usually produced during the mature stage of a thunderstorm's life span.
    c. Large hailstones are composed entirely of clear ice.
    d. Subtropical and tropical thunderstorms contain more hail than thunderstorms in northern latitudes.

25.   _____ air masses are typically dry and stable and are characterized by sparse precipitation and excellent visibilities.
    a. continental Polar
    b. continental Tropical
    c. maritime Polar
    d. maritime Tropical

26.   The weather condition normally associated with unstable air is
    a. continuous precipitation
    b. fair to poor visibility
    c. good visibility except in blowing sand or snow
    d. stratiform clouds

27.   Which of the following would decrease the stability of an air mass?
    a. cooling from below
    b. decrease in water vapor
    c. sinking of the air mass
    d. warming from below

28.   The most severe weather conditions, such as destructive winds, heavy hail, and tornadoes, are generally associated with
   a. fast-moving fronts
   b. slow-moving cold fronts
   c. slow-moving warm fronts
   d. squall line thunderstorms

29.   Tornadoes are more likely to occur with which type thunderstorms?
   a. air mass thunderstorms
   b. squall line thunderstorms that form ahead of warm fronts
   c. steady-state thunderstorms associated with cold fronts or squall lines
   d. tropical thunderstorms during the mature stage

30.   When two air masses are so well balanced that neither one prevails, it is called a/an _____front.
   a. discontinuous
   b. genetic
   c. occluded
   d. stationary

31.   Passage of a warm front is characterized by
   a. a steady or slowly changing barometer
   b. slow dissipation of frontal weather
   c. a wind change from southeast to southwest
   d. all of the above

32.   A pilot planning a long-distance flight from east to west in the conterminous United States would most likely find favorable winds associated with high- and low-pressure systems by flying a course that is
   a. through the center of highs and lows
   b. to the north of a high
   c. to the north of a high and to the south of a low
   d. to the south of a high and to the north of a low

ANSWERS

Key Terms and Concepts, Part 1

1.	k	2.	a	3.	f	4.	n
5.	g	6.	d	7.	q	8.	s
9.	i	10.	e	11.	o	12.	h
13.	c	14.	b	15.	p	16.	r
17.	m	18.	j	19.	l		

Key Terms and Concepts, Part 2

1.	t	2.	a	3.	k	4.	q
5.	o	6.	g	7.	n	8.	f
9.	m	10.	s	11.	l	12.	b
13.	e	14.	r	15.	h	16.	i
17.	c	18.	j	19.	d	20.	p

Key Terms and Concepts, Part 3

1.	i	2.	c	3.	k	4.	o
5.	d	6.	t	7.	m	8.	e
9.	j	10.	p	11.	a	12.	r
13.	b	14.	g	15.	n	16.	f
17.	h	18.	s	19.	q	20.	l

Key Terms and Concepts, Part 4

1.	g	2.	a	3.	k	4.	f
5.	d	6.	i	7.	b	8.	h
9.	c	10.	j	11.	e		

Discussion Questions and Exercises

33. T; due to the ionosphere's electrical properties.
34. F; it loses pressure as altitude increases.
35. F; it is called saturated.
36. F; it depends upon the earth's rotation around the sun as well as the earth's daily rotation and the angle of incidence.
37. T; what more can one say?
38. T; and clockwise around a system of high pressure.
39. T; steep pressure gradients mean rapid pressure changes that are typically associated with high winds.
40. T; precisely!
41. F; hundreds of feet when it is poor and statute miles when it is good.
42. T; that is exactly what it is: moist and thick.
43. F; this is called radiation.
44. F; VMC specifies the weather and VFR specifies the rules that govern actual flight.
45. T; cumuliform clouds produce large water droplets that are especially prone to produce clear ice.
46. T; such conditions may lead to frost.
47. T; mechanically lifted moist air can be particularly unstable.
48. T; at night, water retains heat while the land cools quickly, leading to offshore winds. During the day the land warms more rapidly than the water, leading to onshore breezes as the cold air over the water moves in to replace the warm air.
49. F; it is just the opposite.

50.   T; these are evidence of turbulent mountain waves on the leeward or downwind side of the mountain.
51.   T; that is the definition of an inversion.
52.   T; because the ground cools (loses its heat) at a rapid rate.
53.   F; it points in the direction the storm is moving.
54.   F; they may be thrown upward and outward as far as 5 miles.
55.   F; one should control the airplane's pitch and bank attitude.
56.   T; air masses are defined by the temperature of the mass in relation to the surface over which it travels.
57.   F; it is associated with fast-moving cold fronts.
58.   T; warm fronts typically move slowly and cover a large area.

Review Questions

1.   b; the layers are (closest to farthest) troposphere, stratosphere, ionosphere.
2.   a; this is the ISA standard at sea level in pounds per square inch.
3.   c; this defines relative humidity.
4.   d; this defines the process of sublimation.
5.   a; dew point is the temperature to which the air must be cooled to become saturated, leading typically to low clouds or fog.
6.   c; convective currents are established as hot air rises and cool air descends.
7.   b; how close the isobars are indicates the intensity of the gradient.
8.   c; friction tends to slow the speed of the wind so that the Coriolis force and pressure gradient are no longer balanced. This turns the wind toward the area of lower pressure, and thus the wind travels across the isobars.
9.   a; 0–9 percent, clear; 10–49 percent, scattered; 50–89 percent, broken; 90–100 percent, overcast.
10.   a; high relative humidity and the presence of condensation nuclei are also necessary.
11.   a; advection fog is common along the oceanfront as warm, moist air condenses when it passes over the cooler ground surface.
12.   c; the distance from the nose to the ground is a diagonal line known as the slant range.
13.   a; OAT must also be at or below freezing, and visible moisture must be present.
14.   c; for ice to form, there must be visible moisture, freezing temperatures, and an airfoil that is as cold or colder than freezing.
15.   c; the type of droplet will determine what type of ice will form (clear or rime). Clear ice forms when droplets are large, and rime ice when they are small.
16.   b; drag increases, weight increases, lift decreases, and thrust is reduced.
17.   d; it is more stable and loses heat at a rate of about 3 degrees Celsius per thousand feet as compared to 1.1 to 2.8 degrees Celsius for moist air.
18.   a; lenticular clouds are signs of a mountain wave, and offshore winds are common at night.
19.   a; these clouds are strong evidence that turbulent mountain waves exist.

20.   a; wind shear involves a rapid change in direction or speed or both in a short distance. It is associated with temperature inversions and frontal activity and may occur in clear air.

21.   b; cumulonimbus clouds are associated with all kinds of violent weather, including thunderstorms and hail.

22.   d; this defines stratus clouds.

23.   c; the squall line typically precedes a front and contains the most severe weather conditions.

24.   b; it is produced during the mature stage and may be thrown miles from the parent cell.

25.   a; continental Polar air masses have cold surface temperatures, low moisture content, and great stability in lower layers, especially in the source region.

26.   c; although strong updrafts and cumulus clouds may exist, visibilities are typically good except near storm centers.

27.   d; generally, anytime air rises, it becomes less stable (for example, convection currents).

28.   d; these produce the most severe storms, particularly when associated with fast-moving cold fronts.

29.   c; they are associated with squall lines and steady-state storms.

30.   d; such fronts do not move more than 5 miles per hour.

31.   d; all of these happen when a warm front passes.

32.   d; winds blow clockwise around high-pressure systems and counterclockwise around low-pressure systems in the Northern Hemisphere. Thus, flying to the south of highs and to the north of lows would produce the most favorable winds going from east to west.

9/USING AVIATION WEATHER SERVICES

MAIN POINTS

1. The **National Weather Service (NWS)** gathers information about the weather from such sources as direct observations, balloons, radar, and pilot reports.

2. Automated weather information is available from several sources: pilot briefings: **Pilot's Automatic Telephone Weather Answering Service (PATWAS);** airports: **Automatic Terminal Information Service (ATIS),** identified by a letter from the phonetic alphabet; and en route information: **Transcribed Weather Broadcasts (TWEB)** for 250 miles around a navigational aid such as a VOR station. **En Route Flight Advisory Service (EFAS)** provides a weather specialist on 122.0.

3. FAR 91.5 requires you to familiarize yourself with weather information prior to any flight outside the local area. When you contact the weather facility (FSS, if one is available, or NWS), give them your name, aircraft type and call number, destination, route of flight and altitude, rating, type of flight (VFR), estimated time of departure (ETD), estimated time en route (ETE), estimated time of arrival (ETA), and any stops en route.

4. **Surface analysis charts (SAs)** depict pressure patterns, fronts, surface winds, temperatures and dew points, and visibility restrictions. Fortunately, SA maps have legends so you will not have to memorize the many symbols that appear on them. Cloud cover is represented by a circle that is progressively filled for greater amounts of cover. Wind direction is represented by a wind arrow whose tail points into the wind; wind velocity is indicated by feathers (10 knots per) or a pennant (50 knots). Isobars are represented in millibars (last two digits) and are spaced at 4-millibar intervals.

5. **Weather depiction charts** connect all IFR areas (visibility below 3 miles and/ or a ceiling of less than 1000 feet) with a solid line, and marginal VFR areas (visibility 3 to 5 miles and/or a ceiling of 1000 to 3000 feet) with a scalloped line.

6. A **significant weather prognosis chart** (prog) is a *prognosis* (estimate) of how the weather may change. It contains two successive 12-hour estimates for both surface and low-level conditions. In addition to solid lines for IFR and scalloped lines for marginal VFR, broken lines represent areas of moderate or greater turbulence, dotted lines depict surface freezing, and dashed lines represent freezing aloft. Shaded areas on the surface portion indicate areas of precipitation.

7. The **radar summary chart** shows areas of precipitation, not cloud cover, which typically is more widespread. The chart indicates precipitation trends and intensities.

8. Weather reports are important in terms of both time frame *and* difference in relative accuracy between actual observations and a future estimate of those observations. Several reports can be used in flight planning.

9. The **surface aviation weather report,** or sequence report, is given every hour and contains the following information: (1) station identifier, a three-letter code; (2) type of report—for example, hourly or special; (3) time of report, given in GMT or zulu; (4) sky condition and ceiling: measured (M), estimated (E), indefinite (W), or variable (V); (5) visibility, given in statute miles; (6) present weather; (7) sea level pressure, given in millibars (no decimal, initial 9 or 10 omitted); (8) temperature, in Fahrenheit; (9) dew point; (10) wind direction and speed in knots; (11) altimeter setting, last three digits only; and (12) remarks—for example, pilot reports (PIREPs) and *Notices to Airmen (NOTAMs)*. PIREPs alert other pilots to in-flight situations, while *NOTAMs* alert pilots to closed runways, inoperable VOR stations, unusual airspace activity, and so forth.

10. **Terminal forecasts (FTs),** prepared three times daily for selected large airports, contain information similar to sequence reports. Winds are shown only if they are expected to be greater than 10 knots, and visibility only if it is expected to be 6 miles or less. **Area forecasts** are released every 12 hours for 18-hour periods, with an additional 12-hour outlook.

11. **Winds and temperatures aloft forecasts (FDs)** are important for performance and navigation calculations. Wind directions are reported with respect to true (not magnetic) north.

12. **Transcribed weather broadcasts (TWEBs)** provide general area weather forecasts, PIREPs, radar reports, and winds aloft. TWEBs begin at 15 minutes past the hour, every hour, and are updated as changes occur.

13. **En Route Flight Advisory Service (EFAS)** provides weather-related information on 122.0.

14. Several in-flight advisories are issued. A **SIGMET** (*sig*nificant *met*eorological advisory) typically refers to severe weather developments such as turbulence or icing. A **convective SIGMET** refers to thunderstorm activity. An **AIRMET** (*air*men's *met*eorological advisory) is important for light aircraft and of interest to all aircraft. **Hurricane advisories, convective outlooks, severe weather watch bulletins** (for example, tornado watches), and *special flight forecasts* are also issued.

KEY TERMS AND CONCEPTS

Match each term or concept (1–24) with the appropriate description (a–x) below. Each item has only one match.

— 1. TWEB
— 2. winds aloft forecast
— 3. area forecasts
— 4. ceiling
— 5. PIREP
— 6. ATIS
— 7. severe weather watch bulletin (WW)
— 8. remote communication outlet (RCO)
— 9. EFAS
—10. NWS
—11. *NOTAMs*
—12. radar summary chart
—13. AIRMET
—14. PATWAS
—15. SIGMET
—16. station model
—17. echo
—18. Automated Field Observing System (AFOS)
—19. ceilometer
—21. convective SIGMET
—20. isobar
—23. surface aviation weather reports
—22. significant weather prognosis charts
—24. terminal forecasts

a. height of the lowest layer of clouds above the earth's surface when the total coverage is more than 50 percent
b. in-flight pilot report on weather conditions
c. significant meteorological advisory pertaining to all aircraft
d. forecasts of winds at selected altitudes; issued every 6 hours
e. hourly sequence reports
f. short-term forecast of dangerous weather for small aircraft; issued by NWS
g. civilian agency that coordinates weather services in the United States
h. chart that depicts precipitation through "echoes"
i. significant meteorological advisory pertaining to thunderstorms
j. expected weather for the next 12 hours for a geographical area; issued every 6 hours
k. continuous recording of current and forecast weather along certain flight routes
l. continuous broadcast of meteorological information from a VOR facility

m.   forecasts for specific airports issued three times daily
n.   using CRTs to distribute weather information
o.   appearance on a radar indicator of energy returned from a target such as a storm
       cell
p.   remotely controlled air/ground communication facility
q.   four-panel NWS charts for surface and significant weather estimates
r.   publication containing current information essential to flight safety
s.   electronic device that measures cloud bases
t.   provides timely weather information at pilot request on 122.0
u.   lines on an SA chart joining points where barometric pressure is the same
v.   in-flight advisory issued by National Severe Storms Forecast Center
w.   grouping of weather information around a station on an SA chart
x.   continuous broadcast of recorded noncontrol information in selected terminal
       areas

DISCUSSION QUESTIONS AND EXERCISES

1.   State what the initials stand for and briefly describe the weather advisory function
of each of the following:

       a. NWS

       b. FSS

       c. PATWAS

       d. ATIS

e. TWEB

f. EFAS

g. SIGMET

h. AIRMET

i. PIREP

j. *NOTAM*

2.   Outline what you should tell a weather specialist when you call for a briefing.

3.   What is a station model? How is it used on a surface analysis chart (SA)?

4.   What is the chief value to pilots of a weather depiction chart?

5.   How are the significant weather prognosis chart and the surface prognosis chart related? How are they different?

6.   Of what value to pilots is a radar summary chart?

7.   Outline the information obtained in a surface aviation weather report.

8.   What are the three ways of determining a station's ceiling? How are they coded on SA charts?

9.   How are area forecasts different from terminal forecasts?

10.   Of what value to pilots are winds and temperatures aloft forecasts?

REVIEW QUESTIONS

1.   Refer to the surface weather map in Figure 9.1. The front that extends from the low-pressure area southward along the Texas border from El Paso into Mexico is known as a/an
      a. cold front
      b. occlusion
      c. stationary front
      d. warm front

2.   The weather information depicted on the surface weather map in Figure 9.1 indicates that
      a. air circulation around the low-pressure area near El Paso is clockwise
      b. after the front has passed through Texas the surface winds should be from the south
      c. the front appears to have little or no movement in the vicinity of Abilene
      d. the front located in the western half of Texas should move northwesterly out of the state

3.   Refer to the surface weather map in Figure 9.1. From what direction is the wind blowing in Grand Junction, Colorado?
      a. east
      b. north
      c. south
      d. west

4.   Refer to the surface weather map in Figure 9.1. What is the cloud cover in Winslow, Arizona?
      a. clear
      b. broken
      c. overcast
      d. scattered

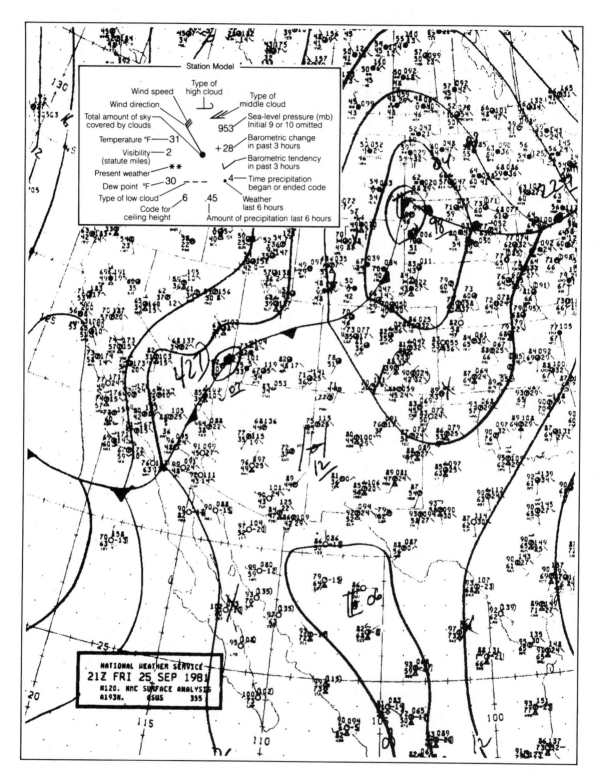

Figure 9.1

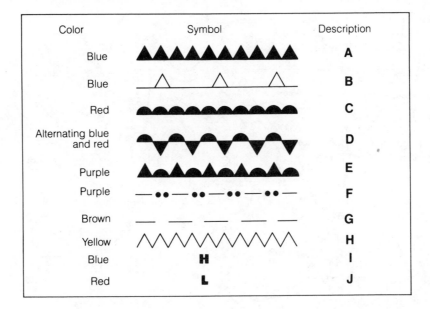

Figure 9.2

5.   Refer to the weather symbols in Figure 9.2. Weather conditions associated with symbol F are
   a. an area of thundershowers
   b. a line of active thunderstorms
   c. rain, drizzle, and fog
   d. stratiform clouds and haze

6.   Refer to the symbols in Figure 9.2. The three principal types of fronts are the cold front, the warm front, and the stationary front. Which of the following symbols are properly identified?
   a. B, cold front; D, warm front; E, stationary front
   b. A, cold front; C, warm front; D, stationary front
   c. C, cold front; D, warm front; E, stationary front
   d. A, warm front; B, stationary front; E, cold front

7.   Refer to the symbols in Figure 9.2. If symbol C is shown on a surface weather map, it indicates that
   a. a cold air mass has caught up with a warm air mass and the air masses have closed together to form an occluded front
   b. a cold air mass is overtaking and replacing a warm air mass
   c. neither a cold air mass nor a warm air mass is being replaced and the front is stationary
   d. a warm air mass is moving in and replacing colder air

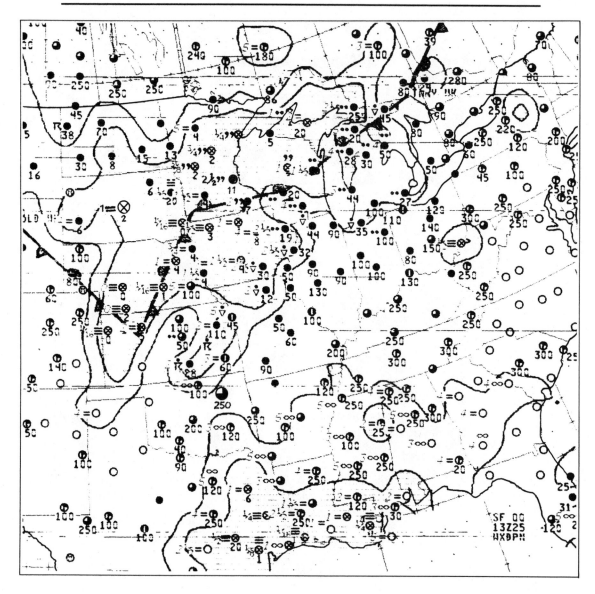

Figure 9.3

8.   When using a weather depiction chart as shown in Figure 9.3, you should know
that the
    a. scalloped area in Kansas and Iowa encloses that portion of the state having
       an overcast below 1000 feet
    b. scalloped lines enclose areas where the ceiling is below 1000 feet and the
       visibility is less than 3 miles

c. smooth solid lines enclose areas containing weather that is below VFR minimums for controlled airspace

d. smooth solid lines enclose areas of constant barometric pressure

9. Refer to the weather depiction chart in Figure 9.3. The weather over most of Oklahoma and Arkansas is
 a. below IFR minimums
 b. below VFR minimums
 c. clear skies with unlimited visibility
 d. marginal VFR

10. A weather depiction chart is useful in determining
 a. areas of equal barometric pressure
 b. areas where weather conditions reported are above or below VFR minimums
 c. the forecast areas of cloud cover and precipitation
 d. the temperature and dew point at selected stations

11. Select the true statement about significant weather prognosis charts (progs).
 a. The charts are designed for use in domestic flight planning to 24,000 feet.
 b. The valid time of the charts corresponds to the time of the plotted observations, and they are not forecasts.
 c. The charts do not depict ceiling, visibility, or turbulence.
 d. The four-panel charts forecast weather for a 48-hour period.

12. Refer to Figure 9.4. The wind for Crazy Woman, Wyoming (CZI), at 6000 feet is forecast to be from
 a. 022° at 16 mph
 b. 220° at 08 knots with gusts
 c. 220° at 16 knots
 d. 240° at 12 knots with gusts

13. Refer to Figure 9.4 for Denver (DEN) at FL 39. The winds and temperature are forecast to be
 a. 230° at 63 mph; 62 degrees Celsius
 b. 230° at 62 knots; 62 degrees Fahrenheit
 c. 230° at 62 mph; −62 degrees Celsius
 d. 230° at 62 knots; −62 degrees Fahrenheit

14. In a winds and temperatures aloft forecast, the coded group 9900+00 means
 a. there is no forecast of wind and temperature at a prescribed level
 b. wind from 90° at 9 knots, temperature 0 degrees Celsius
 c. wind in excess of 90 knots, temperature 90 degrees Fahrenheit
 d. winds light and variable, temperature 0 degrees Celsius

① { FDUS1 KWBC 180545
    DATA BASED ON 180000Z

② — VALID 181200Z FOR USE 0600-1500Z. TEMPS NEG ABV 24000

FT	3000	6000	9000	12000	18000	24000	30000	34000	39000
BFF		2412+08	2715+04	2523-04	2536-20	2541-32	244544	246755	246862
CZI		2216+08	2619+02	2725-05	2531-23	2447-35	245047	256352	256762
DEN		2609+08	2717+03	2722-05	2630-19	2632-31	253543	236056	236262
RAP		2115+07	2415+03	2420-05	2431-21	2445-33	244745	244854	245561
RKS		2315+08	2517+03	2727-05	2439-20	2647-34	254346	237252	238160

(with ③ bracketing the station rows)

① { FD heading specifying date (eighteenth of month), GMT teletype transmission time (0545 Z), and day and time actual observation was made (the eighteenth day of the month at 0000 Z).

② { Winds and temperatures will be as forecast at the "valid" time, however, they may be used during the "use" times indicated. "TEMPS NEG" means that the last two digits of the numbers listed under the columns above 24000 (that is, from 30000 upward) will always be negative.

③ { The column heads represent altitude (3000 to 39,000 feet) with wind and temperature entries below for each station listed on the left. The first entry for any station must be at least 1500 feet AGL, hence the stations shown (all in the high terrain of the Rocky Mountain area) have no entry until the 6000-foot level. The first two digits of each entry represent the true (*not* magnetic) direction from which the winds are blowing, with the last digit deleted. The next two numbers represent the wind speed in knots. "9900" is printed when the winds for that level are light (below 5 knots) and variable. Winds of 100 to 199 knots can be read by *subtracting* 50 from the direction and *adding* 100 to the wind speed shown. Temperatures are given in degrees Celsius.

Figure 9.4

15.   In area forecasts, cloud heights are given in reference to
       a. density-altitude
       b. ground level only
       c. pressure altitude
       d. sea level

16.   Based on the area forecast for Wyoming in Figure 9.5 you determine that
       a. a squall line is expected ahead of the cold front
       b. moderate to severe turbulence is forecast below 16,000 feet in the higher
          mountains and passes
       c. surface winds are forecast to be from 321° at 5 knots with gusts to 25 knots
          with frontal passage in Wyoming
       d. the ceiling in western and central Wyoming is forecast to be 12,000 to 14,000
          feet AGL

17.   Based on the area forecast for Wyoming in Figure 9.5 you determine that
       a. a cold front was located in western Wyoming at 0400 MST

b. icing is decreasing, moving from west to east throughout the state
c. the ceilings in central and western Wyoming are 12,000 to 14,000 AGL (estimated)
d. all of the above

MKC FA 291240
13Z MON TO 07Z TUE (0600 MST MON TO 0000 MST TUE)
OTLK 07Z TUE TO 19Z TUE (0000 MST TUE TO 1200 MST TUE)

WYO. . . . .

HEIGHTS ABOVE SEA LEVEL UNLESS NOTED.

FLIGHT PRECAUTIONS RECOMMENDED DUE TO TURBULENCE AND RESTRICTED VISIBILITIES.

SYNOPSIS. COLD FRONT AT 11Z (0400 MST) LOCATED FROM NORTHEAST MONTANA THROUGH EXTREME WESTERN WYOMING ACROSS CENTRAL UTAH MOVING TO NORTHWEST WISCONSIN CENTRAL IOWA EASTERN KANSAS BY 19Z (1200 MST) TUESDAY. FRONTAL SYSTEM ACCOMPANIED BY GUSTY NORTHWESTERLY SURFACE WINDS.

SIGNIFICANT CLOUDS AND WEATHER.

WYOMING. 12,000 TO 14,000 BROKEN TO OVERCAST WESTERN AND CENTRAL PORTIONS BY 15Z (0800 MST) WITH CHANCE OF LIGHT SHOWERS. SURFACE WIND 3215G25 WITH FRONTAL PASSAGE CENTRAL AND EASTERN PORTIONS AFTER 13Z (0600 MST). HIGHER MOUNTAINS AND PASSES OBSCURED BY CLOUDS OR SHOWERS WITH MODERATE TO LOCALLY SEVERE TURBULENCE BELOW 16,000. OUTLOOK MARGINAL VFR CENTRAL AND WEST, VFR EAST PORTIONS.

ICING. LOCALLY MODERATE MIXED ICING IN CLOUDS ABOVE FREEZING LEVEL. FREEZING LEVEL 2500 EASTERN PORTIONS OF FA AREA SLOPING TO 8000 WYOMING AND COLORADO.

TURBULENCE. MODERATE LOCALLY SEVERE TURBULENCE BELOW 16,000.

Figure 9.5
Area forecast
(plain language interpretation)

FT180940

RAP 181010 100 SCT 250 -BKN 1615. 18Z C80 BKN 1815.
  00Z C50 BKN 3215. 04Z MVFR CIG..

CYS 181010 100 SCT C250 BKN 2512. 16 Z C80 BKN 2815. 22Z C50 OVC 2920G30.
  04Z MVFR CIG WIND..

CPR 181010 140 SCT C250 BKN 2320G30. 17Z C60 OVC 2325G40. 22Z 30 SCT
  C60 OVC 2325G40 SCT V BKN. 04Z MVFR CIG WIND..

BFF 181010 250 -SCT OCNL 100 SCT. 16Z 100 SCT 250 -BKN 2912. 04Z VFR..

SHR 181010 250 SCT. 19Z 60 SCT C180 BKN 3012. 23Z C50 BKN 3012. 04Z
  MVFR..

DEN 181010 250 -BKN. 16Z 120 SCT C250 BKN 2015. 22Z C100 BKN 2115G20.
  00Z CFP C80 OVC 3118G25. 04Z VFR..

Note: The contractions CLR, SCT, BKN, and OVC have replaced the symbols ○, ◐, ◑, and ⊕.

Figure 9.6
Selected terminal forecasts

18.   Based on the terminal forecasts for Casper (CPR) and Rapid City (RAP) in
Figure 9.6 you would expect
    a. Rapid City to have a ceiling of 1000 feet at the beginning of the forecast
       period
    b. the lowest clouds at Casper to be 3000 feet scattered
    c. the lowest layer of clouds at Rapid City to be 8000 feet broken
    d. the surface wind at Casper to be from 250° at 23 knots after frontal passage

19.   Refer to the terminal forecasts for Scottsbluff (BFF) and Rapid City (RAP) in
Figure 9.6. What is the lowest ceiling forecast during this period at either of these
stations?
    a. 2500 feet broken
    b. 4000 feet scattered
    c. 5000 feet broken
    d. 8000 feet broken

20.   Refer to the 1300 aviation weather reports for Casper (CPR) and Salt Lake City
(SLC) in Figure 9.7. Which statement is true?
    a. At Salt Lake City there were wisps or streaks of water or ice particles falling
       out of the clouds in all quadrants.
    b. The altimeter setting at Casper was 30.38 inches of mercury.
    c. The cloud bases were lower at Casper than at Salt Lake City.
    d. The temperature/dewpoint spread was greater at Casper than at Salt Lake
       City.

SA 181300
RAP SA 1251 250 -SCT 15 042/36/21/1909/959
BFF SA 1253 200 -SCT 25 088/27/19/0805/974
SNY RS 1252 CLR 20 088/32/27/2812/975
CPR SA 1253 140 SCT 250 -BKN 15 038/37/21/2418/967 → CPR ↘11/7 11/8
CYS SA 1251 E250 BKN 15 073/42/21/2708/980 → CYS ↘ 10/5 11/1
→ CYS 10/5 CYS RWY LGTS 12-30 OTS
→ CYS 11/1 CYS 12-30 CLSD 15-2300 WKDAY
LAR SA 1252 E120 BKN 250 OVC 15 086/35/22/2313/983
SLC SA 1251 E110 OVC 30 079/53/28/1916G24/981/VIRGA ALQDS

SA 181400
RAP SA 1352 250 -SCT 35 028/45/20/2415/958
BFF SA 1351 80 SCT 200 -BKN 25 090/29/20/0000/975
SNY SA 1354 100 SCT 250 -SCT 20 088/31/24/2608/974
CPR SA 1351 140 SCT 250 -BKN 60 027/38/21/2222G29/964 → CPR ↘ 11/7 11/8
CYS SA 1354 E250 BKN 30 071/40/21/2906/978 → CYS ↘ 10/5 11/1
→ CYS 10/5 CYS RWY LGTS 12-30 OTS
→ CYS 11/1 CYS 12-30 CLSD 15-2300 WKDAY
LAR SA 1355 50 SCT E100 BKN 250 OVC 40 090/33/23/2310/983
SLC SA 1352 E90 OVC 25RW- 096/53/30/2410G21/986/RB52 WND 20V26

Note: The contractions CLR, SCT, BKN, and OVC have replaced the symbols ○, ◐, ◑, and ⊕.

Figure 9.7
Selected surface aviation weather reports

21.   Refer to the 1300 aviation weather reports for Sidney (SNY) and Cheyenne (CYS) in Figure 9.7. Which statement is true?
    a. The altimeter setting at Sidney was 29.75 inches of mercury.
    b. The surface wind at Sidney was from 028° at 12 knots.
    c. The temperature/dew point spread was greater at Sidney than at Cheyenne.
    d. The visibility was greater at Cheyenne than at Sidney.

22.   Which statement is true about in-flight weather advisories?
    a. AIRMETS will be issued about such severe weather phenomena as tornadoes, embedded thunderstorms, squall lines, severe and extreme turbulence, hail of ¾ inch, and severe icing.
    b. In-flight weather advisories are also called PIREPs (pilot reports).
    c. SIGMETs will be issued about weather phenomena that may be potentially hazardous to single-engine and light aircraft.
    d. The purpose of this service is to notify en route pilots of the possibility of encountering hazardous flying conditions.

MKC WA 181250
181250Z-181900Z

AIRMET CHARLIE 1. FLT PRCTN. MTNS WRN WYO AND WRN COLO OCNL
MDT TURBC BLO 180 WITH LCL STG UDDF ERN SLPGS WITH CONDS CONTG
BYD 19Z.

MKC WA 180820
180820-181500Z

AIRMET ALFA 2. FLT PRCTN. ERN AND CNTRL KANS AND SERN NEB CIGS
BLO ONE THSD AND VSBYS OCNL BLO 3MI IN FOG WITH CONDS SPRDG
NWD INTO NERN NEB BY 15Z. CONDS CONTG AFT 15Z.

MKC WA 181435
181435Z-182100Z

AIRMET BRAVO 1. FLT PRCTN. MTNS NWRN WYO OBSCD IN CLDS AND
SNW AOA 70 WITH CONDS SPRDG SWD AND EWD AND CONTG BYD 21Z.
CONT ADVY BYD 21Z.

Figure 9.8
In-flight advisories

23.   Refer to the in-flight advisories in Figure 9.8. Which statement is true about
AIRMET charlie 1?
   a. In western Wyoming the visibilities are occasionally below 3 miles in fog.
   b. Precipitation is occurring over the mountains of western Wyoming.
   c. The weather conditions given are expected to continue beyond 1800 Green-
      wich time.
   d. Western Colorado has mild turbulence below 1800 feet MSL.

24.   Weather specialists available on a nationwide FSS frequency of 122.0 to provide
time-critical weather information such as severe weather en route utilize a service
labeled
   a. ATIS
   b. EFAS
   c. PATWAS
   d. TWEB

25.   FAR 91.5 states that you familiarize yourself with all available weather information before any flight outside the local area. This regulation is a
   a. suggestion for safe flight

b. requirement that applies only when IFR or marginal VFR conditions exist

c. requirement for student pilots and a suggestion for pilots who hold at least a private pilot certificate

d. requirement for all pilots

26.   An IFR flight encounters clear ice at 8000 feet in clouds and the pilot calls FSS to report the situation. FSS prepares a message and broadcasts it to other pilots. This is an example of a/an

a. AIRMET

b. *NOTAM*

c. PIREP

d. SIGMET

27.   When you telephone for a preflight weather briefing, you should

a. identify the radio communications equipment aboard the aircraft

b. identify yourself as a pilot (student, private, or commercial)

c. state the number of hours you have flown within the preceding 90 days

d. all of the above

28.   The advisory that estimates the potential for severe and general thunderstorms over a 24-hour period is called a/an

a. AIRMET

b. convective outlook (AC)

c. severe weather watch bulletin (WW)

d. SIGMET

29.   Which chart would be most useful in preflight planning to identify the movement of a particular thunderstorm cell?

a. prognosis chart

b. radar summary chart

c. surface weather map

d. weather depiction chart

ANSWERS

Key Terms and Concepts

1.	1	2.	d	3.	j	4.	a
5.	b	6.	x	7.	v	8.	p
9.	t	10.	g	11.	r	12.	h
13.	f	14.	k	15.	c	16.	w
17.	o	18.	n	19.	s	20.	u
21.	i	22.	q	23.	e	24.	m
25.	y						

Review Questions

1.   a; this is the symbol for a cold front. In this case it extends south from El Paso. To the north of El Paso it is a stationary front.
2.   c; it has little movement because the front is stationary (moving at 5 miles per hour or less).
3.   a; the arrow's tail points in the direction from which the wind is coming.
4.   b; the sky is covered by about 70 to 80 percent clouds, which is classified as broken.
5.   b; you have a good memory.
6.   b; you have an excellent memory.
7.   d; a warm front is replacing cooler surface air.
8.   c; solid lines enclose areas below VFR minimums (visibility of less than 3 miles and/or a ceiling of less than 1000 feet).
9.   d; scalloped lines enclose marginal VFR areas (1000-to-3000-foot ceilings and/ or visibilities of 3 to 5 miles).
10.   b; they also contain areas, enclosed by scallops, of marginal VFR conditions.
11.   a; they are four-panel and include forecasts for low-level and surface conditions 12 and 24 hours in advance.
12.   c; the first two digits plus a zero represent the direction; the second two digits represent the speed in knots; plus (+) or minus (−) indicates the temperature relative to 0 degrees Celsius; and the last two digits represent the actual temperature.
13.   d; see 12 above. For FL above FL 24, temperatures are negative above 24,000 (TEMPS NEG ABV 24,000).
14.   d; 99 refers to winds less than 5 knots.
15.   d; they are given in reference to sea level unless otherwise noted.
16.   b; read directly from the forecast.
17.   a; read directly from the forecast.
18.   b; read directly from the forecast.
19.   c; read directly from the forecast.
20.   a; read directly from the forecast.
21.   a; read directly from the forecast.
22.   d; definition.
23.   c; read directly from the forecast.
24.   b; this service can be used by pilots en route for weather information.
25.   d; FAR 91.5 *requires* that you familiarize yourself with all available weather information before any flight outside the local area.
26.   c; PIREPs are reports filed by pilots about changing weather conditions or other hazards.
27.   b; you should also give your make, model, aircraft call number, VFR or IFR flight plan expectations, ETD, ETA, ETE, and intermediate stops.
28.   b; definition.
29.   b; a radar summary chart contains the direction and speed of echo movements and precipitation trends and intensities.

10/FLIGHT INFORMATION PUBLICATIONS

MAIN POINTS

1. The FAA expects you to be a knowledgeable and updated pilot. Familiarity with a number of publications will accomplish this task. The critical feature of each publication is its currency.

2. Regulatory and technical information publications of importance to the private pilot include:

Federal Aviation Regulations (FARs) (See Appendix B for how the FAA establishes and enforces aviation safety standards.)

Airman's Information Manual (AIM): the so-called bible for navaids, airspace, ATC, and so forth

Airport/Facility Directory: the airport Yellow Pages

Notices to Airmen (NOTAMs): bulletins about flying conditions

Graphic Notices and Supplemental Data (GNSD): airspace and operational data not subject to frequent change (for example, parachute jumping areas; graphic limits of TRSAs)

Airworthiness Directives (ADs): notices about compulsory maintenance, repair, or inspection

3. Nonregulatory and supplemental publications include:

Advisory Circulars (ACs): diverse information for pilots and aircraft owners

Exam-O-Grams: analyses of questions frequently missed on FAA exams

Flight Standards Safety Pamphlets: operational problems affecting safety and pilot judgment

4. Other publications of importance to private pilots include:

National Transportation Safety Board (NTSB) publications: aviation safety statistics; accident and incident reports

National Ocean Survey (NOS) charts: navigation
Sectional aeronautical charts: primary for VFR navigation
World aeronautical charts: for high-flying, high-performance aircraft
VFR terminal control area charts: large-scale charts that cover the area around a TCA
VFR planning charts: medium-scale charts

5. The *Airman's Information Manual (AIM)* includes chapters on navigational aids (radio navaids, airport markings and lighting aids), airspace restrictions, air traffic control (for example, ARTCC, FSS, and VFR advisory services; radio techniques; airport operations at controlled and uncontrolled airports; ATC clearance procedures; preflight activities such as weather briefings; pilot and controller responsibility; emergency procedures; national security and interception procedures), flight safety procedures, good operating practices, aviation physiology, and a glossary of pilot/controller terms.

6. The *Airport/Facility Directory* is an important tool for cross-country flying. It is published every fifty-six days and covers primarily airports and communication facilities. Refer to Figure 10.1 for an example from the *Airport/Facility Directory*.

7. *Notices to Airmen (NOTAMs),* Class Two, are published every fourteen days and contain current flight safety bulletins. They are available for pilot briefings and are posted in FSS facilities.

8. *Graphic Notices and Supplemental Data (GNSD)* refer to restrictions found on aeronautical charts (for example, from parachute jump areas to civil flight test areas). They are updated quarterly.

9. *Advisory Circulars (ACs)* are informative and explanatory in nature. They are not regulations; rather, they attempt to supplement the letter of the law with some guidance as to its intent and with techniques for operating safely within its framework. *ACs* are numbered to correspond with topics covered by the FARs and are revised when necessary to reflect changing concepts, adoption of new equipment, or the approval of new regulations.

10. *Exam-O-Grams* are produced as needed in response to feedback from pilots. Educational rather than directive, they deal with specific and commonly misunderstood topics.

KEY TERMS AND CONCEPTS
Match each term or concept (1–15) with the appropriate description (a–o) below. Each item has only one match.

___ 1. *NOTAMs*   ___ 2. *Exam-O-Gram*
___ 3. NTSB   ___ 4. *GNSD*
___ 5. *ADs*   ___ 6. TCA charts

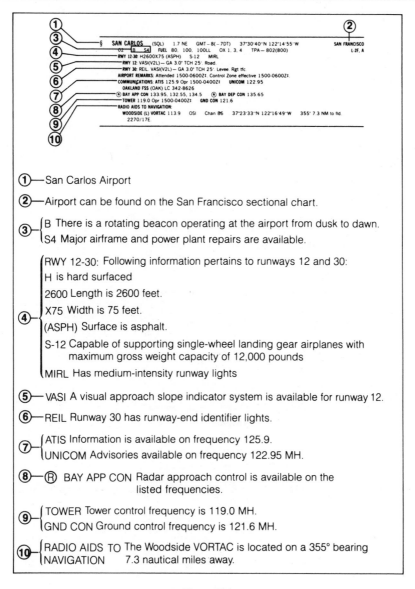

Figure 10.1

① —San Carlos Airport

② —Airport can be found on the San Francisco sectional chart.

③ { B There is a rotating beacon operating at the airport from dusk to dawn.
S4 Major airframe and power plant repairs are available.

④ { RWY 12-30: Following information pertains to runways 12 and 30:
H is hard surfaced
2600 Length is 2600 feet.
X75 Width is 75 feet.
(ASPH) Surface is asphalt.
S-12 Capable of supporting single-wheel landing gear airplanes with
maximum gross weight capacity of 12,000 pounds
MIRL Has medium-intensity runway lights

⑤ —VASI A visual approach slope indicator system is available for runway 12.

⑥ —REIL Runway 30 has runway-end identifier lights.

⑦ { ATIS Information is available on frequency 125.9.
UNICOM Advisories available on frequency 122.95 MH.

⑧ —Ⓡ BAY APP CON Radar approach control is available on the
listed frequencies.

⑨ { TOWER Tower control frequency is 119.0 MH.
GND CON Ground control frequency is 121.6 MH.

⑩ { RADIO AIDS TO The Woodside VORTAC is located on a 355° bearing
NAVIGATION   7.3 nautical miles away.

____ 7. hypoxia   ____ 8. FARs
____ 9. *Airport/Facility Directory*   ____10. *ACs*
____11. sectionals   ____12. hyperventilation
____13. vertigo   ____14. *AIM*
____15. ADIZ

a.   a guidebook of airports

b.   aviation safety statistics and accident/incident reports are published by this
      group

c.   comprehensive publication dealing with navigation, ATC, flight safety, medical
      facts

d.   airspace and other operational data not subject to frequent change are found
      here

e.   large-scale charts covering areas around terminal control areas

f.   publication through which FAA establishes and enforces aviation safety stan-
      dards

g.   spatial disorientation

h.   lack of oxygen

i.   notices of compulsory maintenance, repair, or inspection

j.   mandatory identification point for all aircraft entering the United States

k.   contains bulletin information on flying safety

l.   key medium for FAA to advise the public on a wide variety of subjects; inform-
      ative and explanatory in nature

m.   large-scale charts VFR pilots use for navigation

n.   too much oxygen

o.   contains analyses of questions frequently missed on FAA exams

DISCUSSION QUESTIONS AND EXERCISES

1.   Indicate whether each of the following publications is classified as regulatory
(and/or technical) or nonregulatory in nature:

   a. *NOTAMs*

   b. *GNSD*

   c. NOS aeronautical charts

   d. *ACs*

   e. NTSB reports

   f. *ADs*

   g. FARs

    h. *AIM*

    i. *Airport/Facility Directory*

    j. *Exam-O-Grams*

    k. Flight Standards Safety Pamphlets

2.   What are *Airworthiness Directives* and why should pilots be concerned with them?

3.   In preparing for a trip from Havre, Montana, to Edmonton, Alberta, Canada, you decide to brush up on requirements for international flight. In which publications would you find:

    a. ATC procedures

    b. port-of-entry requirements

    c. navigational aid limitations

    d. operational bulletins

4.   Suppose you want to learn more about the special techniques and hazards of flying at night. What publication would you expect to contain piloting tips and information on the physiology of night flying?

5.   Before using *any* flight information publication for flight planning or navigation, what should you check first?

6.   In what flight information document would you find a list of telephone numbers for an FAA Flight Service weather briefing?

7.   Assume you are planning to arrive at Beals Airport at twilight. The following *NOTAM* is posted for Brule, Nebraska:

BRULE, BEALS ARPT: for rwy lights rwy 8-26 key freq 121.7
(10/81-2)

What does the *NOTAM* say and what operational procedures does it contain that are relevant to your arrival?

8.   Using the entry from the *Airport/Facility Directory* in Figure 10.2, answer the following questions:

a. How would you find out about current conditions and runway use without calling and requesting such information?

b. Is 80 octane fuel available?

SAN DIEGO
§ BROWN FIELD MUNI   (SDM)   13 SE   GMT–8(–7DT)   32°34′20″N 116°58′46″W   **LOS ANGELES**
      524   B   S4   **FUEL** 80, 100, 100LL, JET A   OX 2   TPA— See Remarks   AOE   **L-3C**
         CFR Index Ltd   **IAP**
      RWY 08L-26R: H7999X200 (ASPH-CONC)   S-80, D-110, DT-175   MIRL
         RWY 26R: REIL. Tree. Rgt tfc.
      RWY 08R-26L: H3032X70 (ASPH)   S-12
         RWY 08R: Thld dsplcd 200′. Rgt tfc.   **RWY 26L:** Thld dsplcd 305′.
      AIRPORT REMARKS: Attended 1430-0630Z‡, thereafter for fee call (714) 426-3410 or 421-0873. Parachute
         Jumping. Overngt parking fee. Local Wx observation facility. Rwy 08R-26L dalgt hours only. All asph areas other
         than taxiways and Rwy 08L-26R limited to acft under 12,000 pounds gross weight. TPA— 1524(1000) Rwy
         08L-26R, 1124(600) Rwy 08R-26L. CFR Index Ltd available 1430-0630Z‡. Flight Notification Service (ADCUS)
         available. Control Zone effective 1500-0600Z‡.
      COMMUNICATIONS: ATIS 132.35 opr 1500-0600Z‡   **UN:COM** 122.95
         SAN DIEGO FSS (SAN) LC 291-6381 NOTAM FILE SDM
      ® **SAN DIEGO APP CON** 119.6   ® **SAN DIEGO DEP CON** 125.15
         TOWER 126.9, 128.25 (Rwy 08L-26R) opr 1500-0600Z‡   **GND CON** 124.4   **CLNC DEL** 124.4
      RADIO AIDS TO NAVIGATION:
         MISSION BAY (H) ABVORTAC 117.8   ■ MZB   Chan 125   32°46′56″N 117°13′28″W   120° 17.7 NM to
            fld. 10/15E
         TWEB avbl 1400-0500Z‡.
         VORTAC unusable 300°-310° beyond 20 NM below 5000′   310°-330° beyond 10 NM below 3000′.

Figure 10.2

c. During what hours is the control zone in effect?

d. How would you obtain a weather briefing at this airport?

e. What is the length of the longest runway?

f. What should you know about runway 08R?

g. Why do you suppose runway 26R has a right traffic pattern?

h. If you arrive at Brown Field in the middle of the night and the wind is 330 at 15, on what runway would you land and why?

   i. What is the tower frequency? On what frequency would you contact ground
       control?

   j. What is the field elevation?

9.   T F To determine if UNICOM is available at an airport without a control tower,
you should refer to *Notices to Airmen (NOTAMs)*.

10.   T F Sectional charts for the conterminous United States are updated every six
months.

REVIEW QUESTIONS

1.   *Advisory Circulars* are issued by the Federal Aviation Administration to inform
the aviation public of
       a. projects in the planning stage
       b. proposed rule making
       c. nonregulatory material of interest
       d. regulatory material of interest

2.   Refer to Figure 10.3. VFR aircraft approaching the Denver Stapelton International Airport from the north should, when in the vicinity of Barr Lake, contact
approach control on the frequency of
       a. 120.5 MHz
       b. 120.8 MHz
       c. 124.45 MHz
       d. 125.6 MHz

3.   Refer to Figure 10.3. A VFR aircraft is approaching Denver Stapelton International Airport from the northwest. In the vicinity of Jerrico the pilot should contact
       a. Denver Approach Control for permission to enter the TCA
       b. Denver FSS Arrival Control to obtain a special VFR clearance to enter the
          TCA
       c. Denver Radio for instruction
       d. Denver Stapelton International Airport Control Tower for instructions

4.   Refer to Figure 10.3. How long is runway 17R?
       a. 4864 feet
       b. 7926 feet
       c. 11,500 feet
       d. 12,000 feet

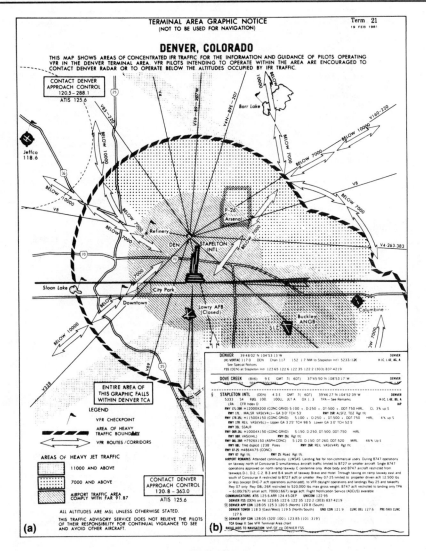

Figure 10.3

5.   The letters VHF/DF appearing in the *Airport/Facility Directory* for a certain airport indicate that

    a. the Flight Service Station has equipment for determining your direction from the station

    b. this airport has a direct-line phone to the Flight Service Station

    c. this airport is a defense facility

    d. this airport is designated as an Airport of Entry

§ **JONESBORO** (JBR) 2.6 E GMT-6(-5DT) 35°49'51''N 90°38'47''W   MEMPHIS
  262   B   S4   **FUEL** 80, 100, JET A+   CFR Index A   H-4F, L-14F
  RWY 05-23: H5599X150 (ASPH) S-80, D-90, DT-140 MIRL   IAP
    RWY 23: VASI
    RWY 14-32: H4101X150 (ASPH) S-30 MIRL
     RWY 14: Thld dsplcd 130'   RWY 32: Railway 700' thld dsplcd 160'
    RWY 18-36: H3943X60 (ASPH) S-30
     RWY 18: Trees 1800'. Thld dsplcd 160'.   RWY 36: Bldg 1400' from thld. Thld dsplcd 347'.
  AIRPORT REMARKS: Attended 1200-0100Z‡. Control Zone effective 1200-0400Z‡.
  COMMUNICATIONS: UNICOM 123.0
    JONESBORO FSS (JBR) on fld 123.6 122.3 122.2 122.1R 108.6T (501) 935-3471
     Opr 1200-0400Z‡. DL- dial 0, ask for ENTERPRISE 0246 O/T ctc Memphis FSS
  RADIO AIDS TO NAVIGATION:
    (T) BVOR 108.6 JBR 35°52'30''N 90°35'18''W   222° 3.1 NM to fld. Unmonitored 0400-1200Z‡

PINE BLUFF   34°14'48''N 91°55'34''W   MEMPHIS
  (L) BVORTAC 116.0 PBF Chan 107   181° 3.9 NM to Grider Fld   L-14F
    VOR unusable 054°-075° beyond 35 NM below 5000'
           170°-185° beyond 30 NM below 2000'
           236°-249° beyond 20 NM below 6000', or beyond 26 NM below 13000'.
    TACAN az unusable 091°-129° beyond 20 NM below 3500'

PINE BLUFF

  GRIDER FLD (PBF) 4.3 SE GMT-6(-5DT) 34°10'32''N 91°56'07''W   MEMPHIS
    206   B   S4   **FUEL** 80, 100, JET A   CFR Index A   H-4F, L-14F
    RWY 17-35: H6000X150 (ASPH) S-50, D-70, DT-110 HIRL   IAP
     RWY 17: MALSR, VASI. Key 118.4 7 times in 5 sec for high, 5 times in 5 sec for med, 3 times in 5 sec
      for low intensity.
     RWY 35: VASI
    AIRPORT REMARKS: Attended 1300-0500Z‡. On call other hrs. Control Zone effective 1200-0400Z‡.
    COMMUNICATIONS:
     LITTLE ROCK FSS (LIT) DL-536-8466
     PINE BLUFF FSS (PBr) 123.6 on arpt (501) 536-8466 Opr 1400-2200Z‡
      Flight planning/briefing svc only
     PINE BLUFF RCO 122.6 122.2 122.1R 116.0T (LITTLE ROCK FSS)
     PINE BLUFF APP/DEP CON 118.4 Opr 1200-0400Z‡
     LITTLE ROCK APP/DEP CON 124.2 0400-1200Z‡
     PINE BLUFF TOWER: 118.4 Opr 1200-0400Z‡   GND CON: 122.7
    RADIO AIDS TO NAVIGATION:
     PINE BLUFF (L) BVORTAC 116.0 PBF Chan 107   34°14'48''N 91°55'34''W   181° 3.9 NM to fld
       VOR unusable 054°-075° beyond 35 NM below 5000'
             170°-185° beyond 30 NM below 2000'
             236°-249° beyond 20 NM below 6000', or beyond 26 NM below 13000'.
       TACAN az unusable 091°-129° beyond 20 NM below 3500'
     ILS 111.7 I-PBF RWY 17 LOC only

LITTLE ROCK   34°40'39''N 92°10'49''W   MEMPHIS
  (H) BVORTAC 113.9 (LIT) Chan 86   315° 3.8 NM to Adams Fld   H-4F, L-14E

LITTLE ROCK FSS (LIT) on Adams Fld   MEMPHIS
  122.55, 122.35, 122.2, 122.1R, 113.9T (501) 376-0721   H-4B, L-14E

LITTLE ROCK

§ **ADAMS FIELD** (LIT) 1.7 E GMT-6(-5DT) 34°43'48''N 92°13'59''W   MEMPHIS
  257 ·   B   S4   **FUEL** 80, 100 JET A   OX 1, 3   LRA   CFR Index C   H-4B, L-14E
  RWY 04-22: H7010X150 (ASPH) S-70, D-90, DT-140 HIRL   IAP
    RWY 04: SSALR Thld dsplcd 127'   RWY 22: MALSR, VASI
  RWY 17-35: H5125X150 (ASPH) S-30, D-45, DT-70 MIRL
    RWY 17: Road 260'. Thld dsplcd 270'   RWY 35: Road 33' AL'SF1
  RWY 14-32: H4032X150 (ASPH) S-26 MIRL
    RWY 14: Road 220'. Thld dsplcd 365'   RWY 32: Trees 3000'
  AIRPORT REMARKS: Landing fee. Rwy 14-32 closed to air carriers.
    Transient acft parking at airline terminal ramp ctc arpt police at airline concourse for reentry to locked
    operations area.
  COMMUNICATIONS: ATIS 125.6 1200-0600Z‡   UNICOM 123.0
    LITTLE ROCK FSS (LIT) on fld. 122.55 122.35 122.2 122.1R 113.9T (501) 376-0721
  ® LITTLE ROCK APP CON: 124.2 042°-221° 119.5 222°-041° 118.1
    TOWER: 118.7 123.85   GND CON: 121.9
  ® LITTLE ROCK DEP CON: 124.2 041°-220° 119.5 221°-040° 118.1
    STAGE III SVC ctc APP CON 20 NM, check ATIS
  RADIO AIDS TO NAVIGATION:
    LITTLE ROCK (H) BVORTAC 113.9 LIT Chan 86   34°40'39''N 92°10'49''W   315° 3.8 NM to fld.
    LASKY NDB (H-SAB) 353 LI   34°57'09''N 92°01'09''W   041° 4.6 NM to fld
    ILS 110.3 J-LIT Rwy 04 LOM LASKY NDB
    ASR 110.3 I-AAY Rwy 22

Figure 10.4

6.   Refer to the *Airport/Facility Directory* data in Figure 10.4. Which statement is true about Jonesboro Airport?

    a. Aircraft and power plant maintenance are not available.

    b. For Airport Advisory Service contact UNICOM on the frequency of 122.8 MHz.

    c. Runway 36 threshold is displaced 347 feet.

    d. The airport elevation is 2620 feet MSL.

7.   Refer to the *Airport/Facility Directory* data in Figure 10.4 for Adams Field at Little Rock and select the true statement.

    a. Grade 115 gasoline is available.

    b. Low-pressure oxygen replacement bottles are available.

    c. Runway 35 threshold is displaced 365 feet.

    d. The longest hard-surfaced runway available for takeoffs is runway 22.

8.   Refer to the *Airport/Facility Directory* data in Figure 10.4 for Adams Field at Little Rock. The proper sequence of radio frequencies for departing this airport southbound using ATIS, ground control, tower, departure control, and the Flight Service Station is

    a. 123.0, 121.7, 118.7, 124.2, and 113.9 MHz

    b. 124.2, 123.86, 121.9, 119.5, and 122.55 MHz

    c. 125.6, 121.9, 118.7, 124.2, and 122.2 MHz

    d. 125.6, 124.2, 121.9, 118.1, and 122.35 MHz

9.   Refer to the *NOTAMs* in Figure 10.5. Select the true statement about an airport in New Jersey.

    a. At Morristown Municipal Airport the runway lights are in service between midnight and 3:00 AM.

    b. Automatic Terminal Information Service is available at Teterboro Airport.

    c. Runway 5-23 is closed at the Wildwood, Cape May County Airport.

    d. The full length of runway 22 is available for landings at Manahawkin Airport.

10.   Refer to the *NOTAMs* in Figure 10.5. Select the true statement about an airport in Nebraska.

    a. At Brule, Beals Airport runway lights are available.

    b. At Trenton Municipal Airport the full length of runway 19 may be used for takeoffs and landings.

    c. Bruning Hawks Field has an operating control tower on the frequency 122.8 MHz.

    d. The facilities and services at Palisade, Rich Field are no longer available; however, the runways may be used for takeoffs and landings.

11.   Refer to the *NOTAMs* in Figure 10.5. Select the true statement about an airport in Nevada or New Hampshire.

NOTICES TO AIRMEN

INFORMATION CURRENT AS OF

THIS SECTION CONTAINS NOTICES TO AIRMEN THAT ARE
EXPECTED TO REMAIN IN EFFECT FOR AT LEAST SEVEN
DAYS.
NOTE: NOTICES ARE ARRANGED IN ALPHABETICAL ORDER
BY STATE (AND WITHIN STATE BY CITY OR LOCALITY).
NEW OR REVISED DATA: NEW OR REVISED DATA ARE
INDICATED BY UNDERLINING THE AIRPORT NAME.
NOTE: ALL TIMES ARE LOCAL UNLESS OTHERWISE
INDICATED.

NEBRASKA

AINSWORTH MUNI ARPT: Rwy 6-24 closed permly. Rwy
    12-30 now 5500 ft x 90 ft. Rwy 17-35 now 6800
    ft. (12/76-2) (12/76-2)
BRULE, BEALS ARPT: For rwy lights rwy 8-26 key
    freq 121.7. (10/76-2)
BRUNING HAWKS FIELD: UNICOM freq 122.8. (10/76-
    2)
CHADRON MUNI ARPT: VASI rwy 20 cmsnd. (11/76-2)
COLUMBUS MUNI ARPT: VASI rwy 14 cmsnd. (1/77-2)
ELLSWORTH, BACKWARD H ARPT: Arpt closed permly.
MCCOOK MUNI ARPT: Rwy 3-21 closed. (11/76-2)
NELIGH ANTELOPE COUNTY ARPT: UNICOM freq 122.8
    cmsnd. (9/76-3)
NORTH LOUP HELIPORT: Helipad 16 ft x 16 ft
    concrete. (12/76-3)
PALISADE, RICH FIELD: Arpt closed permly. (1/77-
    3)
SUPERIOR MUNI ARPT: Rwy 14-32 3700 ft x 60 ft
    asphalt, low intensity rwy lights cmsnd.
    (10/76-2)
TECUMSEH MUNICIPAL ARPT: Rotating beacon cmsnd.
    (10/76-2)
TRENTON MUNICIPAL ARPT: Threshold rwy 19 dsplcd
    200 ft. (11/76-2)

NEVADA

BOULDER CITY MUNI ARPT: Glider operations near
    arpt 0800-1700 Tues-Sun sfc to 6500 ft MSL.
    (1/77-2)
ELY ARPT/YELLAND FLD: For rwy lights rwy 18-36
    key freq 122.8 5 times in 5 seconds 2100-0530.
    (12/76-2)

NEW HAMPSHIRE

GOFFSTOWN COUNTY CLUB AIR PARK: Rwy N-S now 1600
    ft. (10/76-2)
MANCHESTER: VORTAC OTS until Jan 21, 1977 for
    freq change to 114.4. (12/76)
WOLFBORO, LAKE REGION ARPT: For rwy lights key
    freq 123.0 5 times in 5 seconds. (11/76-2)

NEW JERSEY

ALBION ARPT: First 600 ft rwy 22 closed. (2/75)
BELMAR-FARMINGDALE, MONMOUTH COUNTY ARPT: Rwy 14-
    32 now 5500 ft. (12/76-2)
MANAHAWKIN ARPT: Threshold rwy 22 dsplcd 390 ft.
    (4/76-2)
MORRISTOWN MUNI ARPT: Rwy lights 12-30 OTS.
    (6/76)
PITTSTOWN ALEXANDRIA ARPT: For rwy lights rwy 8-
    26 key 121.8 for 3 seconds, lights stay on for
    17 minutes. Rwy 8-26 2400 ft x 120 ft
    asphalt/turf.
TETERBORO: FSS Fast file recorded IFR Flight Plan
    filing service call:
    Teterboro: 201-288-6437 or 201-288-6436 Newark:
    201-624-5352 or 201-624-5353 Morristown: 201-
    539-1581 Caldwell: 201-226-7077 LaGuardia:
    212-898-2323 or 212-898-2339 Rockland County:
    914-352-2569
TETERBORO ARPT: ATIS freq 114.2 cmsnd. (12/76-3)
WEST CREEK, EAGLES NEST ARPT: Arpt closed.
    (3/75)
WEST MILFORD NAIROBI ARPT: Rwy 2 closed landing
    nights. (10/76-2)
WILDWOOD, CAPE MAY COUNTY: S 600 ft rwy 5-23
    closed. Rwy 10-28 closed nights until Feb 1977.
    HIRL rwy 1-19 cmsnd. (12/76-2)

Figure 10.5

a. Goffstown Country Club Air Park now has a 1600-foot displaced threshold on the north-south runway.

b. The Boulder City Municipal Airport is closed to airplane traffic from 0800 to 1700 on Tuesdays and Sundays.

c. The Ely Airport/Yelland Field runway lights may be activated by use of the UNICOM frequency 122.8 MHz.

d. The Manchester VORTAC frequency was changed to 124.4 MHz in January of 1977.

12.   Refer to the *NOTAMs* in Figure 10.5. Select the true statement about an airport in New Jersey.

a. At Belmar-Farmingdale, Monmouth County Airport the length of runway 32 is 5500 feet.

b. At Morristown Municipal Airport runway lights are available for use on runway 12-30.

c. At Pittstown Alexandria Airport the threshold for runway 8 is displaced 120 feet.

d. Runway 22 at Albion Airport is closed.

ANSWERS

Key Terms and Concepts

1. k	2. o	3. b	4. d
5. i	6. e	7. h	8. f
9. a	10. l	11. m	12. n
13. g	14. c	15. j	

Discussions Questions and Exercises

1.   Regulatory publications include a, b, f, g, h, and i.

3.a. *AIM.*

b. *Airport/Facility Directory; AIM.*

c. *GNSD.*

d. *NOTAMs.*

e. VFR planning charts.

4.   *AIM.*

5.   Its currency.

6.   *Airport/Facility Directory.*

7.   For Beals Airport at Brule, Nebraska. Runway lights are available for runway 8-26 by keying the radio mike on 121.7 MHz.

8.   a; listen to ATIS on 132.35.

b; yes, 80 octane is available.

c; 1500–0600 zulu.

d; call San Diego FSS on the phone (291-6381), local call.

e; 7999 feet.

f; it has a 200-foot displaced threshold and uses a right pattern.

g; to keep clear of traffic departing and arriving on runway 26L.

h; you would use 26R since it is lighted; it has the best angle with respect to the wind.

i; 126.9; 121.6.

j; 524 feet MSL.

9. F; you should refer to the appropriate *Airport/Facility Directory*.

10. T; see the sectional chart legend.

Review Questions

1. c; they are just as the name implies, advisory in nature (informative, but not regulatory).

2. a; Barr Lake is a VFR checkpoint as indicated by the flag. Since it is to the north of Denver, aircraft should contact approach control on 120.5.

3. a; all VFR traffic must contact Denver Approach Control for permission to enter the TCA.

4. c; RWY 17R-35L: H11,500 × 150 means the runway is 11,500 feet long by 150 feet wide.

5. a; the VHF direction finder indicates your magnetic direction from the station.

6. c; RWY 36 . . . thld dsplcd 347 means runway 36 has a displaced threshold of 347 feet.

7. d; as listed for runway 04-22.

8. c; as listed.

9. b; Teterboro Airport is directly above the notation for West Creek, and ATIS is 114.2.

10. a; lights are available for Brule on runway 8-26.

11. c; for runway lights key your mike five times in five seconds on 122.8 at Ely Airport/Yelland Field.

12. a; Runway 14-32 is now 5500 at Belmar-Farmingdale, Monmouth County Airport.

13. c; self-explanatory.

11/BASICS OF AIR NAVIGATION

MAIN POINTS

1. A **fix** is made when two **lines of position (LOPs)** intersect. There are five basic methods of navigation: **pilotage,** reference to visual landmarks; **dead reckoning (DR),** figuring one's position from time-distance computations using one or more LOPs; **radio,** observing one's bearings from a radio source; **celestial,** navigation by the stars; and **inertial,** continuous DR computations based on airplane instruments.

2. Straight lines that run between the poles are **lines of longitude,** or **meridians. Lines of latitude,** or **parallels,** form the cross streets. Taken together, they provide a geographic coordinate system or grid. The **prime meridian** runs north and south through Greenwich, England, and lines to the east and west are numbered as compass headings. The **equator** divides Northern and Southern Hemispheres and is 0° latitude. Latitude degrees increase as you approach the two poles. For finer discriminations, latitude and longitude are further subdivided into 60 arc minutes per degree and 60 arc seconds per minute. A **nautical mile (NM)** is one minute of latitude marked off vertically on a meridian. The shortest distance between two points on the earth's surface is along a **great circle**—one whose plane runs through the earth's center. Circles whose plane does not run through the earth's center (for example, latitude lines other than the equator) are called **small circles.**

3. The earth is divided into 24 time zones of approximately 15° longitude each. Most time is reported relative to a standard: **Greenwich mean time (GMT),** or **zulu time.** To convert from local time to GMT, add hours to local time depending on which zone you are in and whether the area is observing standard or daylight savings time. Finally, there are several ways to project or create a map: **Lambert conformal conic projection** (common in air navigation), **Mercator cylindrical projection, azimuthal, gnomonic,** and Goode's **homolosine.**

4. **Sectional charts** are used primarily for low-altitude, low-airspeed flight by reference to visible landmarks. They contain three general types of information: topographical features: cities, roads, towers (MSL with AGL given in parentheses), contour lines, lakes, and so on; aeronautical data: airports, communication information, airspace restrictions, and so forth; and legend and notes: airport directory, VFR flight rules, and so on. Other charts are **terminal area charts** for selected TCAs, **world aeronautical charts (WACs)** for higher altitude flights where less detail is needed, **operational navigation charts (ONCs)** for navigation over long routes outside the United States, **jet charts, planning charts,** and **IFR charts.** All charts are updated frequently, and it is against FARs to use outdated charts.

5. The **navigational plotter** consists of a straightedge, mileage scales, and a protractor. To determine a course, select the appropriate chart, make a general inspection of the terrain, draw a true course line (assuming you select a direct route), determine the **true course,** or **TC** (using a meridian line nearest the center of your course and your plotter), measure the distance, divide the course into equal intervals every 10 to 20 miles, and select prominent landmarks (plainly visible ones that suggest direction as well as position) on both sides of the course line (called **bracketing**).

6. **Dead reckoning (DR)** begins with determining a true course line and then making corrections for wind (**wind correction angle,** or **WCA**). When the value of the WCA is added to or subtracted from the true course, the result is called the **true heading (TH).** Angular **variation (VAR)** between magnetic and geographic north is shown on the chart and must be inserted in the equation to obtain **magnetic heading (MH).** Magnetic heading needs to be corrected for **compass deviation (CD)** to obtain **compass heading (CH).** Another facet of DR involves computing time en route and fuel consumption. First, convert *indicated airspeed (IAS)* to *calibrated airspeed (CAS)*. Next, determine **true airspeed (TAS)** and adjust for wind effects to arrive at **ground speed (GS),** which is crucial in determining how fast you will travel from fix to fix.

7. Once you complete all steps normally involved in simple pilotage, you do a number of other steps for dead reckoning, all of which are facilitated by using a **flight computer** or **electronic flight calculator.** First, to determine true heading, you use the wind face of the flight computer to calculate both WCA and GS for any given TC, TAS, and wind condition (obtained from winds aloft forecast). Any crosswind component will affect your TC, and the effect is magnified as the crosswind component increases. Second, to determine the magnetic heading, you need to correct for the magnetic variation shown on the chart. **Isogonic lines** are lines of equal variation. The line of no variation is referred to as the **agonic line.** If the variation is to the west, you add it to the true heading; if it is to the east, you subtract it. To remember this, use the rhyme: "East is least ($-$) and west is best ($+$)." *Magnetic course* (MC) is true course corrected for variation *without* taking wind into account; it is used by the FAA to regulate cruising altitudes. Magnetic heading corrected for compass deviation error gives the compass heading you will need to hold in order to fly a desired track.

8. Your flight computer or electronic calculator will greatly simplify solving dead reckoning problems, but you should also understand the concepts behind each calculation. Most calculations are based on the relationship between distance (D), time (T), and rate (R) such that R = D/T. Endurance can be calculated by dividing fuel on board by fuel flow (gallons per hour). The computer can be used to solve these and similar proportion problems. You will need to spend time with your computer to learn to read the scales accurately.

9. In addition to ground speed, endurance, fuel flow, and time, the computer also has a scale to convert calibrated airspeed to true airspeed (corrected for the effects of less dense air at higher altitudes). TAS must be determined before WCA or GS can be computed. To compute TAS, you need to know the pressure altitude, temperature, and indicated airspeed. The flight computer also allows you to compute true altitudes for nonstandard temperatures, density-altitude for a given temperature and pressure altitude, and to make conversions such as statute miles to nautical miles, pounds of fuel to gallons, and Fahrenheit to Celsius.

10. The wind correction angle is the number of degrees you must add or subtract from your true course to obtain a true heading that compensates for drift. Ground speed is affected by both the speed and the direction of the wind. Both ground speed and true heading can be derived from the computer by following specific instructions written on most computers. After you have done many practice exercises, these computations will be routine.

11. The choice of a flight computer or electronic calculator is an individual one. In either case, it is wise to understand the concepts and relationships so that you can intuitively arrive at an estimate. The computer or calculator can then give a precise answer.

12. If you use a calculator during the FAA written test, information relating to regulations, ATC signals, and so forth must be obscured; memory circuits must be cleared before and after the test; and tape printout if produced must be surrendered at the end of the test. Further, you cannot use the operations manual, nor can you use calculators with permanent memories or prewritten programs related to the test.

13. As with the flight computer, if you use an electronic calculator, it is wise to become familiar with its accurate operation. Again, it is important to understand the concepts and relationships so that you can detect unexpected answers.

KEY TERMS AND CONCEPTS, PART 1
Match each term or concept (1–20) with the appropriate description (a–t) below. Each item has only one match.

__ 1. zulu   __ 2. inertial
__ 3. pilotage   __ 4. protractor

___ 5. equator
___ 7. bracketing
___ 9. longitude
___11. compass heading
___13. great
___15. true heading
___17. dead reckoning
___19. sectional chart

___ 6. latitude
___ 8. terminal control area chart
___10. fix
___12. magnetic heading
___14. celestial
___16. plotter
___18. small
___20. prime meridian

a.   TH plus or minus VAR
b.   navigation by reference to visual landmarks
c.   typical one has a straightedge, mileage scales, and protractor
d.   circle whose plane does not run through the center of the earth
e.   straight lines that run between the poles
f.   selecting landmarks on both sides of a course line
g.   MH corrected for compass deviation
h.   navigation by reference to the sun
i.   chart that depicts a TCA (scale of 1 inch = 4 miles)
j.   parallel lines that circle the earth
k.   point where two lines of position intersect
l.   semicircular compass rose used to measure angles
m.   line that divides North and South Hemispheres
n.   TC plus or minus the WCA
o.   time used for most weather reports and flight planning
p.   navigation by making time-distance computations along a LOP
q.   navigation by reference to motion sensors mounted on the aircraft
r.   chart used primarily for low-altitude, low-airspeed flight by reference to visual landmarks
s.   line that runs through Greenwich, England
t.   circle whose plane runs through the center of the earth

KEY TERMS AND CONCEPTS, PART 2

Match each term or concept (1–14) with the appropriate description (a–n) below. Each item has only one match.

___ 1. agonic line
___ 3. pressure altitude
___ 5. true airspeed
___ 7. true altitude
___ 9. magnetic course
___11. calibrated airspeed
___13. wind correction angle

___ 2. indicated airspeed
___ 4. compass heading
___ 6. magnetic variation
___ 8. easterly
___10. westerly
___12. isogonic line
___14. ground speed

a.   IAS corrected for instrument position errors
b.   true course corrected for magnetic variation but not wind effects
c.   number of degrees added to or subtracted from TC to yield TH

d.   lines of equal variation
e.   airspeed corrected for density-altitude
f.   difference between true north and magnetic north
g.   variation added to TH to obtain MH
h.   altitude read from the altimeter with 29.92 set in the Kollsman window
i.   airspeed read directly from the airspeed indicator
j.   actual height above MSL
k.   TAS corrected for wind effects
l.   magnetic course corrected for compass deviation
m.   line of no variation
n.   variation subtracted from TH to obtain MH

DISCUSSION QUESTIONS AND EXERCISES

1.   What is the relationship between a line of position and a fix?

2.   Name and define the three basic methods of navigation commonly used by private pilots.

3.   What does the expression 55°40'N, 104°20'W represent and how would it be interpreted by a pilot or navigator?

4.   T F The prime meridian runs east and west while the equator runs north and south.

5.   T F Longitude lines are of the same length, whereas latitude lines decrease in length as the distance from the equator increases.

6.   T F Longitude lines converge at the poles, whereas latitude lines converge at the equator.

7.   What are great circles and how are they important to pilots?

8.   How are surface obstructions and terrain relief depicted on sectional charts? What information about them would you expect to find in a sectional chart?

9.   Refer to your San Francisco sectional chart. What is the highest obstruction (above ground level) within a 5-nautical mile radius of Hanford Airport (approximately 120°30′N, 36°30′W)? What kind of obstruction is it? How high is it above ground level?

10.   Locate the quadrangle on your San Francisco sectional chart in which the city of Stockton is located (approximately 121°N, 38°W). At a quick glance, can you tell how high above sea level the highest obstruction is? How is this reported on the map?

11.   Find the Fresno Air Terminal on your San Francisco sectional chart (approximately 120°N, 37°W). Explain what each of the various numbers and symbols above and below the name mean.

12.   Name two major limitations to pilotage as a primary means of air navigation.

13.   What is bracketing? Explain why it is an important procedure to follow in pilotage.

14.   Why is dead reckoning considered a means of coordinating other methods of navigation?

15.   Given:

True course	280°
Variation	15° east
Cruising altitude	8500 feet MSL
Winds at 9000 feet	240° at 35 knots
True airspeed	110 knots

Find the magnetic heading, the wind correction angle, and the ground speed.

16.   Suppose you plan a flight of 225 statute miles at an anticipated ground speed of 123 mph. The airplane has 36 gallons of usable fuel on board and a fuel consumption rate of 9 gallons per hour. How much fuel will you have left when you land at your destination? How much flying time does this represent?

17.   Assume you depart Hays, Kansas, at 1330 CDT for a 2-hour flight to Colorado Springs, Colorado. What would be your landing time, expressed in GMT, or zulu time?

18.   Suppose the OAT is 68 degrees Fahrenheit and you are flying at a CAS of 120 knots at a pressure altitude of 6500 MSL. What is your TAS in knots? What is your TAS in mph?

19.   What special limitations does the FAA put on the use of electronic calculators during the FAA Private Pilot's Written Test?

20.   For the next problem, refer to your San Francisco sectional chart. You are going to fly a cross-country trip from Salinas Airport (approximately 36°50′N, 122°30′W) to Fresno Chandler Airport. Given:

Usable fuel	29 gallons
Fuel consumption	5.3 gallons per hour
Cruise altitude	7500 feet
TAS	91 knots
Winds at 6000 feet	210° at 25 knots
Winds at 9000 feet	230° at 35 knots

a. How far is it from Salinas to Fresno?

b. What is your true course?

c. What is your magnetic course?

d. What is the wind correction angle? What is the magnetic heading?

e. What will your ground speed be? How long will it take you to fly the trip?

f. How much fuel will you burn?

21.   Given the same conditions as in question 20, answer the following questions for a return trip to Salinas. Use a cruise altitude of 6500 feet and assume the winds at 6000 feet are representative.

a. What is your true course?

b. What is your magnetic course?

c. What is the wind correction angle? What is the magnetic heading?

d. What will your ground speed be? How long will it take you to make the trip?

e. How much fuel will you burn?

REVIEW QUESTIONS

1.   Navigation by figuring one's position through reference to lines of position and time-distance computations is called
   a. celestial navigation
   b. dead reckoning
   c. inertial navigation
   d. pilotage

2.   The intersection of a longitude line and a latitude line is called a/an
   a. azimuth
   b. coordinate
   c. grommet
   d. rhumb

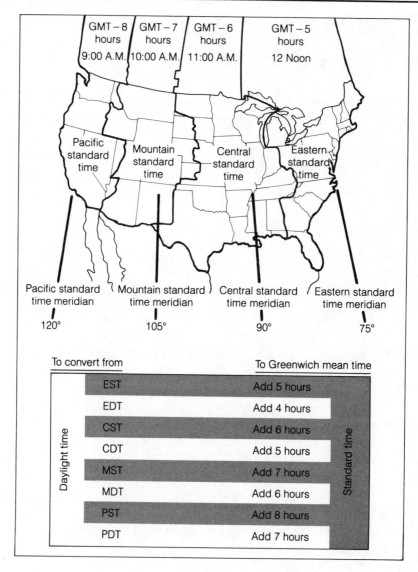

Figure 11.1

3.   Refer to Figure 11.1. Assume that you depart an airport in the central standard time zone at 0930 CST for a 2-hour flight to an airport located in the mountain standard time zone. What would be the landing time?

    a. 0930 MST

    b. 1030 MST

    c. 1130 MST

    d. 1230 MST

4.   Refer to Figure 11.1. Assume that you depart an airport in the central daylight
time zone at 0845 CDT for a 2-hour flight to an airport located in the mountain daylight
time zone. At what Greenwich mean time would you expect to land?
   a. 1345Z
   b. 1445Z
   c. 1545Z
   d. 1645Z

5.   Refer to Figure 11.1. Assume that you depart an airport in the pacific standard
time zone at 1230 PST for a 3-hour flight to an airport located in the central standard
time zone. At what Greenwich mean time would you expect to land?
   a. 0030Z
   b. 1630Z
   c. 2130Z
   d. 2330Z

6.   Refer to Figure 11.2. The maximum elevation of the terrain and obstructions
(towers, antennas, and so on) within the quadrangle bounded by the ticked lines of
latitude and longitude is
   a. 495 AGL
   b. 880 MSL
   c. 1600 AGL
   d. 1600 MSL

7.   Refer to the obstruction near the town of Tranquility in Figure 11.2. The top of
the obstruction is
   a. 253 AGL
   b. 253 MSL
   c. 418 AGL
   d. 1600 MSL

8.   Refer to the obstructions near Madera in Figure 11.2. Which of the following
statements is correct?
   a. Each of these is a single obstruction, neither of which is more than 1000 feet
      MSL.
   b. This is a group obstruction; the base of one is 213 AGL and the base of the
      other is 314 AGL.
   c. This is a group obstruction; the tops are less than 1000 feet AGL.
   d. This is a group obstruction; the maximum top is 587 feet MSL.

9.   Which statement is true about a national wildlife refuge such as that shown in
Figure 11.2?
   a. A minimum altitude of 3000 feet above the terrain is required while flying
      over these areas.

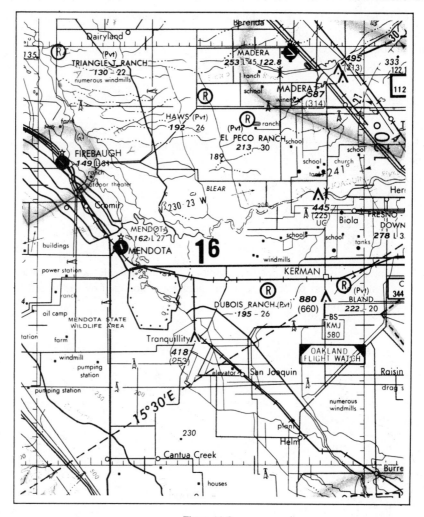

Figure 11.2

b. Pilots are requested to maintain a minimum altitude of 2000 feet above the terrain while flying over these areas.

c. Prior approval is required to fly over these areas.

d. There are no restrictions for such areas.

10.   The following notation appears on a sectional chart:

JUNCTION MOA, 12,000 to but not incl FL 180.
Hours of use 0800–1900 daily, other times by *NOTAM*.
Contact nearest FSS.

Select the true statement about the Junction MOA and a proposed flight that would take you through it.

a. IFR traffic may be cleared through the MOA, and VFR pilots should exercise caution while flying within the area.
b. The appropriate military authority having jurisdiction over the area must be contacted to obtain permission to fly within the area.
c. You should circumnavigate the MOA by flying around it.
d. You should contact the nearest FSS for rerouting around the area.

11.   An asterisk (*) at the top of an airport symbol on a sectional chart indicates that
a. high-performance aircraft are permitted to land
b. the airport has a rotating beacon in operation from sunset to sunrise
c. services and fuel are available
d. this is a military airport

12.   Refer to Figure 11.2. Assume that you are flying over the city of Madera from east to west. According to regulations, which altitude is the minimum safe altitude required to fly over the highest obstruction shown?
a. 600 feet AGL
b. 1000 feet MSL
c. 1400 feet AGL
d. 3000 feet AGL

13.   Refer to Figure 11.2. What statement about Madera Airport is correct?
a. FSS at this airport operates on 122.8.
b. Landing lights are available on request.
c. The airport is 253 AGL.
d. None of the above is correct.

14.   Refer to Figure 11.2. Suppose the following surface aviation weather report has been issued for Madera:

MAD SA 1351 80 BKN 25 090/29/20/0000/975

At what indicated altitude above Madera would you expect to find the base of the clouds?
a. 253 feet MSL
b. 800 feet MSL
c. 1053 feet MSL
d. 8000 feet MSL
e. 8253 feet MSL

15.   Flight through a restricted area with continuous hours of operation should not be accomplished unless the pilot has
a. an airplane that is transponder equipped
b. filed a VFR flight plan
c. received prior permission from the appropriate authority
d. received prior permission from the commanding officer of the restricted area

16.   True course measurements on a sectional aeronautical chart should be made using a meridian near the midpoint of the course because the

    a. geographic North Pole, from which direction is measured, is not located at the magnetic North Pole

    b. isogonic lines are not parallel

    c. lines of latitude vary from point to point

    d. meridians converge toward the poles and the angles formed by lines of longitude and latitude vary from point to point

17.   Given the following data for a cross-country flight with two legs:

Leg AB	TC 070°, 100 statute miles
Leg BC	TC 120°, 107 statute miles
Wind	325° at 25 knots
TAS	156 miles per hour
Variation	7° east
Fuel consumption	11.3 gallons per hour

What is the *magnetic course* for leg BC?

    a. 108°

    b. 113°

    c. 123°

    d. 127°

18.   Using the data in question 17, the *magnetic heading* for leg BC is

    a. 108°

    b. 113°

    c. 122°

    d. 127°

19.   According to the data in question 17, how much fuel will be used for the entire trip?

    a. 11.8 gallons

    b. 13.8 gallons

    c. 14.9 gallons

    d. 16.8 gallons

20.   Assume that an airplane is serviced with 38 gallons of usable fuel and an average ground speed of 138 mph is anticipated on a flight of 260 statute miles. At a fuel consumption rate of 12 gallons per hour, what will be the maximum flying time available with the fuel remaining after reaching the destination?

    a. 1 hour, 2 minutes

    b. 1 hour, 17 minutes

    c. 2 hours, 5 minutes

    d. 2 hours, 30 minutes

21.   Given:

Distance	260 statute miles
True course	110°
Cruise altitude	7500 feet MSL
Wind at 7500 feet	010° at 30 knots
True airspeed	115 mph
Fuel consumption	8 gallons per hour

What will be the approximate ground speed and amount of fuel consumed?
  a. 95 mph; 21.8 gallons
  b. 112 mph; 19.6 gallons
  c. 116 mph; 17.9 gallons
  d. 128 mph; 15.3 gallons

22.   Given:

Pressure altitude	8000 feet
Outside air temperature	+ 10° Celsius
Indicated airspeed	120 mph

What is the true airspeed?
  a. 104 mph
  b. 118 mph
  c. 138 mph
  d. 148 mph

23.   Given:

Distance	380 statute miles
True course	360°
Cruise altitude	8500 feet MSL
Wind at 8500 feet	230° at 40 knots
True airspeed	139 mph
Fuel consumption	10 gallons per hour

What will be the approximate ground speed and amount of fuel consumed?
  a. 115 mph; 28.6 gallons
  b. 127 mph; 25.0 gallons
  c. 158 mph; 22.1 gallons
  d. 162 mph; 23.4 gallons

24.   Given:

Flight duration	4 hours, 10 minutes
Fuel consumption rate	9.6 gallons per hour

How much fuel will be used?
    a. 25.6 gallons
    b. 36.6 gallons
    c. 40.0 gallons
    d. 65.5 gallons

25.   How many statute miles would 160 nautical miles be?
    a. 129 statute miles
    b. 139 statute miles
    c. 172 statute miles
    d. 184 statute miles

26.   The magnetic heading plus or minus the compass deviation yields the
    a. compass heading
    b. magnetic course
    c. true course
    d. true heading

27.   _____ represents how fast you are actually moving through the air.
    a. Calibrated airspeed
    b. Ground speed
    c. Indicated airspeed
    d. True airspeed

28.   A line of zero magnetic variation is called a/an
    a. agonic line
    b. isobar
    c. isogonic line
    d. rhumb line

29.   Where does one typically find weather information pertaining to wind conditions
at various flight levels?
    a. surface aviation weather reports
    b. terminal forecasts
    c. weather depiction charts
    d. winds aloft forecasts

30.   Refer to Figure 11.3. Given a variation of 17° east in this area, what is the
magnetic course from Olivehurst (A) to Yolo Co (B)?
    a. 180°
    b. 186°
    c. 197°
    d. 203°

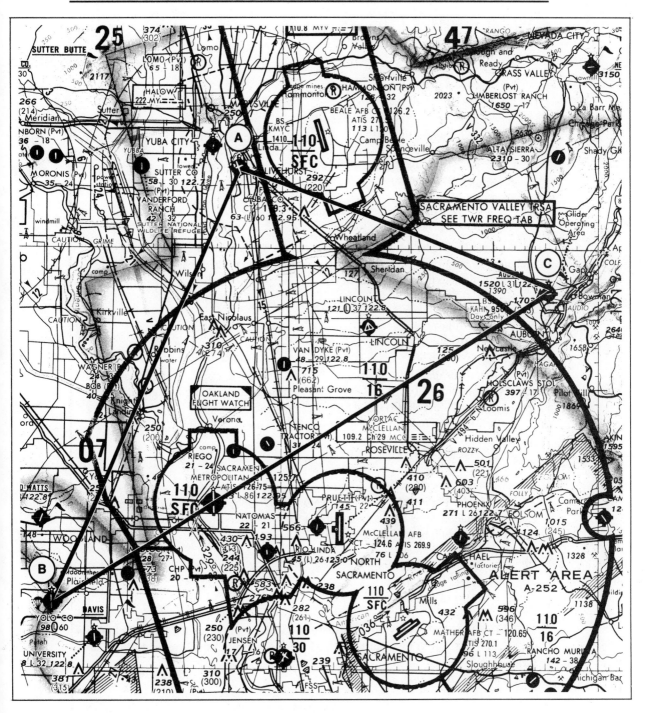

Figure 11.3

31.   Refer to Figure 11.3. Given a variation of 17° east in this area, what is the true course from Yolo Co (B) to Auburn (C)?
       a. 41°
       b. 44°
       c. 58°
       d. 61°

32.   Refer to Figure 11.3. What is the approximate distance from Olivehurst (A) to Auburn (C)?
       a. 25 nautical miles
       b. 28 nautical miles
       c. 50 nautical miles
       d. 57 nautical miles

33.   Refer to Figure 11.3. Suppose you fly the traffic pattern at 1000 feet AGL at Auburn (C) Airport. If the altimeter is properly adjusted to the latest altimeter setting, it would indicate a pattern altitude of
       a. 1000 feet
       b. 2390 feet
       c. 2520 feet
       d. 2710 feet

34.   Refer to Figure 11.3. Given a TAS of 130 mph, a variation of 17° east, and forecast winds from 110° at 15 knots, find your magnetic heading and ground speed from Auburn (C) to Yolo Co (B).
       a. 215°; 140 mph
       b. 218°; 144 mph
       c. 238° at 147 knots
       d. 252° at 138 knots

35.   Refer to Figure 11.3. Given a TAS of 109 mph, a variation of 17° east, a compass deviation of +1°, and winds from 210° at 20 knots, calculate the compass heading and time en route from Olivehurst (A) to Auburn (C).
       a. 83°; 18 minutes
       b. 107°; 15 minutes
       c. 111°; 25 minutes
       d. 141°; 18 minutes

36.   Refer to Figure 11.3. What is the true course from Olivehurst (A) to Yolo Co (B), from Yolo Co (B) to Auburn (C), and from Auburn (C) to Olivehurst (A)? The variation is 17° east.
       a. 185°; 45°; 274°
       b. 195°; 55°; 284°
       c. 202°; 62°; 291°
       d. 219°; 79°; 308°

ANSWERS

Key Terms and Concepts, Part 1
1.	o	2.	q	3.	b	4.	l
5.	m	6.	j	7.	f	8.	i
9.	e	10.	k	11.	g	12.	a
13.	t	14.	h	15.	n	16.	c
17.	p	18.	d	19.	r	20.	s

Key Terms and Concepts, Part 2
1.	m	2.	i	3.	h	4.	l
5.	e	6.	f	7.	j	8.	n
9.	b	10.	g	11.	a	12.	d
13.	c	14.	k				

Discussion Questions and Exercises

4. F; it is just the opposite.

5. T; longitude lines are all the same length and converge at the poles, latitude lines are parallel to one another and become shorter as they approach the poles.

6. F; latitude lines do not converge: they run parallel to one another.

9. The highest obstruction, a tower (KNGS radio), is 305 feet AGL and 553 feet MSL.

10. 3700 feet, as indicated by the maximum elevation figures (MEF). MEFs use large numbers to represent thousands and small numbers to represent hundreds of feet above MSL.

11. The control tower frequency is 118.2. Automatic Terminal Information Service (ATIS) is broadcast on 110.3 and 119.3. The field is 332 feet above sea level (MSL), the longest runway is 9200 feet, and UNICOM is available on 122.95. The FSS above the name indicates that there is a Flight Service Station located on the field.

15. Magnetic heading is 280° (TC). Wind correction angle is (15° VAR), or 253°. Ground speed is 80 to 81 knots.

16. On your trip, you will travel about 1.83 hours (225 ÷ 123), or about 110 minutes (1 hour, 50 minutes), and burn 16.5 gallons (1.83 × 9) of fuel. The fuel remaining is 19.5 gallons (36 − 16.5), which represents about 2.17 hours (19.5 ÷ 9), or 2 hours, 10 minutes. To convert from a decimal representation of hours, such as 2.17, to hours and minutes, you need to multiply the decimal portion (.17) times 60 to determine the number of minutes.

17. Your zulu departure time from Hays would be 1330 + 5 hours, or 1830. You would land at Colorado Springs 2 hours later, or 2030 zulu. To look at it another way, when you land at Colorado Springs, the local time would be 1330 + 2 hours (flying time) − 1 hour (time zone change), or 1430. Adding 6 hours gives you 2030 zulu.

18. Converting 68 degrees Fahrenheit to Celsius yields 20 degrees Celsius. TAS is 136 knots, which converts to 156 mph.

20.a.   87 NM; use your plotter (nautical miles on the sectional chart side).

   b.   87°; use your plotter and a true course.

   c.   87°; 16° = 71° is the magnetic course, so 7500 feet MSL is an appropriate altitude.

   d.   To get the winds at 7500, you need to interpolate between 6000 and 9000 feet. In this example it is easy, since 7500 is right in the middle. Use 220° at 30 knots. The wind correction angle will be about 14° to correct for the effects of the southwesterly winds. So, to obtain your magnetic heading, you compute 87° + 14° (WCA) − 16° (VAR) to get 85° (MH).

   e.   Use your navigation computer or calculator to calculate your ground speed, 109 knots. Divide 85 knots by 109 to give an estimated time en route of .78 hours, or about 47 minutes.

   f.   Multiply .78 hours times 5.3 gallons per hour to arrive at total fuel consumption, 4.1 gallons.

21.a.   267°.

   b.   267° − 16° = 251°, so 6500 feet is an appropriate altitude.

   c.   WCA = 14°; MH = 267° (TC) − 14° (WCA) − 16° (VAR), or 237°.

   d.   75 knots; 1.16 hours, or 1 hour, 10 minutes.

   e.   6.1 gallons.

Review Questions

1.   b; an important procedure for VFR pilots.

2.   b; it also defines a fix; in geographical terms it is a coordinate.

3.   b; you departed at 0930 CST, or 1530Z; your flight of 2 hours made it 1730Z; this converts to 1030 MST. Or, knowing that you lose an hour going one time zone west, you can see how a two-hour flight would add only one hour to your destination time.

4.   c; departure time is 1345Z; arrival is 1545Z.

5.   d; departure time is 2030Z; arrival is 2330Z.

6.   d; the large number in the center of the quadrangle (referred to as the maximum elevation figure) indicates that the highest elevation is 1600 MSL.

7.   a; MSL is indicated in bold figures; AGL is indicated in parentheses.

8.   a; these are separate obstructions: one is 495 MSL and 213 AGL; the other is 587 MSL and 314 AGL.

9.   b; as outlined in *AIM*.

10.   a; when an MOA is in use, IFR traffic may be cleared, if ATC can provide IFR separation. VFR pilots should exercise extreme caution within an active MOA.

11.   c; the * means that the airport has a rotating beacon in operation from sunset to sunrise.

12.   c; the minimum altitude over an obstruction is 1000 feet (FARs). The tallest obstruction is 314 feet AGL, so 1400 AGL would satisfy the requirement.

13.   d; there is no FSS facility at this airport (it would be indicated by the letters FSS); landing lights are in operation from sunrise to sunset at Madera and do not need to be requested; the airport is 253 feet MSL.

14.   e; the report indicates that the clouds are at 8000 feet broken. This measure is of the base of the clouds above ground level and must be added to the height of the airport above sea level.

15.   c; VFR traffic *must* request permission to fly through a restricted area; sectional charts specify whom to contact.

16.   d; midcourse measurements minimize errors due to magnetic variation.

17.   b; MC = TC − VAR. In this problem MC (113°) = TC (120°) − VAR (7°). Remember, "East is least (−) and west is best (+)."

18.   a; convert 25 knots to 29 mph. *Note: Always* check to see what is stated and what is asked when knots and mph occur in the same problem. Given the wind at 325°, the wind correction angle (WCA) is − 5 degrees left at 29 mph. TC (120°) − WCA (5°) yields TH (115°). Subtract VAR (7°) to get MH (108°).

19.   b; for the total trip you need to calculate each leg separately. For segment AB, ground speed is 160 mph for a time of .625 hours (37.5 minutes). For segment BC, ground speed is 181 mph for a time of .591 hours (35 minutes). Total time is 1.22 hours (1 hour, 13 minutes). This requires 13.8 gallons (1.22 hours × 11.3 gallons per hour).

20.   b; divide distance (260 miles) by speed (138 mph) to get time (1.83 hours). Multiply time (1.88 hours) by consumption rate (12 gallons per hour) to get total consumption (22.6 gallons). This leaves 15.4 gallons, which divided by 12 gallons per hour leaves 1.28 hours of fuel. Converting .28 hours to 17 minutes (.28 × 60) makes the answer 1 hour, 17 minutes. Another way to solve the problem is to figure total endurance (38 hours ÷ 12 gallons per hour), or 3.16 hours (3 hours, 10 minutes). Subtract 1.88 from 3.16 to get 1.28 hours remaining.

21.   c; since this problem is done in mph, convert 30 knots to 34.5 mph (30 × 1.15, or use your computer or calculator) for the wind speed. Ground speed is 116 mph. Divide distance (260 miles) by speed (116 mph) to yield time (2.24 hours), which if multiplied by consumption rate (8 gallons per hour) yields total consumption (17.9 gallons).

22.   c; use your calculator or computer for this problem. True airspeed is 138 mph.

23.   d; convert wind speed to mph (40 × 1.15 = 46 mph). Ground speed is 163 mph under these conditions, which if divided into distance (380 miles) yields an elapsed time of 2.33 hours. Elapsed time (2.33) times consumption rate (10 gallons per hour) yields total consumption (23.3 gallons).

24.   c; convert 4 hours, 10 minutes to 4.17 hours. To do this, divide 10 minutes by 60 minutes to get the decimal part of the hour. Multiply 4.17 times 9.6 gallons per hour to get total consumption (40.0 gallons). Or use your calculator or computer.

25.   d; multiply 160 nautical miles times the conversion factor (1.15) to get 184.

26.   a; definition.

27.   d; definition.

28.   a; definition.

29.   d; review.

30. b; this one is a little more difficult since you will probably have to turn your plotter to read the scale.
31. c; 58° (TC).
32. a; using your plotter (sectional chart side), you can measure 25 nautical miles, or 29 statute miles.
33. c; the field elevation is 1520 feet, to which you add 1000 feet.
34. a; your TC is 238°; wind speed is 17.25 mph; ground speed is 140 mph; WCA is $-6°$. 238° (TC) $-$ 6° (WCA) $-$ 17° (VAR) = 215° (MH).
35. a; TC is 111°; 20 knots is 23 mph; the WCA is 12°; ground speed is 110 mph. 111° (TC) + 12° (WCA) $-$ 17° (VAR) yields 106° (MH). CH is 106° (MH) + 1° (DEV), or 107°. Ground speed (110 mph) divided into distance (28 miles) yields roughly .25 hours, or 15 minutes.
36. c; use your plotter to figure the true course for each segment.

12/RADIO NAVIGATION AIDS

MAIN POINTS

1. Radio navigation allows airplanes to track prepositioned LOPs and to fly toward (home) a radio source. A prepositioned radio LOP is called a **bearing.**

2. **Very-high-frequency (VHF) omnidirectional ranges,** or **VORs,** broadcast bearings for all 360 degrees of the compass. Stations using ultra-high frequencies (UHF) are called **tactical air navigation** stations, or **TACAN,** and are used by the military. They also have **distance measuring equipment,** or **DME.** Most VOR and TACAN stations have been combined and are called **VORTACs.** Stations such as commercial radio stations that use low and medium frequencies are called **nondirectional beacons,** or **NDBs,** and are part of the **automatic direction finding (ADF)** system.

3. IFR approaches made using VOR, TACAN or NDBs that provide only bearing information are referred to as **nonprecision approaches.** When a glide slope is also provided, as with an **instrument landing system (ILS)** or **precision approach radar (PAR),** it is referred to as a **precision approach.** Both types of approaches are of primary use to IFR pilots, although VFR procedures (for example, traffic patterns) may be affected by their existence.

4. VORs transmit between 108 and 117.95 MHz. Bearings (called **radials**) radiate from the station; each bearing is named for its magnetic course *from* the station. Magnetic course and the VOR radial are the same only when flying outbound; when flying inbound, the magnetic course is the reciprocal of the VOR radial. VHF airways, called **victor airways,** connect VOR stations.

5. VOR cockpit controls include a tuning knob to obtain the desired frequency, an **omni bearing selector (OBS)** to select the desired radial, a **course deviation indicator (CDI)** to measure deviations from the radial, a **To-From indicator** to designate whether the course selected takes you *to* or *from* the VOR, and an **Off flag** to indicate when the station level is too weak (the station is off, you are too far away, you are passing directly overhead—the *cone of confusion*—or you are 90 degrees off the radial selected in the OBS). VOR receivers also have an audio channel with Morse code or voice identifier, and many stations broadcast weather and *NOTAMs* 15 minutes past the hour. You should always verify that the station is operating and is correctly tuned by listening for its identifier. Some cockpit displays also feature a **radio magnetic indicator (RMI),** a gyrocompass that receives directional signals from a magnetic compass.

6. VOR navigation provides great flexibility with its omnidirectional characteristics. Furthermore, it is relatively free from atmospheric interference and it is relatively accurate (within $\pm 1°$ of the magnetic course). The main disadvantage is that its signals operate on a line-of-sight basis, thus giving them a fairly limited range and necessitating a large network of stations.

7. There are a number of ways to use a VOR:
Always tune and identify the station by selecting the desired frequency and listening to the Morse code or voice identifier. Monitor the station as long as you are using it. Select the desired OBS position and check the Off flag.
If you simply want to fly to the station **(homing),** turn the OBS until the CDI is centered and you have a To indication. Then fly the magnetic heading indicated. When the needle moves off center, recenter it and select a new course with the OBS. Homing is not very efficient since it involves a curved flight path unless you have a direct headwind or tailwind.
If you wish to **proceed direct** to the station, center the CDI with a To indication, fly the indicated heading, and then keep the CDI indicator centered. When the CDI moves off center (due to crosswind), turn the airplane into the wind (toward the CDI needle); make minor changes until you have figured out the amount of crosswind correction needed to keep the needle centered.
To *intercept a radial* you need a heading called the **intercept heading.** The angle the aircraft makes with the radial is called the **angle of interception,** and how fast you approach it is called the **rate of interception.** After setting the inbound course on the OBS with a To indication, turn to the same heading as the inbound course. Note if the CDI points to the left or right and turn toward the needle to establish an intercept angle. If the CDI moves slowly, proceed until you intercept it; if it moves rapidly, cut the intercept angle to slow the needle's movement.
To *intercept an outbound radial,* set the course and check for a From indication. Fly the heading of the outbound course to an intercept heading and follow the intercept procedures already outlined.
Station passage occurs when you pass through the **cone of confusion** above the station. Station passage is confirmed when the To-From indicator makes its first positive change from To to From.

Time-distance checks can also be made using the VOR by timing how long it takes to fly a 10° bearing change. The time in seconds between bearings divided by the degree of bearing change (in this procedure, 10) tells you how many minutes you are from the station. Multiply this figure by your speed per minute and you can calculate how far away the station is.

To *establish a VOR fix* once you have established a course with the CDI centered, tune and verify a second station. Turn the OBS until the CDI is centered and the To-From indicator states From. Read the radial from the OBS and use it to establish your fix. You can use any two stations to obtain a fix, but the fix may not be totally accurate unless you can use two VORs simultaneously. If you know the distance from the station, you can use a single VOR to obtain a **single-station fix.** Since you know the distance to the station, you can also calculate ground speed by dividing the distance by how long it takes you to fly there. Finally, to preflight your VOR equipment, many airports have **VOR test (VOT)** facilities (published in the *Airport/Facility Directory*). Turn the OBS until the CDI is centered; it should read 000° with a From indication or 180° with a To indication (±4° tolerance). If VOT is not available, refer to the *Airport/Facility Directory* for airborne or ground checkpoints (tolerance, ±6°).

8. *Distance measuring equipment (DME)* uses UHF distance-fixing information from the VORTAC system. It measures the slant range, not the linear distance, from the source to the aircraft and is subject to line-of-sight restrictions. DME is valuable not only for distance readings but also as a source for ground speed calculations.

9. **Radio direction finding (RDF)** and **automatic direction finding (ADF)** are radio compasses that use low frequencies (190 to 1750 kHz) to provide bearing information. Unlike VDR and UHF signals, they are not limited to line-of-sight transmission. A serious drawback, though, is their susceptibility to interference.

A homing station that broadcasts a low-frequency navigational signal is called a *nondirectional beacon,* or *NDB*. Many commercial radio stations can also be used for navigational purposes. However, they too are subject to interference and need identify themselves only once every 30 minutes. Radio compass instruments have a **bearing indicator,** an On-Off and volume control knob, and a selector knob.

The first step in ADF navigation is to tune and identify the station. Magnetic bearing to the station is equal to the relative bearing indicated on the ADF plus the magnetic heading. ADF homing is similar to VOR homing; it also involves a curved track to the station if there is any crosswind.

To intercept an inbound course (fixed compass card), fly the magnetic heading of the desired course to the station. Note the number of degrees (must be within 90°) the bearing pointer is deflected from the top index. Turn toward the pointer plus 30° to arrive at the angle of interception. When the pointer has deflected the same number of degrees from the top index as the angle of interception (30°), you will be on the inbound course. Turn to the desired course and make corrections as needed for wind effects. To intercept an outbound course, fly the magnetic heading of the desired outbound course and note the position of the tail of the bearing pointer. Turn away from the tail of the bearing pointer. Beware, however, because outbound tracking can lead to considerable track displacement (outbound homing error). ADF is usually used as a supplement to VOR navigation, for example, to establish fixes.

10. Airway navigation does not always represent the shortest distance between two destinations. An alternative is **area navigation (RNAV),** which involves creating phantom stations (way points) using VOR and/or DME information.

11. Radar allows controllers to monitor traffic visually on a radar screen. The system can provide direct vectors to a destination, but the VFR pilot still has navigational responsibility (important if a transponder fails or if the pilot's service is terminated due to heavy IFR traffic). Radar navigation, rather than being a passive system on the pilot's part, involves several specific procedures, not the least of which is maintaining VFR cloud and visibility minimums. The transponder has 4096 four-digit codes available for broadcast and several switches (Standby, to warm it up; On; Alt, if it has an encoding altimeter; Reply, which responds when the unit replies to the ground; Ident, to broadcast a special signal to the controller). Controllers use the word *squawk* to refer to airborne transponder transmission (for example, *squawk* means to turn to the code the controller tells you to select; *squawk ident* means to push the Ident button, *squawk standby* means to turn the selector knob to Standby, and so on). General transmission codes are 1200 for VFR, 7500 for hijacking, 7600 for loss of two-way radio communication, and 7700 for airborne emergency. Use of precision approach radar (PAR) or airport surveillance radar (ASR) is reserved for IFR pilots (or for use with a CFI).

12. Several other avionic aids and displays are available, including integrated navigation and communication controls, and automatic pilots.

13. Some safety factors to consider in flight planning when using radio navigation include: checking minimum en route altitudes, since VOR transmits line-of-sight; checking the *Airport/Facility Directory* and *NOTAMs;* and checking equipment (for example, use a VOT facility if one is available). Using one method of navigation to complement another (composite navigation) is both practical and, for many VFR flights, almost a necessity.

KEY TERMS AND CONCEPTS, PART 1
Match each term or concept (1–18) with the appropriate description (a–r) below. Each item has only one match.

__ 1. VOR	__ 2. home
__ 3. rate of intercept	__ 4. victor airway
__ 5. NDB	__ 6. course deviation indicator (CDI)
__ 7. radio navigation	__ 8. precision
__ 9. Off flag	__10. TACAN
__11. airways	__12. radial
__13. angle of intercept	__14. To-From
__15. nonprecision	__16. VORTAC
__17. omni bearing selector (OBS)	__18. bearing

a.   approach made with both bearing and glide slope information (for example, ILS)
b.   difference between an airplane's heading and a desired course
c.   part of the VOR cockpit display that shows the aircraft's deviations from a radio
d.   how fast you encounter a radial or desired course
e.   approach made with bearing information only (for example, NDB or VOR)
f.   very-high-frequency omnidirectional range station
g.   establishing courses and fixes by reference to radio signals broadcast from ground stations
h.   part of the VOR cockpit display that designates where the selected radial will take you relative to the VOR
i.   a VHF airway connecting two VOR stations
j.   LOP derived from a radio source
k.   to fly toward a radio source
l.   ultra-high-frequency tactical air navigation station
m.   part of the VOR cockpit display that indicates a weak signal
n.   a LOP sent out by a VOR station
o.   combination of f and l above
p.   part of the VOR cockpit display that allows you to select a radial
q.   station that uses low or medium radio frequencies
r.   bearings that run from one ground station to another

KEY TERMS AND CONCEPTS, PART 2

Match each term or concept (1–12) with the appropriate description (a–l) below. Each item has only one match.

___ 1. 1200   ___ 2. cone of confusion
___ 3. ADF   ___ 4. 7600
___ 5. squawk ident   ___ 6. area navigation
___ 7. station passage   ___ 8. nondirectional beacon
___ 9. DME   ___ 10. 7700
___ 11. composite navigation   ___ 12. intercept heading

a.   navigational system not limited by line-of-sight transmission
b.   using one method of navigation to complement another
c.   this is confirmed when the To-From indicator makes its first positive change from To to From
d.   homing beacon that offers low-frequency navigation signal
e.   activate the transponder to broadcast a special signal to the controller
f.   VFR transponder frequency
g.   heading used to get to a desired radial or course
h.   area above a VOR station where radial signals are blocked
i.   uses UHF to fix distance from a VORTAC system
j.   transponder frequency to indicate an airborne emergency
k.   navigation in which phantom stations are created using VOR and/or DME information
l.   transponder frequency to indicate loss of two-way radio communication

DISCUSSION QUESTIONS AND EXERCISES

1.   What are two major differences between VOR and TACAN radio transmission?

2.   How are broadcast signals from a VOR station radiated relative to actual headings? What is the difference between To and From headings?

3.   Briefly describe the VOR cockpit controls and their functions.

4.   What is the difference between *tracking* a radio bearing and *homing* to the radio station? Why is the latter considered poor piloting technique?

5.   Name two advantages and two disadvantages of VOR as a navigation aid.

6.   Outline the VOR procedure for each of the following:

        a. homing to the station

b. flying direct to the station

c. intercepting a course inbound to the station

d. intercepting a course outbound from the station

7.   A fix is any intersection between two or more LOPs. Outline three ways fixes can be made by reference to a single VORTAC station.

8.   What is the cockpit indication that you have passed over a VOR station?

9.   Outline how you can use a single VOR to obtain a time and distance check.

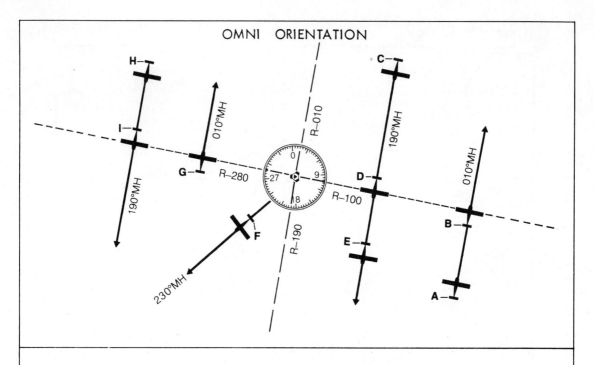

OMNI ORIENTATION

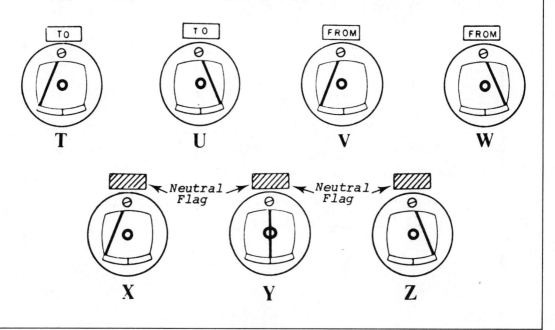

OMNI INDICATIONS

NOTE: ASSUME ALL OMNI BEARING SELECTORS ARE SET TO 190°.

Figure 12.1

10.   Refer to Figure 12.1. Match each VOR indicator in the bottom of the figure with the appropriate airplane in the top of the figure. Some indicators may have more than one correct match. Assume the omni bearing selector (OBS) in all airplanes is set to read 190°.

11.   Briefly explain how distance measuring equipment (DME) works, when it derives radio information, and how station passage is indicated.

12.   What is the one major advantage of a low-frequency (ADF) navigation over a VOR? What is a low-frequency station's biggest disadvantage?

13.   Will ADF homing work in reverse (that is, when flying outbound from the station)? Why or why not?

14.   Refer to Figure 12.2. Match the correct ADF (fixed compass card) indication in the bottom of the figure with the airplanes shown in flight in the top of the figure for flight in the vicinity of a typical nondirectional radio beacon (NDB). Indicators may have no match, one match, or two matches.

15.   Given an ADF pointing to 190° and a magnetic compass indicating 135°, what is the magnetic bearing to the station? Assume 0° deviation for the heading.

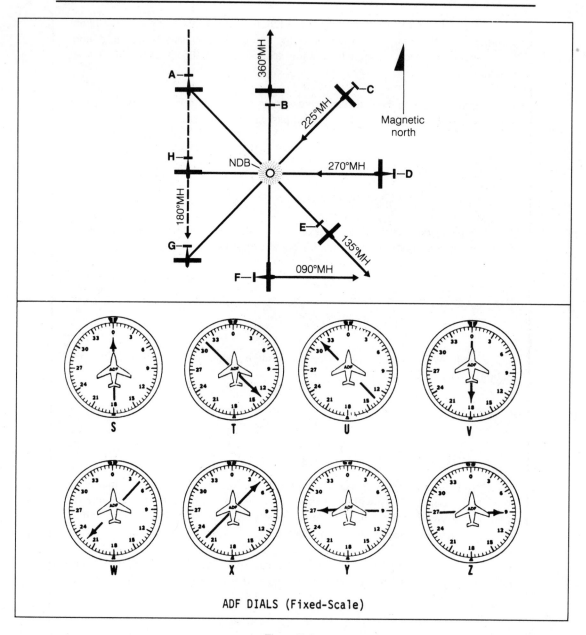

Figure 12.2

16.   For each of the ADF headings in Figure 12.3, calculate the magnetic bearing to the station given the compass shown in the figure. Assume 0° deviation for the heading. Also figure how far and in what direction you would have to turn to fly to the station.

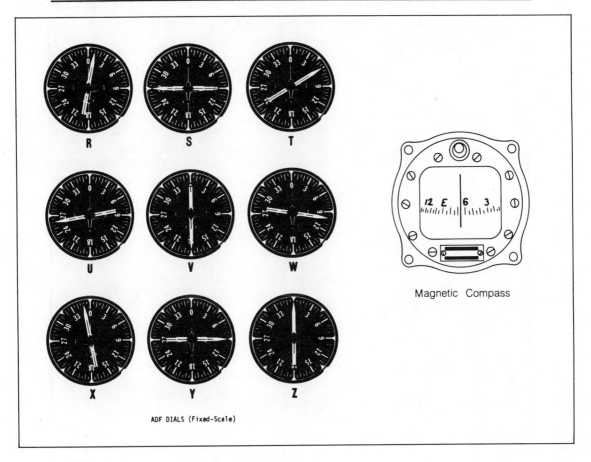

ADF DIALS (Fixed-Scale)

Magnetic Compass

Figure 12.3

17.   Briefly describe radar navigation and explain your responsibilities and options as a VFR pilot.

18.   Explain each of the following as they relate to radar navigation:

    a. 4096

    b. Ident

    c. Standby

    d. squawk code 0413

    e. code 1200

    f. code 7500

    g. code 7600

    h. code 7700

    i. PAR and ASR for VFR pilots

19.   Outline at least three things safety-conscious VFR pilots do as part of preflight planning when radio navigation is to be used.

REVIEW QUESTIONS

1.   TACAN stations operate at _____frequency.
    a. low
    b. medium
    c. very high
    d. ultra-high

2.   Approaches that provide bearing information and a glide slope are called ____
approaches.
    a. controlled
    b. IFR
    c. nonprecision
    d. precision

3.   Which of the following is not a frequency on which VORs transmit?
    a. 107.8
    b. 113.2
    c. 116.0
    d. 117.85

4.   When you are flying inbound to a VOR station, the magnetic course is _____
the VOR radial.
    a. parallel to
    b. perpendicular to
    c. the same as
    d. the reciprocal of

5.   Which of the VOR cockpit controls is the first to indicate passage over a VOR
station?
    a. an interruption in the auditory signal broadcast by the station
    b. course deviation indicator (CDI)
    c. omni bearing selector (OBS)
    d. To-From indicator

6.   Under which of the following conditions will the Off flag of a VOR receiver appear? When
    a. the To indicator is used for an outbound radial
    b. the From indicator is used for an inbound radial
    c. you are 90° off the radial selected on the OBS
    d. all of the above

7.   Which of the following is a disadvantage of VOR navigation?
    a. its inaccuracy
    b. its omnidirectionality
    c. its susceptibility to atmospheric interference
    d. none of the above

8.   Keeping the CDI centered to fly to a VOR station is a navigational procedure called
    a. homing
    b. intercepting an inbound radial
    c. intercepting an outbound radial
    d. proceeding direct

9.   At VOR test facilities (VOTs), VORs should agree with the VOT within a range of plus or minus _____degrees.
    a. 1
    b. 4
    c. 6
    d. 10

10.   Refer back to Figure 12.1. The omnireceiver indications at airplane positions H and I would be, respectively,
    a. T and X
    b. T and Y
    c. U and Z
    d. V and X

11.   Refer back to Figure 12.1. The omnireceiver indications for airplane positions C, D, and E would be, respectively,
    a. T, X, V
    b. U, Y, V
    c. U, Y, W
    d. U, Z, W

12.   Refer back to Figure 12.1. Which of the airplanes shown would have omni indication X?
    a. I only
    b. B and D

c. B and I

d. G and I

13.   Refer back to Figure 12.1. At which airplane position(s) would you receive omni indication X or Z?

a. F only

b. B and G

c. D and I

d. B, D, G, and I

14.   Refer back to Figure 12.2. At which of the aircraft position(s) would you expect to receive the ADF indication S?

a. F only

b. B and D

c. B and E

d. C and D

15.   Refer back to Figure 12.2. Which ADF indication would you most likely have at aircraft position B?

a. S

b. V

c. Y

d. Z

16.   Refer back to Figure 12.2. Which aircraft would most likely depict your position if the ADF is indicating as illustrated by dial W?

a. A

b. C

c. G

d. H

17.   According to ADF dial indication U (Figure 12.2), you would be headed directly toward the station if you turned

a. 45° to the left

b. 45° to the right

c. 135° to the right

d. 330° to the left

18.   Refer back to Figure 12.2. Which ADF dial indication would the pilot most likely have at aircraft positions C and D?

a. S

b. W

c. X

d. Y

19.   Refer back to Figure 12.2. Which aircraft would most likely depict your position if the ADF indicated as illustrated by dial Y?
   a. D only
   b. A and G
   c. D and H
   d. F and H

20.   If ADF dial Y in Figure 12.3 is observed and the magnetic heading is 180°, what is the *magnetic bearing* to the station?
   a. 090°
   b. 180°
   c. 270°
   d. 360°

21.   Refer to ADF dial Z and the magnetic compass in Figure 12.3. The *magnetic bearing* to the station is
   a. 065°
   b. 180°
   c. 295°
   d. 360°

22.   Refer to ADF dial V and the magnetic compass in Figure 12.3. The *magnetic bearing* to the station is
   a. 115°
   b. 180°
   c. 245°
   d. 360°

23.   Refer to Figure 12.4. On course from airport B to airport A, you tune in Fresno VOR to check your progress. If the omni bearing selector is set to 241° and the receiver shows a From indication with the CDI needle deflected to the left, you have
   a. a malfunctioning omnireceiver since the Fresno VOR is to the right of course
   b. already crossed the 241 radial (V 230–23 W)
   c. already crossed the Fresno 061 radial
   d. not crossed the 241 radial (V 230–23 W)

24.   Refer to Figure 12.4. While on course from airport C to airport B, you tune the VOR to Fresno VOR to check your progress along the route. With the omni bearing selector set to 141° (V 23) and the To-From indicator reading From, the course deviation indicator (CDI needle) shows a full-scale deflection to the right. This means that you
   a. are not using a proper method of determining your position
   b. have a malfunction in your omni equipment since Fresno VORTAC is to the left of course
   c. have already crossed the 141 radial (V 23)
   d. have not crossed the 141 radial (V 23)

25.   Refer to Figure 12.4. To check your progress on course from airport A to airport B, you tune to the Fresno VOR. With the omni bearing selector set to 241° (V 230–23 W) and the To-From indicator reading From, the course deviation indicator (CDI needle) shows a full-scale deflection to the right. This means that you
     a. are not using a proper method of determining your position
     b. are presently on the 241 radial (V 230–23 W)
     c. have already crossed the 241 radial (V 230–23 W)
     d. have not crossed the 241 radial (V 230–23 W)

26.   Refer to Figure 12.5. Assume that you are flying outbound from McAlester VORTAC (X) on the 025 radial. Which radial of Okmulgee VOR (Z) intersects your course at point C?
     a. 100 radial
     b. 110 radial
     c. 115 radial
     d. 295 radial

27.   Refer to Figure 12.5. While flying westbound, you notice that one omnireceiver indicates you are crossing the 025 radial of McAlester VORTAC (X). Another receiver tuned to Okmulgee VOR (Z) indicates you are on the 130 radial of this VOR. Your position is
     a. at point C
     b. at point D
     c. at point E
     d. directly over McAlester VORTAC

28.   Refer to Figure 12.5. Assume that you are flying outbound on the 025 radial of McAlester VORTAC (X). You have another VOR tuned to Okmulgee VOR (Z), with the omni bearing selector set to 105°; the CDI needle is centered, and the To-From indicator reads From. Your position is between points
     a. A and B
     b. B and C
     c. C and D
     d. D and E

29.   Refer to Figure 12.5. While flying eastbound, one omnireceiver indicates you are crossing the 025 radial of McAlester VORTAC (X). Another receiver tuned to Okmulgee VOR (Z) indicates you are on the 145 radial of this VOR. Your position is at point
     a. B
     b. C
     c. D
     d. E

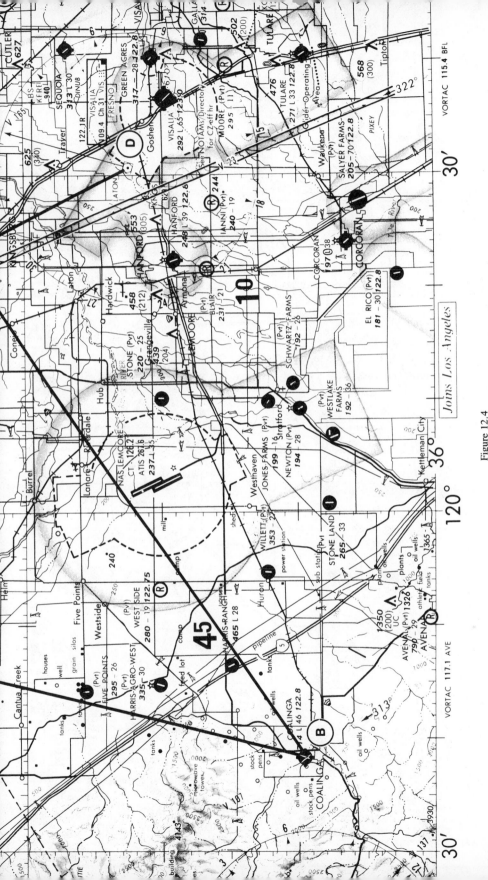

Figure 12.4

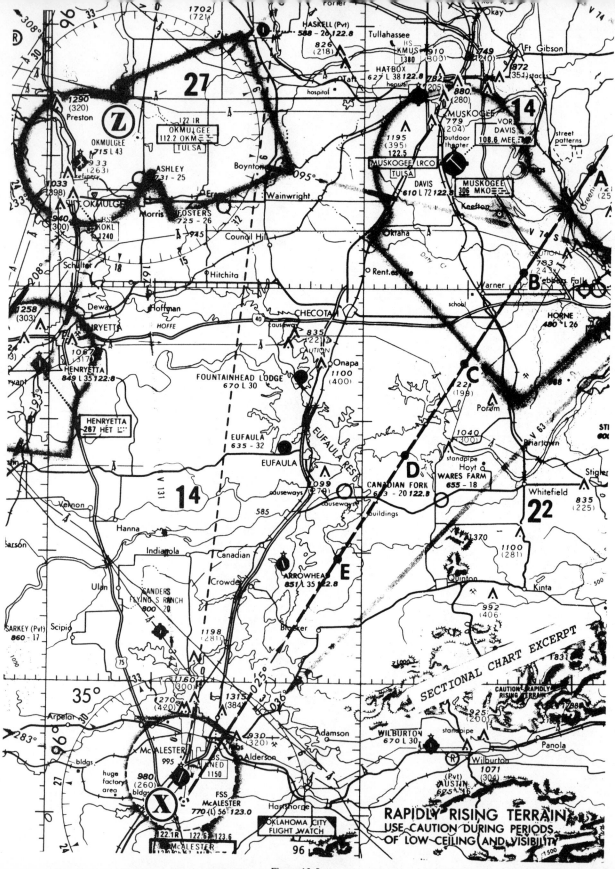

Figure 12.5

30.   Refer to Figure 12.6. While on course from airport A to airport B, you note
that you crossed the 030 radial of Maxwell VOR at 1408 CST and the 060 radial 5
minutes later. By maintaining the same ground speed, you should arrive over airport
B at approximately
     a. 1413 CST
     b. 1424 CST
     c. 1427 CST
     d. 1430 CST

31.   Refer to Figure 12.6. While on course from C to D, you tune one omnireceiver
to Maxwell VOR. You note that you crossed the 030 radial of Maxwell VOR at 0810
CST and the 060 radial 13 minutes later. By maintaining the same ground speed, you
should arrive over airport D at approximately
     a. 0823 CST
     b. 0830 CST
     c. 0837 CST
     d. 0844 CST

32.   Refer to Figure 12.6. While on course from airport B to A, you tune one
omnireceiver to Maxwell VOR. You note that you crossed the 060 radial of Maxwell
at 1103 CST and the 030 radial 8 minutes later. By maintaining the same ground speed,
you should arrive over airport A at approximately
     a. 1111 CST
     b. 1117 CST
     c. 1124 CST
     d. 1131 CST

33.   Assume that you desire to fly inbound to a VOR station on the 300 radial. The
recommended procedure is to set the course selector to
     a. 120° and make heading corrections away from the course deviation indicator
       (CDI needle)
     b. 120° and make heading corrections toward the course deviation indicator
       (CDI needle)
     c. 300° and make heading corrections away from the course deviation indicator
       (CDI needle)
     d. 300° and make heading corrections toward the course deviation indicator
       (CDI needle)

34.   While flying on a north heading, assume that you are using Radar Traffic Information Service and the wind is calm. You receive the following traffic advisory:

    Traffic 9 o'clock, 2 miles, southbound. . . .

You should look for this traffic
     a. ahead of your left wing tip
     b. behind your right wing tip

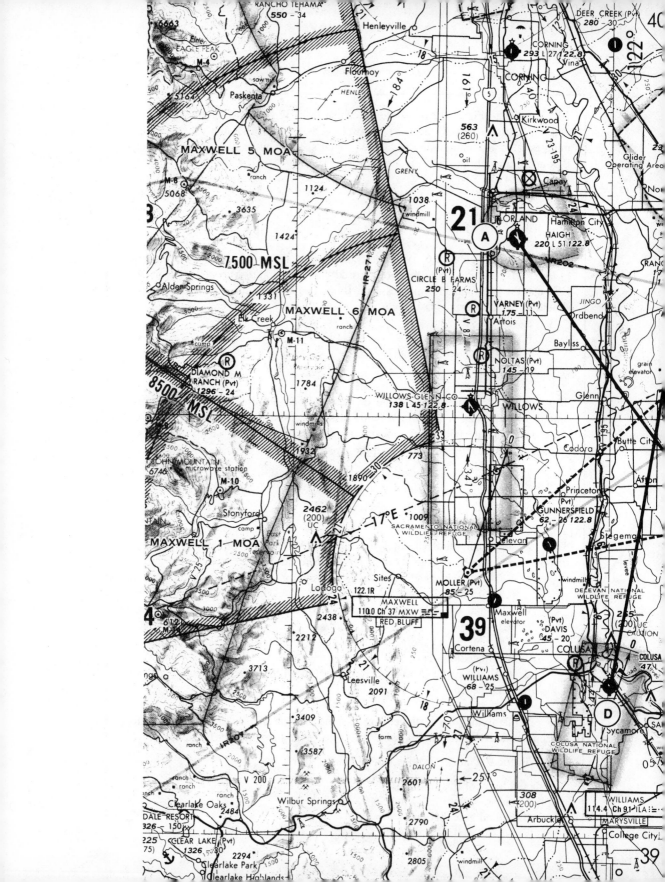

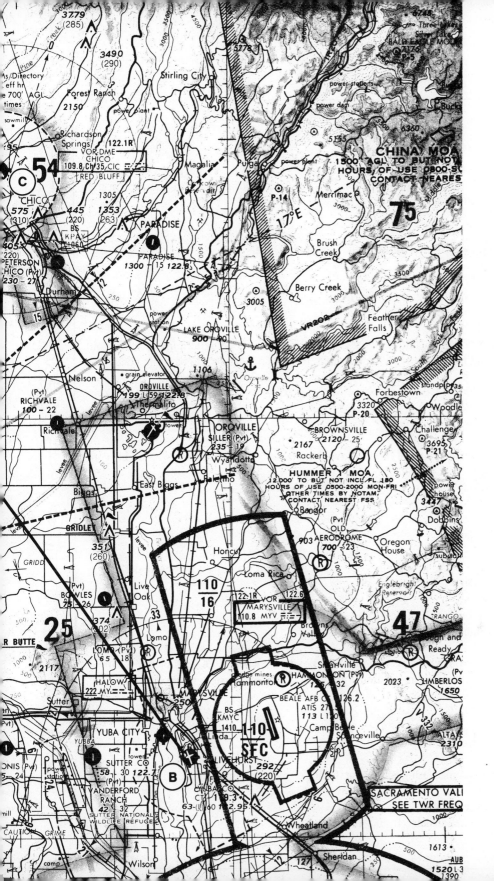

Figure 12.6

c. off your left wing tip
d. off your right wing tip

35.   Assume that you are flying on an east heading in the vicinity of a busy airport and obtain Radar Traffic Information Service. The wind is calm and you receive the following traffic advisory:

Traffic 3 o'clock, 2 miles, westbound. . . .

You should look for this traffic in the direction of your
a. left wing tip
b. left wing tip and ahead of you
c. nose and slightly to the right
d. right wing tip

36.   If Air Traffic Control advises that radar service is being terminated when you are departing a terminal radar service area, the transponder should be set to code
a. 0000
b. 1200
c. 4096
d. 7700

37.   To indicate that you have lost two-way radio communication during flight, you should turn your transponder to
a. 1200
b. 4096
c. 7500
d. 7600

38.   Which of the following is not a typical cockpit display on a transponder?
a. CDI
b. Ident
c. Reply
d. Standby

39.   The use of phantom stations (way points) in which VOR and/or DME information is calculated for navigational purposes is part of a system referred to as
a. area navigation
b. ARTCC
c. TACAN
d. victor airways

40.   Distance measuring equipment (DME) displays the airplane's _____ a VORTAC station.
a. distance above
b. ground distance from

c. slant range distance from
d. both a and b

41.   Which of the following is an advantage of ADF radio navigation?
       a. It is omnidirectional.
       b. It is not subject to line-of-sight restrictions.
       c. It can be used to measure distance from a station accurately.
       d. All of the above are correct.

ANSWERS

Key Terms and Concepts, Part 1

1.	f	2.	k	3.	d	4.	i
5.	q	6.	c	7.	g	8.	a
9.	m	10.	l	11.	r	12.	n
13.	b	14.	h	15.	e	16.	o
17.	p	18.	j				

Key Terms and Concepts, Part 2

1.	f	2.	h	3.	a	4.	l
5.	e	6.	k	7.	c	8.	d
9.	i	10.	j	11.	b	12.	g

Discussion Questions and Exercises

10.   T—H.
       U—C.
       V—F.
       W—A, E (remember, it does not matter where the nose of the airplane is pointed).
       X—G, I (remember, you are 90° off the radial).
       Y—no match (you would have to be directly over the station in the zone of confusion to get this reading).
       Z—B, D.
14.   S—C, D.
       T—no match.
       U—A.
       V—B, E.
       W—G.
       X—no match.
       Y—F, H.
       Z—no match.
15.   325°; the magnetic bearing to the station is equal to the magnetic heading plus the relative bearing.

16.   The magnetic bearing to the station is equal to the magnetic heading plus the
       relative bearing.
       R, 75° (turn 10° right).
       S, 335° (turn 90° left).
       T, 125° (turn 60° right).
       U, 325° (turn 100° left).
       V, 245° (turn 180° in either direction).
       W, 165° (turn 100° right).
       X, 55° (turn 10° left).
       Y, 155° (turn 90° right).
       Z, 65° (steer on course).

Review Questions
  1.   d; they transmit UHF, or ultra-high frequency.
  2.   d; precision approaches are of most interest to IFR pilots, although they may
        affect traffic patterns at some airports.
  3.   a; VORs transmit on frequencies between 108 and 117.95.
  4.   d; the radial is its magnetic course *from* the station; all radials are *from* the
        station.
  5.   d; the To-From indicates station passage when it makes its first positive change
        from To to From.
  6.   c; it will also appear when you are passing directly over the station (the cone
        of confusion), when the station is off, when it is out of the line of sight (you
        are too far away or there is an obstruction), and when you are 90° off the radial
        selected on the OBS.
  7.   d; VOR is characterized by accuracy, omnidirectionality, and freedom from
        atmospheric interference. The major drawback is its restriction to line-of-sight
        transmission and reception.
  8.   d; definition.
  9.   b; definition; other airborne and ground checkpoints are accurate within ±6°.
 10.   a; see review question answer 10.
 11.   d; see review question answer 10.
 12.   d; see review question answer 10.
 13.   d; see review question answer 10.
 14.   d; see review question answer 14.
 15.   b; see review question answer 14.
 16.   c; see review question answer 14.
 17.   a; see review question answer 14.
 18.   a; see review question answer 14.
 19.   d; see review question answer 14.
 20.   c; see review question answers 15, 16.
 21.   a; see review question answers 15, 16.
 22.   c; see review question answers 15, 16.

23.   b; since the needle is to the left with a From indication, you have already crossed the radial. A memory aid for intersection problems goes like this: If the needle and the station are on the same side, you are not there yet.

24.   d; same logic as in the answer to review question 23.

25.   c; same logic as in the answer to review question 23.

26.   c; you need a plotter or a ruler to find the intersection of the 115° radial and point C. Remember, radials are named for their magnetic heading *from* the station.

27.   b; same logic as in the answer to review question 26.

28.   b; same logic as in the answer to review question 26.

29.   d; same logic as in the answer to review question 26.

30.   b; you need to use your plotter. You traveled 11 miles in 5 minutes, or about 2.2 miles per minute. To cover the remaining 24 miles will take 11 additional minutes. So, 1408 + 5 (the time for your calculation) + 11 = 1424. The closest answer is 1432 CST.

31.   c; the 11.8 miles from fix to fix took 13 minutes, or 0.91 miles per minute. The remaining 12.5 miles should take 13.7 minutes (11.8 ÷ 0.91). 0810 + 13 (the time it took to make your distance computation) + 13.7 yield an estimated time of arrival of about 0837 CST.

32.   c; use the same logic as in review questions 30 and 31.

33.   b; fly To the station on the reciprocal of the heading from the station.

34.   d; traffic is reported by giving the other aircraft's direction of flight and position relative to positions on the clock, with 12 o'clock representing the nose of your airplane and 6 o'clock representing your tail. Your right wing would be 3 o'clock and your left wing 9 o'clock.

35.   d; same logic as in review question 34.

36.   b; definition.

37.   d; definition.

38.   a; a course deviation indicator (CDI) is part of the VOR navigational equipment.

39.   a; definition.

40.   c; DME measures slant range or line-of-sight distance.

41.   b; one of its major advantages is that it is *not* limited to line-of-sight transmission; its major disadvantage is its susceptibility to interference.

13/COMPOSITE NAVIGATION: GOING CROSS-COUNTRY

MAIN POINTS

1. This chapter, which describes the process of planning and executing a cross-country flight, draws on all the knowledge you have accumulated in the preceding chapters of this book, including preflight planning, weight and balance, dead reckoning, radio navigation, FARs, and weather.

2. One of your tasks during this chapter will be to prepare a *flight log* for a proposed cross-country flight. The phases you will consider are general planning; preflight planning, including navigational computations; weather briefings and airport data; airplane preflight preparation; departure procedures; en route procedures; en route replanning; arrival procedures; and postflight activities, including such items as closing your flight plan.

CROSS-COUNTRY EXERCISE

For this exercise, you will need a flight computer or electronic calculator, plotter, navigation log, weight and balance graphs (Chapter 6 of the Pilot's Operating Handbook), landing and takeoff charts (Chapter 5 of the *POH*), San Francisco sectional chart, and excerpts from the *Airport/Facility Directory* (provided in Figure 13.1). Routing and weather information will be provided.

Your aircraft is a pink and yellow Beechcraft Skipper 77. You and your instructor will be going on a round-robin cross-country flight from Fresno (37°N, 120°W) to Pine Mountain Lake near Groveland (38°N, 120°W), then on to Carmel Valley (36°30'N, 122°30'W), and finally back to Fresno. It is a Thursday in August; pacific daylight time is in effect.

----

§ **FRESNO-CHANDLER DOWNTOWN**   (FCH)   1.7 W   GMT−8(−7DT)   SAN FRANCISCO
        36°43'56"N 119°49'08"W   H-2F, L-2E
        278   B   S4   FUEL 80, 100   OX 3, 4   TPA−1078(800)   IAP
    RWY 12L-30R: H3475X75 (ASPH)   S-17
        RWY 12L: Thld dsplcd 460'. Road.   RWY 30R: Thld dsplcd 527'. Road. Rgt tfc.
    RWY 12R-30L: H3441X75 (ASPH)   S-17   MIRL
        RWY 12R: REIL. Thld dsplcd 474'. Pole. Rgt tfc.
        RWY 30L: REIL. VASI(V2L)— GA 3.42° TCH 21'. Thld dsplcd 536'. Road.
    AIRPORT REMARKS: Attended 1500-0630Z‡. Fee for acft over 12,500 pounds gross weight. Fuel avbl Mon-Sat
        1500Z‡-dusk & Sun 1500-0100Z‡, later thru ATCT. Control Zone effective 1500-0600Z‡.
    COMMUNICATIONS: UNICOM 123.0
        FRESNO FSS (FAT) LC 251-8269
    Ⓡ APP CON 132.35, 119.6   Ⓡ DEP CON 132.35
        CHANDLER TOWER 121.1 opr 1600-0400Z‡   GND CON 121.9
    RADIO AIDS TO NAVIGATION:
        (H) ABVORTAC 112.9   ■ FAT   Chan 76   36°53'12"N 119°48'11"W   167° 9.3 NM to fld. 361/17E.
        CHANDLER NDB (H-SAB) 344   ■ FCH   36°43'26.4"N 119°49'57.7"W   036° 0.8 NM to fld
            NDB unusable 095-120° beyond 40 NM   200-235° beyond 35 NM

GROVELAND

PINE MOUNTAIN LAKE   (Q68)   2.6 NE   GMT−8(−7DT)   37°51'45"N 120°10'40"W   SAN FRANCISCO
    2900   B   TPA−3700(800)   L-2F
    RWY 09-27: H3640X50 (ASPH)   S-2   MIRL
        RWY 09: Trees.   RWY 27: Tree. Rgt tfc.
    AIRPORT REMARKS: Unattended
    COMMUNICATIONS: UNICOM 123.0
        STOCKTON FSS (SCK)
    RADIO AIDS TO NAVIGATION:
        MODESTO (H) VOR/DME 114.6   MOD   Chan 93   37°37'39"N 120°57'25"W   052° 39.7 NM to fld.
        90/17E.

CARMEL VALLEY   (O62)   0 NE   GMT−8(−7DT)   36°28'55"N 121°43'45"W   SAN FRANCISCO
    450   TPA−1500(1050)
    RWY 11-29: 2475X35 (TRTD-GRVL)
        RWY 11: P-line. Rgt tfc.   RWY 29: Trash piles.
    AIRPORT REMARKS: Unattended. No touch & go lndgs. Straight out departure Rwy 29, no turns below 1000'. First
        600' runway 11-29 overgrown with 3' weeds.
    COMMUNICATIONS:
        SALINAS FSS (SNS) LC 372-6050

§ **LOS BANOS MUNI**   (LSN)   .9 W   GMT−8(−7DT)   37°03'43"N 120°52'05"W   SAN FRANCISCO
    119   B   S4   FUEL 80, 100   TPA−919(800)   H-2F, L-2F
    RWY 14-32: H3000X75 (ASPH)   S-23   MIRL   IAP
        RWY 14: VASI(V4L)— GA 3.0° TCH 30'. Rgt tfc.   RWY 32: VASI(V4L).— GA 3.0° TCH 30'. Road.
    AIRPORT REMARKS: Attended 1600-0130Z‡. ACTIVATE VASIs Rwy 14/32-122.8.
    COMMUNICATIONS: UNICOM 122.8
        FRESNO FSS (FAT) Toll free dial 0, ask for ENTERPRISE 14598.
        PANOCHE LRCO 122.1R, 112.6T (FRESNO FSS)
    RADIO AIDS TO NAVIGATIONS:
        PANOCHE (L) VORTAC 112.6   PXN   Chan 73   36°42'56"N 120°46'40"W   333° 21 NM to fld.
        2060/16E.
            VOR unusable 230-280° beyond 7 NM below 9000'   280-290° beyond 6-10 NM below 10,000'

Figure 13.1

Given

Aircraft identification	N7118Q
Your weight (seat forward)	135 pounds
Your instructor's weight (seat forward)	165 pounds
Luggage weight	10 pounds
Total fuel capacity	30 gallons
Total usable fuel	29 gallons
Maximum ramp weight	1680 pounds
Maximum takeoff weight	1675 pounds
Maximum landing weight	1675 pounds
Maximum weight in baggage compartment	120 pounds
Basic empty weight	1190 pounds
Moment for basic empty condition	1023
Maximum useful load	490 pounds
Total oil capacity	6 quarts
Cruise	2400 rpm
Proposed departure time	9 A.M.

Routing

Leg 1: Fresno Chandler Downtown (FCH) direct at 6500 MSL to Pine Mountain Lake at Groveland (Q68); one-hour stopover.

Leg 2: Pine Mountain Lake (Q68) direct at 6500 MSL to Los Banos (LSN); fly over checkpoint.

Leg 3: Los Banos (LSN) direct at 6500 MSL to Carmel Valley (062); two-hour stopover.

Leg 4: Carmel Valley (062) direct at 7500 MSL to Panoche VOR (PXN); checkpoint.

Leg 5: Panoche VOR (PXN) at 7500 MSL direct to Fresno Chandler Downtown (FCH).

Weather Information (summarized)

Winds and temperatures aloft:
3000 feet: 240 at 15 knots; 20 degrees Celsius
6000 feet: 260 at 25 knots; 15 degrees Celsius
9000 feet: 260 at 25 knots; 10 degrees Celsius

Fresno current: 8000 broken, 10,000 overcast, visibility 10 miles, OAT 27 degrees Celsius, dew point 19 degrees Celsius, barometer 29.76, surface winds 240 at 10 knots.

Modesto current: 12,000 scattered, visibility 12 miles, OAT 28 degrees Celsius, dew point 19 degrees Celsius, barometer 29.86, surface winds 200 at 20 knots.

Modesto forecast: clear, visibility 12 miles, OAT 31 degrees Celsius, dew point 19 degrees Celsius, barometer 29.82, surface winds 240 at 20 knots.

Monterey current: field obscured, fog, visibility restricted, OAT 17 degrees Celsius, dew point 17 degrees Celsius, barometer 29.62, winds calm.

Monterey forecast: clear, visibility 6 miles and haze, OAT 21 degrees Celsius, dew point 17 degrees Celsius, barometer 29.76, winds 210 at 10 knots.

Fresno forecast: 6000 scattered, visibility 10 miles, OAT 28 degrees Celsius, dew point 19 degrees Celsius, barometer 29.86, winds 270 at 20 knots.

1. Complete the flight navigation log in Figure 13.2 for this trip.

Aircraft number: ______

FLIGHT LOG

Proposed takeoff: ______
Actual takeoff: ______

Route/Fix/Checkpoint	Alt. / Temp.	IAS / TAS	TC	Wind Dir. / Vel.	WCA / TH	Var. / MH	Dev. / CH	Ground Speed	Dist. / Dist. Rem.	Time ETE / ATE	Time ETA / ATA	Fuel (GPH: ___) Used	Fuel Rem.
								Totals					

Airport Frequencies				
Airport				
ATIS				
Cl. Del.				
Gnd.				
Twr.				
Dep.				
App.				
FSS				
UNICOM				

Airport/ATIS Advisories		
Airport		
Cig.		
Vsby.		
Temp.		
Wind		
Alt.		
Rwy.		
NOTAMs		

Time in	
Time out	
Total Time	

Field Elevation MSL	
Departure	Destination

Remarks:

REMEMBER:
CLOSE YOUR FLIGHT PLAN
Freq. ______
Phone no. ______

Figure 13.2

a. Are the altitudes appropriate for the routing and weather conditions? Why or why not?

b. Calculate the headwind and crosswind components for takeoffs and landings at:

Fresno (FCH); assume you will use runway 30L or 30R.

Pine Mountain Lake (Q68) current and forecast; use Modesto for an approximation; assume you will use runway 27.

Carmel Valley (062) forecast; use Monterey for an approximation; assume you will use runway 29.

Fresno (FCH) forecast; assume you will use runway 30L or 30R.

c. Have you exceeded the demonstrated crosswind component in any of the above? Which, if any?

d. Pine Mountain Lake, as you discovered above, may present a problem on landing since the current Modesto conditions suggest that the demonstrated crosswind component might be exceeded. Should you change your flight plan at this point? Analyze the situation.

2.   Complete the weight and balance landing form below.

Item	Weight	MOM/100
Basic empty condition	_____	_____
Occupant, left	_____	_____
Occupant, right	_____	_____
Baggage	_____	_____
Subtotal, zero fuel condition	_____	_____
Fuel loading: 29 gallons	_____	_____
Subtotal, ramp condition	_____	_____
Less fuel for start, taxi, runup	_____	_____
Subtotal, takeoff condition	_____	_____
Less fuel to destination (FCH)	_____	_____
Landing condition (FCH)	_____	_____

a. How close to maximum takeoff weight are you?

b. Are you within the moment limits versus weight limits for takeoff?

c. Will you be within CG limits on your return to FCH? How close to either extreme will you be?

d. Calculate your takeoff distance for:

Fresno Chandler (FCH), current conditions

Pine Mountain (Q68), based on the Modesto forecast

Carmel Valley (O62), based on the Monterey forecast

e. Once you leave Fresno, how long will it take to reach altitude? How much fuel will you consume during the climb? How many miles will you be from Fresno when you reach altitude?

3.   Your flight plan:

a. With whom will you file the plan? How will you contact them? Where are they located?

b. Using the form in Figure 13.3, complete a flight plan for the trip.

c. How will you activate your flight plan on your departure from FCH?

						Form Approved: OMB No. 04-R0072	

DEPARTMENT OF TRANSPORTATION
FEDERAL AVIATION ADMINISTRATION

FLIGHT PLAN

CIVIL AIRCRAFT PILOTS. FAR Part 91 requires you file an IFR flight plan to operate under instrument flight rules in controlled airspace. Failure to file could result in a civil penalty not to exceed $1,000 for each violation (Section 901 of the Federal Aviation Act of 1958, as amended). Filing of a VFR flight plan is recommended as a good operating practice. See also Part 99 for requirements concerning DVFR flight plans.

1. TYPE	2 AIRCRAFT IDENTIFICATION	3 AIRCRAFT TYPE/ SPECIAL EQUIPMENT	4 TRUE AIRSPEED	5 DEPARTURE POINT	6 DEPARTURE TIME		7 CRUISING ALTITUDE
VFR					PROPOSED (Z)	ACTUAL (Z)	
IFR							
DVFR			KTS				

8. ROUTE OF FLIGHT

9 DESTINATION (Name of airport and city)	10 EST. TIME ENROUTE		11 REMARKS
	HOURS	MINUTES	

12 FUEL ON BOARD		13 ALTERNATE AIRPORT(S)	14 PILOT'S NAME, ADDRESS & TELEPHONE NUMBER & AIRCRAFT HOME BASE	15 NUMBER ABOARD
HOURS	MINUTES			

16. COLOR OF AIRCRAFT

CLOSE VFR FLIGHT PLAN WITH_____ FSS ON ARRIVAL

FAA Form 7233-1 (5-77)

Figure 13.3

4.   Departure and leg 1:

a. Given your proposed flight route, to which runway will you probably be directed for takeoff? Why?

b. After your runup, you are ready for takeoff. It is 8:55 A.M. What do you do next?

c. How would you use your VOR to obtain a fix exactly 21 nautical miles from Fresno Chandler (FCH)? What visual landmarks are also available at this point?

d. Use the road heading northwest out of Mariposa-Yosemite Airport as another checkpoint. A crosscheck is the 025° radial from the Merced (MCE) VOR. If it takes you 20 minutes to get from the checkpoint in question 4c to the Mariposa-Yosemite checkpoint, what is your actual ground speed? Why do you suppose it is different from your estimated ground speed?

e. How would you call Pine Mountain to get an advisory?

f. Suppose the Pine Mountain UNICOM reports that winds are 230° at 20. Are you going to land?

g. Describe how you would enter and fly the pattern at Pine Mountain, including directions on the various legs of the pattern and compensation for the surface winds to keep the airplane in a rectangular pattern relative to the runway.

5. Leg 2:

a. What should you know about the *alert area* that lies between Pine Mountain and Los Banos?

b. Since you will be flying over Castle Air Force Base, are you required to report your position to them? If so, where should you report?

c. Shortly after passing Castle Air Force Base, you glance at the oil temperature indicator and notice to your amazement that it is near red line. What should you do?

d. Suppose as you approach Los Banos, the oil temperature has risen further and is now on the red line. You and your instructor decide to land and have it checked. As you begin your descent, you need to check Los Banos. The winds are reported as 180° at 15 and runway 14 is the active runway. Describe how you will enter and fly the pattern, the directions on the various legs of the pattern, and what crabbing you will have to do to fly a square pattern.

e. Suppose you decide to use VASI to aid you on final approach. How would you get it turned on?

f. As your instructor and a mechanic analyze the situation (a faulty gauge), you decide to call FSS and file an amended flight plan that will allow you an extra hour for lunch at Carmel Valley. How would you contact FSS and where is the station located?

g. After departing Los Banos, you climb to 6500 and proceed to Carmel Valley. Assume it takes you 12 minutes to travel from V 107 to V 485. What is your ground speed?

6.   Leg 3:

a. How would you set your VOR to fly from Carmel Valley to Panoche?

b. How would you set your VOR to fly from Panoche to Fresno Chandler?

c. Assume you decide to contact Fresno Chandler Tower over Kerman. What frequency would you use and what would you say?

d. With whom will you close your flight plan?

ANSWERS

Cross-Country Exercise
1.   See Figure 13.4.
    a. Yes, they meet FAA standards as far as routes are concerned and they keep you away from adverse weather (assuming that Monterey clears as forecast).
    b. Your headwind and crosswind components for takeoff at:
        Fresno current: headwind, 5 knots; crosswind, 8.5 knots.
        Pine Mountain Lake (assume you will use runway 27): current: headwind, 7 knots; crosswind, almost 19 knots; forecast: headwind, 17 knots; crosswind, 10 knots.
        Carmel Valley (assume you will use runway 29): forecast: headwind, 2 knots; crosswind, almost 10 knots.
        Fresno forecast (assume you will use runway 30L or 30R): headwind, 17 knots; crosswind, 10 knots.

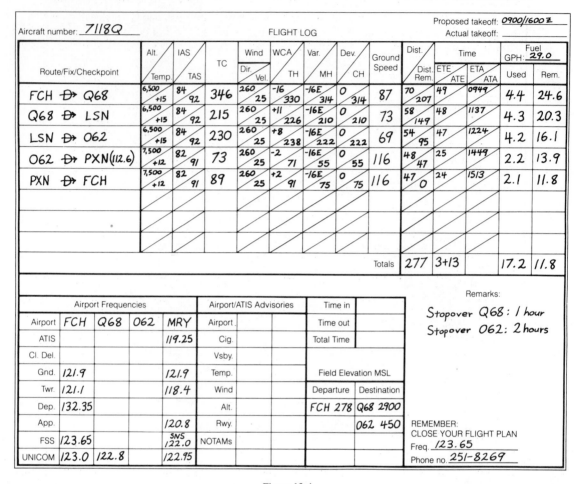

Route/Fix/Checkpoint	Alt. / Temp.	IAS / TAS	TC	Wind Dir. / Vel.	WCA / TH	Var. / MH	Dev. / CH	Ground Speed	Dist. / Dist. Rem.	Time ETE / ATE	Time ETA / ATA	Fuel Used	Fuel Rem.
FCH ➡ Q68	6,500 / +15	84 / 92	346	260 / 25	-16 / 330	-16E / 314	0 / 314	87	70 / 207	49	0949	4.4	24.6
Q68 ➡ LSN	6,500 / +15	84 / 92	215	260 / 25	+11 / 226	-16E / 210	0 / 210	73	58 / 149	48	1137	4.3	20.3
LSN ➡ 062	6,500 / +15	84 / 92	230	260 / 25	+8 / 238	-16E / 222	0 / 222	69	54 / 95	47	1224	4.2	16.1
062 ➡ PXN(112.6)	7,500 / +12	82 / 91	73	260 / 25	-2 / 71	-16E / 55	0 / 55	116	48 / 47	25	1449	2.2	13.9
PXN ➡ FCH	7,500 / +12	82 / 91	89	260 / 25	+2 / 91	-16E / 75	0 / 75	116	47 / 0	24	1513	2.1	11.8
								Totals	277	3+13		17.2	11.8

Aircraft number: **7118Q**   FLIGHT LOG

Proposed takeoff: **0900/1600 Z**
Actual takeoff: _____

Fuel GPH: **29.0**

Airport Frequencies

Airport	FCH	Q68	062	MRY
ATIS				119.25
Cl. Del.				
Gnd.	121.9			121.9
Twr.	121.1			118.4
Dep.	132.35			
App.				120.8
FSS	123.65			SNS 122.0
UNICOM	123.0	122.8		122.95

Airport/ATIS Advisories

Airport		
Cig.		
Vsby.		
Temp.		
Wind		
Alt.		
Rwy.		
NOTAMs		

Time in	
Time out	
Total Time	

Field Elevation MSL

Departure	Destination
FCH 278	Q68 2900
	062 450

Remarks:
Stopover Q68: 1 hour
Stopover 062: 2 hours

REMEMBER:
CLOSE YOUR FLIGHT PLAN
Freq. _123.65_
Phone no. _251-8269_

Figure 13.4

c.   Yes, Pine Mountain may have winds that exceed the demonstrated crosswind component, assuming Modesto is representative.

d.   According to the Modesto forecast, the winds should become more favorable throughout the morning. It might be wise to call Pine Mountain, but the airport is unattended. You might also ask FSS for any pilot reports. The winds are a factor to monitor as your flight progresses but at present are not serious enough to warrant canceling that portion of your flight.

2.   Weight and balance loading form:

Item	Weight	MOM/100
Basic empty condition	1,190	1,023
Occupant, left	135	121
Occupant, right	165	146
Baggage: 10 pounds	10	12
Subtotal, zero fuel condition	1,500	1,302
Fuel loading: 29 gallons	174	142
Subtotal, ramp condition	1,674	1,444
Less fuel for start, taxi, run up	− 5	− 4
Subtotal, takeoff condition	1,669	1,440
Less fuel to destination: 17.2 gallons	− 103	− 84
	1,566	1,356

a. Six pounds less than gross.

b. Yes; use 1670 as your approximation for 1669.

c. Yes; interpolate between 1550 and 1560. You are well within the limits.

d. Takeoff distance computations:

Fresno Chandler, current. Pressure altitude is 278 + ([29.92 − 29.76] × 100) = 438 feet. OAT is 27 degrees Celsius. Headwind is 5 knots. Gross takeoff weight is 1669 pounds. Surface condition, hard. Approximate takeoff distance, 800 feet.

Pine Mountain based on Modesto forecast. Pressure altitude is 2900 + ([29.92 − 29.82]) = 3000 feet. OAT is 31 degrees Celsius (it will probably be cooler in the mountains, and you might even use the winds aloft for 3000 feet as your reference, 20 degrees Celsius). We will use 31 degrees Celsius for this exercise. Headwind is 17 knots. Gross takeoff weight is 1669 − (6.0 pounds × 4.4 gallons) = 1643 pounds. Surface condition, hard. Approximate takeoff distance, 800 feet. To clear obstacles at the end of the runway, you will need about 1200 feet. You have plenty of runway.

Carmel Valley based on forecast for Monterey. Pressure altitude is 450 + ([29.92 − 29.76]) = 610 feet. OAT is 21 degrees Celsius. Headwind is 2 knots. Gross takeoff weight is 1643 − (6.0 pounds × 8.5 gallons) = 1592 pounds. Surface condition: use grass surface. Approximate takeoff distance, 750 feet. To clear obstacles at the end of the runway, you will need a little over 1200 feet. You have plenty of runway.

e. Pressure altitude at Fresno is 438 feet and the OAT is 27 degrees Celsius. At 6500 feet the OAT is about 14 degrees Celsius. Time to altitude is about 11 minutes (12 − 1), during which you will use about 1.4 (1.5 − 0.1) gallons of fuel. Assuming no wind, you will be about 12 (13 − 1) nautical miles from the Fresno Chandler Airport (when you reach altitude). Since you are flying slightly into the wind, however, you will actually be less than 12 nautical miles from the airport. You can figure this exactly by subtracting the headwind component from your climb speed (adjusted for changes in TAS as you climb), but this is tedious and usually unnecessary.

3.a.   Fresno FSS, located at Fresno Air Terminal, can be reached by calling 251-
        8269 (local call). See Figure 13.1, the *Airport/Facility Directory*.
  b.   See Figure 13.5.

<table>
<tr><td colspan="4">DEPARTMENT OF TRANSPORTATION
FEDERAL AVIATION ADMINISTRATION

FLIGHT PLAN</td><td colspan="5">Form Approved: OMB No. 04-R0072

CIVIL AIRCRAFT PILOTS. FAR Part 91 requires you file an IFR flight plan to operate under instrument flight rules in controlled airspace. Failure to file could result in a civil penalty not to exceed $1,000 for each violation (Section 901 of the Federal Aviation Act of 1958, as amended). Filing of a VFR flight plan is recommended as a good operating practice. See also Part 99 for requirements concerning DVFR flight plans.</td></tr>
<tr><td>1 TYPE
☒ VFR
☐ IFR
☐ DVFR</td><td>2 AIRCRAFT IDENTIFICATION
N7118Q</td><td>3 AIRCRAFT TYPE/ SPECIAL EQUIPMENT
BE 77/u</td><td>4 TRUE AIRSPEED
92
KTS</td><td>5 DEPARTURE POINT
FCH</td><td colspan="2">6 DEPARTURE TIME
PROPOSED (Z) | ACTUAL (Z)
1600</td><td colspan="2">7 CRUISING ALTITUDE
6500</td></tr>
</table>

8. ROUTE OF FLIGHT

↝ Q68 ↝ LSN ↝ 062 ↝ PXN ↝ FCH

<table>
<tr><td>9 DESTINATION (Name of airport and city)
Fresno Chandler Downtown Fresno</td><td colspan="2">10 EST TIME ENROUTE
HOURS | MINUTES
3 | 13</td><td>11 REMARKS
Stopovers at
Q68 (1+), 062 (2+)</td></tr>
<tr><td colspan="2">12 FUEL ON BOARD
HOURS | MINUTES
4 | 30</td><td>13 ALTERNATE AIRPORT(S)
N/A</td><td>14 PILOT'S NAME, ADDRESS & TELEPHONE NUMBER & AIRCRAFT HOME BASE
V. Fraser
309 South Willard
Fresno   555-0324</td><td>15 NUMBER ABOARD
2</td></tr>
<tr><td>16 COLOR OF AIRCRAFT
Blue</td><td colspan="3">CLOSE VFR FLIGHT PLAN WITH Fresno FSS ON ARRIVAL</td></tr>
</table>

FAA Form 7233-1 (5-77)

Figure 13.5

  c.   Call Fresno FSS on 123.65 or 122.3; see your sectional chart for frequencies.
  4.   Departure:
  a.   Since you will be departing to the northwest, you will probably be assigned to
        runway 30R to take into account the right traffic pattern. Runway 30L has left
        traffic, which would take you away from your proposed flight route.
  b.   Call the tower on 121.1 and tell them you are ready to take off.
  c.   Use Fresno VOR (FAT, 112.9), From 316°
            Merced VOR (MCE, 114.2), From 274°
        Landmarks include a canal and small lake.
  d.   27.5 nautical miles in 20 minutes (.333 hours) yields a ground speed of 82.6
        knots, considerably less than you estimated. Perhaps the winds are not as fore-
        cast or perhaps you are not following your course precisely. Over relatively
        short distances, rounding errors will account for some variance in your calcu-
        lations.
  e.   The sectional says the UNICOM frequency is 122.8 and the *Airport/Facility
        Directory* says it is 123.0. Use 123.0, as the *Airport/Facility Directory* was
        updated more recently.
  f.   You will be able to land, since the crosswind component is 13 knots, which is
        below the demonstrated component of 15 knots. Since this component is close
        to the airplane's limits, you must be sure to consider your own proficiency
        before deciding to land.

g. You should plan a pattern altitude of 3700 feet (800 feet AGL), as described in the *Airport/Facility Directory*. Since you will be landing on runway 29, you should plan for a right-hand traffic pattern. Fly over the field, make a circle to the west, and enter downwind at a 45° angle midway along the runway. On downwind, you will be flying 090°, keeping in mind that you will have to crab to the south to maintain a straight downwind path. When you turn base (180°), the wind will retard you somewhat and also push you to the east, which means you will have to crab to the right. On final (270°), you will have to crab to the left to maintain a straight final approach.

5. Leg 2:

   a. The alert area is in effect from 0700 to 0200 Monday through Friday from 1000 to 4000 feet MSL. You will overfly the area, so there is no need for alarm. If you were flying through it, you would exercise extreme caution.

   b. You are not required to contact them since the ATA extends from ground level to 3000 feet AGL. You are well above the ATA.

   c. You might be tempted to land at Merced or Atwater, but since it is a hot day the oil temperature may not be abnormal. You might check frequently to see if the temperature continues to rise or if it is stable.

   d. You are northeast of the field and will land on runway 14, which has right traffic. As at Pine Mountain, you should fly over the field so you can enter the right pattern on the southwest side of the field. Pattern altitude is 800 feet, so you will fly the pattern at 919 feet MSL. The downwind leg will be 320° with a crab to the left; base will be 50° with crab to the right. Final (140°) will also necessitate a crab to the right.

   e. Call on 122.8 and ask for it to be activated.

   f. Use the telephone; ask the operator for Enterprise 14598, which will connect you with Fresno FSS (FAT).

   g. It is 14 nautical miles and it took you 0.2 hours, for a ground speed of 70 knots, only slightly more than you estimated.

6. Leg 3:

   a. Set 112.6, check for the identification (PXN), and fly To 057°.

   b. Fly From 072°.

   c. Contact Chandler tower on 121.1 and tell them where you are (over Kerman) and what your intentions are.

   d. Fresno FSS.

14/THE PHYSIOLOGY OF FLIGHT

MAIN POINTS

1. Flight has many effects on the human body, some of which are easy to understand and cope with and others of which can produce serious consequences in a short time. This chapter explores both.

2. **Respiration** is the exchange of gases between your body and the environment. In particular, your body derives oxygen from the environment and expels carbon dioxide. The amount of carbon dioxide in your body governs your involuntary breathing rate. As the amount of carbon dioxide increases, breathing becomes deeper and more frequent, and vice versa. Furthermore, as altitude increases and atmospheric pressure decreases, less oxygen is available to the body. Gases inside the body also expand as altitude increases since they exert more pressure than is being exerted from the outside atmosphere. Thus it is sometimes necessary to clear your ears by yawning or blowing gently through your nose while pinching your nostrils (the **Valsalva technique**). Pilots should also remember that because underwater diving reverses the pressure gradient, diving should not be mixed with piloting—the body takes time to readjust.

3. The motion produced in an airplane also affects the body, in particular the motion associated with **acceleration** (changes in **velocity**). These changes are measured in gravity-level equivalents, or Gs. Forward- and aft-working Gs are called **transverse Gs;** side-force Gs are called **lateral Gs;** and up-and-down Gs are referred to as positive (those that push you down) and negative (those that push you up). Gs produced in varying combinations are called *asymmetric* Gs. Positive Gs tend to deprive blood from the head and upper extremities, while negative Gs do just the opposite. Excessive positive Gs can lead to **grayout** or **blackout** due to the extreme lack of blood, while negative Gs have an opposite effect.

4. The dynamics of flight can have a dramatic effect on spatial orientation. We receive spatial cues from three sources: eyes; motion sensors (the vestibular system) in the semicircular canals of the inner ears; and proprioceptive feedback (the postural system of touch, pressure, and tension). False cues may begin to develop, however, due to the motion produced in the cockpit, especially under conditions of low visibility. For the most part, we have learned to trust our eyes, and as long as VMC conditions prevail, they provide the quickest way to correct any false cues from the vestibular or postural senses.

5. Noise and vibration also affect pilots, particularly over a long period of time. Sound, measured in **decibels,** can become so intense that it produces pain or, in extreme cases, physical damage to the middle and inner ears.

6. Stress, or psychological and bodily tension, is a natural consequence of living. Not all stress is bad, nor is it necessarily produced from unpleasant things. Stress compels us to resolve certain situations and pushes us on to new endeavors. Extremely high (such as panic) or low (for example, sleep) levels of stress lead to low or ineffective performance. As stress increases (as in landing an airplane), our ability to perform increases up to a maximal level, after which performance capability decreases.

7. Stress has three sources: the environment, the body, and psychological processes. As you have probably experienced, the three sources frequently overlap and affect one another. **Environmental stresses** of importance to pilots are apprehension, anxiety, and frustration. **Body stress** includes fatigue, both **acute** (short-lived) and **chronic** (continued). Chronic fatigue can have serious physiological effects on the body, such as slowed reactions and an ambivalent attitude. Diet also affects body stress, as do drugs and alcohol. Drugs, even readily available cold remedies and pain relievers, should not be taken until cleared by an aviation medical examiner since many contain substances that dramatically affect bodily functions, effects that may be exaggerated at high altitudes. Alcohol, a depressant drug, should be avoided twenty-four hours before flight time, even though FARs only prohibit its use eight hours before flight. In addition to reduced judgment and a false sense of capability, the effects of alcohol increase dramatically with altitude. The third type of stress, **psychological stress,** includes worry, job difficulty, and anxiety. Reactions to stress, regardless of its source, include increases in pulse rate, blood pressure, perspiration, respiration, and muscle tension, all of which can produce harmful outcomes if they occur over a long period of time.

8. Two oxygen-related disorders of interest to pilots are **hypoxia** (too little oxygen) and **hyperventilation** (too much oxygen). Hypoxia, or oxygen deficiency, is a progressive condition characterized by impaired vision, euphoria, dizziness, hot and cold flashes, breathlessness, repeated thought patterns, headaches, slowed reaction time, tingling sensation, and perspiration. The time available from the onset of hypoxia to unconsciousness is called **time of useful consciousness (TUC).** As exposure to oxygen

deficiency continues, the effects become more pronounced and may include increased respiration, inability to perform even simple computations, bluing of the skin (cyanosis), and finally, unconsciousness. The *rate* of onset increases dramatically with altitude. From sea level to 10,000 feet (indifferent stage) vision may be affected, particularly at night. From 10,000 to 15,000 feet (compensatory stage) pulse, respiration, and blood pressure increase. From 15,000 to 20,000 feet (disturbance stage) TUC is 20 to 30 minutes, and from 20,000 to 25,000 feet (critical stage) TUC can be as short as 3 to 5 minutes. Rapid decompression in a pressurized cabin can produce extremely rapid (less than a minute) TUC. Furthermore, anything that affects the body's ability to get oxygen to the brain, such as hypertension or smoking, can increase the rate of onset. One way to counteract the effects of hypoxia during flight is to descend at once to a lower altitude since recovery is rapid in an oxygen-rich environment. Oxygen should be used above 10,000 feet during the day and above 5,000 feet at night.

9. Hyperventilation, or overbreathing, is an excessively fast rate of respiration that often occurs unknowingly in response to stress. Hyperventilation can cause the individual to pass out due to a severe shortage of carbon dioxide available to the voluntary respiration center. Symptoms include dizziness, tingling sensations, nausea, muscle tightness (tetany), and fainting. Hyperventilation can begin rapidly, particularly in highly anxiety-producing situations. The first countermeasure is to reduce the rate of breathing or, in more extreme cases, to breathe into an enclosed space, such as a bag, to increase the carbon dioxide content in the blood.

10. **Carbon monoxide poisoning** can be particularly insidious because the gas is odorless. Carbon monoxide (CO) deprives the brain of oxygen; symptoms include a vague uneasy feeling, inability to concentrate, headaches, and, if uncorrected, unconsciousness and death. Effects can last for days because the blood's oxygen-carrying ability has been altered. Carbon monoxide usually enters the cabin through the heating system. If CO poisoning is suspected, close all heating vents, flood the cabin with air, and land at the nearest facility available.

11. **Spatial disorientation,** sometimes referred to as vertigo, occurs when a pilot cannot orient the aircraft to the natural horizon. The condition is physiological, not learned, but understanding it will help you cope with it. There are several motion-related disorientations. The **graveyard spiral** is a result of illusions in which the vestibular and postural systems adjust and stabilize to a spiral (power-on descending turn). Without reference to the appropriate instruments, you may be led to aggravate the situation by adding power and increasing the angle of bank. The **Coriolis illusion** occurs when you move your head quickly once the vestibular system has adjusted to constant condition, such as a constant turn. It is your head that has moved, however, not the airplane. The **leans** may occur when you roll the airplane to level out of a turn, producing the illusion of a turn in the opposite direction. The **oculogyral illusion** may occur during the leans when you perceive the visual field as also moving, a condition that can be overcome by holding your head still and concentrating on the instrument

panel. The **acceleration illusion** may occur when you experience transverse Gs due to a change in velocity. The sensation is that you are climbing, which may lead you to lower the nose of the airplane. *Indefinite horizons* can be a problem at night when you confuse stars and ground lights or when angled cloud decks suggest a horizon. Staring at a stationary light may lead to **autokinesis,** in which the light source appears to move. This effect is why many aviation lights such as beacons rotate, flash, or are arranged in patterns. Finally, **postural illusions** ("seat of the pants") can result from the various motions and G forces that act on the body. To prevent spatial disorientation, trust your eyes when you can see the horizon and your flight instruments when you cannot.

12. *Airsickness,* a sympathetic reaction to conflicting sensations, may have both physical (for example, a warm, stuffy cockpit or changes in velocity) and psychological (anxiety or anticipation of the possibility of becoming sick) components. The best way to cure airsickness is to prevent it. If it occurs or begins to occur, it is wise to scan the horizon or administer fresh air (or oxygen if available).

13. The effects of positive Gs (pushing blood to the lower extremities) can be counteracted by tightening the calf, thigh, and abdominal muscles. The effects of negative Gs (pushing blood to your head) are rare in general aviation and have no easy remedy. Persons who fly more than eight hours a week may want to wear ear plugs to help avoid hearing loss. One way to deal with stress is to learn to accommodate through relaxation. *Panic,* a sudden overpowering and unreasoning fright, can seriously impede your ability to function and can be avoided by limiting your susceptibility to stress (for example, by relaxation exercises, by gaining more knowledge about your airplane, and by expanding your aviation experience).

14. Keeping your body in a general state of good health, knowing you are under stress or in a state of fatigue, and observing regulations about medication, alcohol, and drugs all contribute to being a safe pilot.

KEY TERMS AND CONCEPTS, PART 1
Match each term or concept (1–16) with the appropriate description (a–p) below. Each item has only one match.

— 1. hyperventilation
— 2. the leans
— 3. carbon dioxide
— 4. graveyard spiral
— 5. positive
— 6. aviation physiology
— 7. acceleration illusion
— 8. stress
— 9. time of useful consciousness
—10. eustachian tube
—11. airsickness
—12. negative
—13. Valsalva technique
—14. hypoxia
—15. respiration

a.   tube that connects the space behind your eardrum to the throat
b.   time from the onset of oxygen deficiency to a state of unconsciousness
c.   perceiving a turn in the opposite direction when rolling out of a prolonged turn
d.   blood begins to accumulate in the lower extremities when exposed to these Gs
e.   science that deals with body functions in the flying environment
f.   an excessively fast rate of respiration
g.   measure of your body's need for oxygen
h.   illusion caused by transverse Gs
i.   sympathetic reaction of the stomach to conflicting vestibular, visual, and postural sensations
j.   pinching your nostril and blowing gently through your nose
k.   psychological or body tension
l.   constant descending turn that is the result of disorientation
m.   condition in which the brain and body tissues receive too little oxygen
n.   exchange of gas between you and the environment
o.   blood begins to accumulate in the upper extremities when exposed to these Gs

KEY TERMS AND CONCEPTS, PART 2

Match each term or concept (1–18) with the appropriate description (a–r) below.
Each item has only one match.

— 1. vertigo   — 2. transverse
— 3. acceleration   — 4. oculogyral illusion
— 5. alcohol   — 6. fatigue
— 7. vestibular   — 8. oxygen
— 9. panic   —10. Coriolis illusion
—11. carbon monoxide   —12. aviation medicine
—13. autokinesis   —14. lateral
—15. alveoli   —16. cyanosis
—17. tetany   —18. decibel

a.   branch of medicine that deals with body functions in the flying environment
b.   perceptual system located in the semicircular canals
c.   believing that your field of vision is also moving when you are suffering from the leans
d.   a depressant drug that may lead to a false sense of confidence
e.   the belief that the airplane is spinning in space
f.   forward- and aft-working Gs
g.   muscle tightness
h.   bluing of the skin
i.   apparent movement of a stationary light after you have been staring at it
j.   colorless, odorless, poisonous gas given off by internal combustion engines
k.   air sacs in the lungs where oxygen and carbon dioxide are exchanged

l.   gas your body needs to convert food to energy
m.   any change in velocity
n.   side-force Gs
o.   illusion caused by a rapid head movement when in a constant-rate turn
p.   measure of sound intensity
q.   sudden, overpowering, and unreasoning fright
r.   lack of sleep

DISCUSSION QUESTIONS AND EXERCISES

1.   What is respiration? How does the blood's chemistry regulate normal respiration?

2.   Shortly after leveling off at 9500 feet, a passenger with a mild cold begins to complain of a severe headache. What physiological disorder might you suspect and what action should you take?

3.   Outline the effects of positive and negative Gs on the body's circulatory system.

4.   What three body systems provide cues for spatial orientation? Which is most reliable in VMC conditions?

5.   Name three sources of stress. What special types of flight-related stress may student pilots encounter? What effects do very high and very low levels of stress have on our ability to perform?

6.   Briefly explain what effect each of the following may have on your ability to perform as a pilot:

    a. fatigue

    b. diet

    c. alcohol

7.   Explain the difference between acute fatigue and chronic fatigue. Which is more dangerous? Why?

8.   What is the FAA regulation concerning the time between consuming alcohol and acting as a pilot-in-command?

9.   Name at least five symptoms associated with hypoxia. How does the rate of onset vary with increasing altitude? What countermeasures can be taken against it?

10.   What is hyperventilation? Name at least four symptoms. How is it related to stress and how can it be counteracted?

11.   What is carbon monoxide poisoning? Why is it so dangerous? What should you do if you suspect it while in flight?

12.   What is airsickness? If a passenger begins to complain of nausea, what action should you take?

13.   Briefly characterize each of the following motion-related disorientations:

   a. graveyard spiral

   b. Coriolis illusion

   c. the leans

   d. oculogyral illusion

e. acceleration illusion

f. autokinesis

g. postural illusion

14.   What are two general rules for minimizing the occurrence and effects of spatial disorientation?

REVIEW QUESTIONS

1.   Air sacs in the lungs where carbon dioxide and oxygen are exchanged are called
  a. alveoli
  b. capillaries
  c. eustachian tubes
  d. Valsalva

2.   The Valsalva technique is used to counteract
  a. differential pressure in the eustachian tube
  b. hyperventilation
  c. hypoxia
  d. spatial disorientation

3.   A change in velocity
  a. is defined as acceleration
  b. is measured in decibels
  c. can occur only one direction at one time
  d. all of the above

4.   A _____G force will push blood toward your head while you are flying an airplane.
  a. lateral
  b. negative
  c. positive
  d. transverse

5.   The motion-sensing semicircular canals in the middle ear are part of the _____ perceptual system.
      a. auditory
      b. proprioceptive (postural)
      c. vestibular
      d. visual

6.   Continued exposure to fatigue is referred to as _____fatigue.
      a. acute
      b. active
      c. chronic
      d. delayed

7.   Which of the following is *not* a common reaction to alcohol?
      a. improved reaction time
      b. increased self-confidence
      c. loss of visual acuity
      d. poor reasoning capability

8.   Which statement is true regarding alcohol in the human system?
      a. A common misconception is that coffee alters the rate a body metabolizes alcohol.
      b. An increase in altitude decreases the adverse effect or influence of alcohol.
      c. Alcohol increases judgment and decision-making abilities.
      d. Aspirin increases the rate the body metabolizes alcohol.

9.   Which of the following statements about hypoxia is correct?
      a. Hypoxia is a singular condition that typically strikes all at once.
      b. Hypoxia symptoms occur more rapidly as altitude increases, particularly above 10,000 feet MSL.
      c. One of the most effective countermeasures for the effects of hypoxia is the Valsalva technique.
      d. All of the above are correct.

10.   Hypoxia is considered to be an in-flight hazard. Which statement is true about this hazard?
      a. Alcohol increases the brain's tolerance of hypoxia.
      b. Carbon monoxide increases the brain's tolerance of hypoxia.
      c. Heavy smokers may experience symptoms of hypoxia at lower altitudes than nonsmokers.
      d. A built-in alarm system in the body warns a person that insufficient oxygen is being received.

11.   Which statement concerning hypoxia is true?
      a. A built-in alarm system in the body warns a person that insufficient oxygen is being received.

b. Carbon monoxide has no effect on a person's tolerance of hypoxia.

c. Night vision can be impaired when a person receives insufficient oxygen.

d. Without supplemental oxygen a nonsmoker will experience hypoxia at a lower altitude than a heavy smoker.

12.   A pilot should be able to overcome the symptoms or avoid future occurrences of hyperventilation by
    a. closely monitoring flight instruments to control the airplane
    b. increasing the breathing rate in order to increase lung ventilation
    c. refraining from the use of over-the-counter remedies and drugs such as anti-histamines, cold tablets, tranquilizers
    d. slowing the breathing rate, breathing into a bag, or talking aloud

13.   Breathing carbon monoxide is considered to be an in-flight hazard. Which statement is true about this hazard?
    a. Carbon monoxide forces oxygen to be attached to the hemoglobin.
    b. Even small amounts of carbon monoxide breathed over a long period of time may be harmful.
    c. Remaining below 10,000 feet diminishes the chance of becoming poisoned by carbon monoxide.
    d. Small amounts of carbon monoxide in the human system increase judgment and decision-making abilities.

14.   Suppose a pilot experiences vertigo in a restricted visibility condition (dust, smoke, or snow showers). The best way to overcome the effects of vertigo is to
    a. concentrate on any yaw, pitch, and roll sensations
    b. consciously slow the breathing rate until symptoms clear and then resume a normal breathing rate
    c. depend on sensations received from the fluid in the semicircular canals of the inner ear
    d. rely on the aircraft instrument indications

15.   After a long period of turning flight, a pilot rolls the wings to a level configuration but perceives a turn in the opposite direction. This is known as the
    a. acceleration illusion
    b. Coriolis illusion
    c. graveyard spiral
    d. leans

16.   Which of the following techniques is a common way to combat the effects of position Gs?
    a. administer fresh air
    b. breathe gently through your nose while pinching your nostrils
    c. tighten your abdominal, thigh, and calf muscles
    d. all of these are common, effective techniques

ANSWERS

Key Terms and Concepts, Part 1

1.	f	2.	c	3.	g	4.	1
5.	d	6.	e	7.	h	8.	k
9.	b	10.	a	11.	i	12.	o
13.	j	14.	m	15.	n		

Key Terms and Concepts, Part 2

1.	i	2.	f	3.	m	4.	c
5.	d	6.	r	7.	b	8.	1
9.	q	10.	o	11.	j	12.	a
13.	i	14.	n	15.	k	16.	h
17.	g	18.	p				

Review Questions

1. a; these are little sacs inside the lungs.
2. a; this technique helps reduce the pressure difference; it is used when yawning does not work.
3. a; a decibel is a measure of sound intensity; acceleration can occur in an airplane in many directions and combinations simultaneously (asymmetric).
4. b; negative Gs are most commonly encountered in general aviation during turbulent conditions (for example, turbulent weather or when one encounters wing tip vortices).
5. c; they are filled with fluids that respond to acceleration.
6. c; short exposures are referred to as acute.
7. a; reaction time increases—that is, your reactions are slower.
8. a; your body metabolizes (burns) alcohol at a constant rate; there are no known ways to increase how fast it is metabolized.
9. b; hypoxia is a progressive condition (not a single event); symptoms occur more rapidly at high altitudes.
10. c; the carbon monoxide in cigarettes decreases the blood's capacity to carry oxygen; thus the effects of hypoxia will be more pronounced in a heavy smoker.
11. c; night vision is adversely affected since a lack of oxygen impairs visual acuity.
12. d; slowing one's breathing rate helps to overcome the condition, as does breathing into an enclosed area such as a paper bag (this increases the amount of carbon dioxide in the blood).
13. b; the effects of carbon monoxide may also persist for a long period of time; its effects include hazy thinking, an uneasy feeling, and dizziness.
14. d; vertigo refers to a condition of spatial disorientation in which the pilot believes the aircraft is spinning in space; relying on the airplane's instruments is the best way to combat it.
15. d; definition.
16. c; this helps prevent blood from collecting in the lower extremities.

15/HANDLING AIRBORNE EMERGENCIES

MAIN POINTS

1. Emergency procedures are no different from normal operating procedures; they are simply encountered less frequently.

2. Three general rules apply to airborne emergencies: keep the airplane flying and under control; analyze the situation and take proper action; and land as soon as conditions permit. Specific procedures are found in your airplane's Pilot's Operating Handbook (POH). Learn them as if your life depended on your knowing them.

3. Three factors cited most frequently in general aviation accidents are: inadequate preflight procedures and/or planning, failure to maintain flying speed, and improper in-flight decision making.

4. Unless you are confronted with a bona fide emergency (for example, an engine fire), you should first confirm a suspected emergency with at least one other verifying indication. Pilot experience and confidence also play a factor in identifying and declaring emergency situations. When more than one emergency exists at once (for example, a radio/navigation failure in marginal weather conditions), it is called a **compound emergency.**

5. Equipment malfunctions can be diagnosed more easily if you are familiar with each instrument and how it is powered. For example, if you suspect an electrical malfunction, you should check the proper circuit breaker before taking further action.

6. Safety begins at home, in particular during preflight planning and inspections. Two important aspects of flight preparation are filing a flight plan and using flight following services. Once you file a flight plan, follow it, or advise the nearest FSS if

you make changes. When the flight is complete, close your flight plan. If an overdue airplane is not located by obvious measures such as a ramp check or telephone search, the nearest **Rescue Coordination Center (RCC)** is notified.

7. Emergency landings can be grouped into four categories: as soon as practicable—the nearest suitable airport; as soon as possible—nearest airport regardless of facilities; immediately—continued flight is inadvisable (for example, because of fire) although possible; and forced—the airplane will land very soon whether the pilot wishes it to or not (for example, because of total engine failure).

8. Forced landing procedures include five phases. First, as outlined in the POH, are the immediate actions, including restarting procedures, you should take in case of engine malfunction. In any event, maintain altitude and airspeed; establish a glide path, if necessary, aimed at maintaining as much altitude as possible. If restart fails, set most light trainers as follows: mixture, full lean; fuel selector, off; ignition system, off; master switch, on (for radio, flaps, and so forth). Second, select a landing site, preferably one with a hard surface that will allow you to land into the wind. Third, report your position and situation to the nearest facility, or use the standard emergency frequency. Fourth, in preparation for landing, secure seat belts and shoulder harnesses (if provided) and stow loose items in the cabin. Fifth, maintain airspeed, avoid improvising at the last minute, and hold back pressure as long as possible after touchdown.

9. Know and use your **emergency locator transmitter (ELT)** if you have one.

10. You should be familiar with ground-to-air signals in the event you land in a remote location. Stay near or in your airplane until you are located, unless you see a source of assistance. If you regularly fly in remote areas, you should carry a survival kit.

11. Being lost *is* an emergency situation. If you are lost, remember the **"four Cs"**: confess, communicate, climb, and comply. Confess your problem. Communicate your situation, precisely, over the appropriate radio channel. Climb when possible to improve radio communication, but be sure to maintain VFR conditions. Comply with controller instructions, again with VFR conditions and your airplane's safety as top priorities. Radio assistance may include ATC directions if you have a transponder or a **direction-finding (DF) steer.**

12. The VHF emergency frequency, 121.5, is to be used *only* by aircraft in distress. In an emergency communicate your situation in plain English. State **mayday** three times (or **pan** if you are uncertain about the situation). Next, repeat your airplane identification number three times. Give your type of aircraft, position, heading, TAS, altitude, fuel remaining, nature of distress, intentions, and request. Finally, hold your mike button open for two consecutive ten-second intervals and then repeat your airplane ID and say "over." If you have a transponder, squawk 7700 to indicate an emergency.

13. If your communications receiver fails, you may still be able to transmit and you may be able to receive over your navigation radio. If neither appears to solve the problem, use the information you have already learned about responding to controller signals. If you have a transponder, squawk 7700 for one minute, then switch to 7600 for 15 minutes. Repeat as necessary until you land or solve the problem.

14. The FAA has several guidelines for safe piloting: know your limits, both physiological and technical; use a checklist, particularly for routine tasks; preplan your flight: prepare, file, open, fly, and close; preflight your airplane; know your airplane; and know your airplane's performance limits.

KEY TERMS AND CONCEPTS
Match each term or concept (1–13) with the appropriate description (a–m) below. Each item has only one match.

— 1. land as soon as possible
— 2. confess
— 3. 7700
— 4. compound emergency
— 5. 121.5
— 6. mayday
— 7. land as soon as practicable
— 8. maintain airplane control
—10. land immediately
— 9. pan
—12. 7600
—11. POH
—13. forced landing

a.   land at nearest airport with suitable facilities
b.   first thing you should do in an emergency situation
c.   words to use to notify the ground of an actual airborne emergency
d.   the airplane will land at once whether the pilot wishes it or not
e.   more than one emergency condition occurring at the same time
f.   continued flight is inadvisable although possible
g.   VHF emergency frequency
h.   where you find specific emergency procedures for your airplane
i.   transponder code to squawk to declare an airborne emergency
j.   what you should radio first when you are lost
k.   words to use to notify the ground of a probable airborne emergency
l.   land at nearest airport at once regardless of available facilities
m.   transponder code to squawk to declare a failure in two-way radio communication capability

DISCUSSION QUESTIONS AND EXERCISES
1.   Outline the three general rules for handling any airborne emergency.

2.   What are the three factors cited most frequently in general aviation accidents?

3.   What is the primary way to distinguish between a suspected malfunction and an actual malfunction?

4.   What are compound emergencies? Give an example illustrating how a pilot might help to create a compound emergency.

5.   Suppose you have tried unsuccessfully several times to contact a nearby FSS station. Do you have a malfunctioning radio? How would you troubleshoot this situation?

6.   Identify, describe, and give an example of each of the four types of emergency landings:

        a.

        b.

c.

d.

7.   Outline three immediate actions you should take in case of sudden engine failure.

8.   Name three criteria you should use in selecting a forced landing site.

9.   What are the four Cs and how do they apply to being lost?

10.   Identify the appropriate frequencies, code, or word for each of the following:

a. VHF guard frequency

b. ATC transponder code for an airborne emergency

c. ATC transponder code for two-way radio failure

d. international code word for an airplane in distress

e. international code word for a probable emergency

11.   Refer to your San Francisco sectional chart. Suppose you are en route from Los Banos direct to Carmel at 6500 feet. You are 30 nautical miles from Los Banos on course when your oil pressure suddenly skyrockets and the engine begins to run exceedingly rough. Use the data from the cross-country exercise in Chapter 13 to aid in your planning. Your Beechcraft Skipper has a glide speed of 63 knots, which translates to about 1.3 nautical miles per 1000 feet above the terrain.

a. Where would you attempt to land? Why?

b. What characteristics would you look for in a landing site?

c. Describe in detail what you would communicate over your radio.

12.   Briefly outline the six steps in the FAA Accident Prevention Program.

REVIEW QUESTIONS

1. Which of the following should you do *first* in any airborne emergency?
    a. analyze the situation and take proper action
    b. contact air traffic control (ATC) and confess your predicament
    c. maintain aircraft control
    d. stay in VFR conditions

2. Which of the following is cited least often in general aviation accidents?
    a. engine failure
    b. failure to obtain or maintain flying speed
    c. improper inflight decision making or planning
    d. inadequate preflight preparation and/or planning

3. Where do you find specific procedures for emergency situations?
    a. *AIM*
    b. *Airport/Facility Directory*
    c. Pilot's Operating Handbook
    d. Rescue Coordination Handbook

4. _____means to locate the nearest airport and land at once regardless of available facilities.
    a. Forced landing
    b. Land as soon as practicable
    c. Land as soon as possible
    d. Land immediately

5. The four Cs refer to: (1) climb, (2) communicate, (3) comply, (4) confess. Put them in their proper order.
    a. 1, 4, 2, 3
    b. 1, 4, 3, 2
    c. 4, 2, 1, 3
    d. 4, 1, 3, 2

6.   What is the transponder code for an airborne emergency?
        a. 1200
        b. 4096
        c. 7600
        d. 7700

7.   What is the international word to notify the ground of a probable airborne
emergency?
        a. help
        b. mayday
        c. pan
        d. ouch

8.   The *most* important rule to remember in the event of power failure after becoming airborne is to
        a. determine wind direction to plan for forced landing
        b. maintain safe airspeed
        c. quickly check the fuel supply for possible fuel exhaustion
        d. turn back immediately to the takeoff runway

ANSWERS

Key Terms and Concepts
1.	l	2.	j	3.	i	4.	e
5.	g	6.	c	7.	a	8.	b
9.	k	10.	f	11.	h	12.	m
13.	d						

Discussion Questions and Exercises
11.a.   Given the winds aloft (240° at 25), it makes sense to turn around and glide to
        either Christensen ranch (7.5 nautical miles to the north) or Hollister (9.0 naut-
        ical miles to the north). The glide ratio gives you 1.3 × 5.5, or about 7 nautical
        miles, in a no-wind situation with 1000 feet to spare when you reach your
        destination. Given the moderately favorable winds, you should be able to glide
        to Christensen ranch. Furthermore, the topography between your present posi-
        tion and Christensen ranch is relatively flat, which should give you even more
        options.
     b. If you do not make it to Christensen ranch, refer back to main point 8 for
        detailed forced landing techniques.
     c. mayday, mayday, mayday.
        Beech 7118Q, Beech 7118Q, Beech 7118Q.
        Beech Skipper.
        30 nautical miles southwest of Los Banos, 7 south of Christensen.
        steering 51° true.

true airspeed 97 knots.

6500 feet and descending.

with over 2 hours' fuel.

engine out.

proceeding direct to Christensen ranch.

notify Christensen ranch.

hold mike button for 10 seconds.

Beech 7118Q.

over.

If you have recently contacted FSS, call on that frequency. Otherwise use 121.5, the VHF guard frequency, or 243.0, the UHF guard frequency.

Review Questions

1. c; first and foremost, keep the airplane flying.
2. a; equipment malfunctions (for example, engine failure) play a minor role in general aviation accidents.
3. c; your POH contains *specific* emergency procedures.
4. c; safety requires that the airplane be put on the ground at once, without regard to available facilities.
5. c; confess, communicate, climb, and comply.
6. d; 7700 is the emergency code.
7. c; pan is the word to indicate a probable emergency.
8. b; maintain aircraft control.

APPENDIX B/ FEDERAL AVIATION REGULATIONS

MAIN POINTS

1. FAR Part 1, Definitions and Abbreviations.

Airport: area of land or water used for takeoffs and landings.

Airport traffic area (ATA): airspace from the ground up to but not including 3000 feet AGL; 5-mile radius from the center of an airport with an operating control tower.

Air traffic clearance: authorization to proceed within controlled airspace.

Calibrated airspeed: airspeed corrected for position and installation error.

Ceiling: height AGL of the lowest layer of broken or overcast clouds.

Controlled airspace: ATAs, control zones, transition areas, navigation routes, the continental control area are examples.

Flight crewmember: pilot, navigator, or engineer with assigned duty during flight time.

Flight time: the time from the first movement under the aircraft's own power for the purpose of flight until it comes to rest at the next point of landing.

Flight visibility: forward horizontal distance.

IFR: weather conditions below the minimums for VFR.

Indicated airspeed: pitot-static airspeed less standard pressure, uncorrected for airspeed system errors.

Positive control: control of all air traffic within designated airspace by air traffic control.

Prohibited area: no flight allowed.

Restricted area: restrictions to flight apply.

True airspeed: airspeed relative to undisturbed air.

2. Alphabet soup. See how many of these you can recall: AGL, ATC, CAS, DME, IAS, IFR, MSL, NDB, TAS, Va, Vs, Vx, Vy, VFR, VHF.

3. FAR Part 61, Certification: Pilots and Flight Instructors; Subpart A, General.

61.3 (a)	You must have your pilot certificate in your possession to act as pilot-in-command.
(b)	The same applies for the medical certificate.
61.15	Convicted drug dealers and users can have certificates or ratings revoked and are ineligible for certification for one year following conviction.
61.17	Temporary certificates are valid for 120 days.
61.19	Student pilot certificates expire at the end of the 24th month after issue.
61.23	Medical certificates for student and private pilots expire at the end of the same calendar month in which they were issued, 24 months after the exam.
61.33	In general, one must receive instruction and hold a category and class rating for an airplane to act as pilot-in-command.
61.39	To qualify for the flight test, one must have passed the written test within two years, hold a current medical certificate, and have a CFI's statement (issued within 60 days) that one is prepared.
61.51	Reliable records of required flight time and experience must be kept. Student pilots must carry logbooks on solo cross-country flights.
61.57 (a, b)	Flight reviews (the Biennial Flight Review, or BFR) by a CFI or other person designated by the Administrator are mandatory at least every 24 months to act as pilot-in-command. They expire exactly 24 months after they are issued. The BFR includes questions on general operating procedures, flight rules, and flight maneuvers selected by the person giving the BFR.
61.57 (c)	To act as a pilot-in-command carrying passengers, one must have made at least three takeoffs and landings in the same category and class of aircraft during the prior 90 days.
61.57 (d)	To act as pilot-in-command during the period from one hour after sunset to one hour before sunrise, a person must have made at least three takeoffs and three full-stop landings during the preceding 90 days.

4. FAR Part 61, Subpart B, Aircraft Ratings and Special Certificates.

61.63	To receive additional ratings, the pilot must present a logbook endorsed by an authorized instructor and pass a flight test.

5. FAR Part 61, Subpart C, Student Pilots.

61.83	The minimum age is 16, and English language competency and at least a third-class medical certificate are required.
61.87	Solo flight requires endorsement by a CFI that appropriate training has been given; it is good for 90 days.
61.89	Student pilots cannot carry passengers or act as required crewmembers.
61.93	Cross-country flights (more than 25 nautical miles) require a CFI's endorsement on the student pilot certificate and in the logbook for each cross-country flight.

6. FAR Part 61, Subpart D, Private Pilots.

61.103   The minimum age is 17, and one must have English language competency and at least a third-class medical certificate, and must pass the written test and the oral and flight tests.

61.109   To take the test, the applicant must have at least 20 hours of flight instruction and 20 hours of solo time, as outlined in Chapter 1.

61.118   Private pilots may not act as a pilot-in-command of an aircraft that is carrying passengers or property for compensation or hire. A private pilot may share operating expenses with passengers or act as pilot-in-command to demonstrate an aircraft if he/she is an aircraft salesperson with at least 200 hours of logged flight time.

7. FAR Part 67, Medical Standards and Certification. The Administrator may request medical records if a situation warrants it.

8. FAR Part 91, General Operating and Flight Rules; Subpart A, General.

91.3   The pilot-in-command has responsibility for the aircraft. Deviations from a rule to meet an emergency must be reported to the Administrator in writing upon request.

91.5   Weather information and runway lengths must be considered before any flight not in the vicinity of an airport.

91.7   Seat belts and, when available, shoulder harnesses are required of crewmembers when at stations.

91.11   Alcohol cannot be consumed by the pilot-in-command within 8 hours of a flight, nor can the pilot carry passengers who are obviously under the influence of alcohol or drugs.

91.14   The pilot-in-command is responsible for ensuring that each person knows how to fasten and unfasten his/her safety belt, and for instructing each person to fasten that belt prior to takeoff and landing.

91.21   Simulated instrument flights require the presence of an appropriately rated safety pilot.

91.22   Minimum fuel reserves are 30 minutes for a day VFR flight and 45 minutes for a night VFR flight.

91.24   Group I TCAs require a transponder as well as altitude reporting equipment. Group II TCAs generally require only a transponder.

91.27   An airworthiness certificate must be openly displayed inside the aircraft.

91.31   The pilot must comply with the aircraft's operating limitations and have the following required documents on board: airworthiness certificate, registration, radio station operator's permit, operating limitations, weight and balance data. A convenient way to remember these is to use the acronym ARROW.

91.32   Supplemental oxygen is required for the flight crew for flights of more than 30 minutes between 12,500 and 14,000 MSL. For any flight above 14,000 MSL, the crew must have oxygen, and passengers must have it for flights above 15,000.

91.52	An operable emergency locator transmitter is required for flights outside the local area.

9. FAR Part 91, Subpart B, Flight Rules.

91.67 (a)	Vigilance shall be maintained (VFR, and IFR when weather permits) to see and avoid other aircraft.
91.67 (b)	Aircraft in distress have the right-of-way over all other aircraft.
91.67 (c)	The aircraft to the right has the right-of-way when two aircraft of the same category are converging.
91.67 (d)	When approaching head-on, alter course to your right.
91.67 (e)	Overtaking aircraft shall give right-of-way and pass on the right.
91.67 (f)	Aircraft on final approach have the right-of-way over aircraft on the ground; also, aircraft at lower altitudes have the right-of-way on landing.
91.70 (a)	The speed limit below 10,000 MSL and in TCAs is 250 knots (288 mph).
91.70 (b)	The ATA speed limit is 156 knots (180 mph) for reciprocating engine aircraft and 200 knots (230 mph) for turbine-powered aircraft.
91.70 (c)	The speed limit under TCA airspace is 200 knots (230 mph).
91.71	Acrobatic flight is prohibited over congested areas or open-air assemblies, within control zones, on federal airways, below 1500 AGL, or when visibility is less than 3 miles.
91.73	Position lights are required for night operation (ground and flight operation); anticollision lights are required for night flight.
91.75	Except in an emergency, the pilot must comply with ATC instructions. ATC should be notified of any deviations as soon as possible. ATC may request that a written report of any emergency be sent to the facility chief within 48 hours.
91.77	ATC light signals are covered in Chapter 7. If you cannot remember them, go back for review.
91.79 (a)	Aircraft must always be operated at an altitude that would allow an emergency landing without undue hazard to people and property on the surface.
91.79 (b)	Over congested areas, aircraft must be at least 1000 feet above the highest obstacle within 2000 feet of the aircraft.
91.79 (c)	Over sparsely populated areas, aircraft must stay at least 500 feet away from people, structures, vessels, or vehicles.
91.81 (a)	For flights below 18,000 MSL, altimeters must be set to a station within 100 nautical miles along the route, or if no station is within the prescribed area, to an appropriate current reported altimeter setting. If no radio is available, use the altimeter setting at the departure airport.
91.83 (a)	Flight plans shall include aircraft ID number; type of aircraft; pilot's name and address; time and point of departure; proposed route, altitude, and TAS; point of first landing and ETE; radio frequencies to be used; fuel on board; alternate airport (IFR only); and number of persons

on board. (*Note:* VFR flight plans are optional but *highly* recommended, particularly for cross-country flights.)

91.87   Pilots going to or from or operating on an airport with a control tower are to follow instructions issued by the controller. Two-way radio communication is mandatory unless other arrangements have been made in advance or the radio fails in flight. (*Note:* A clearance to "taxi to" the takeoff runway is a clearance to cross other runways but not to taxi onto the active runway.)

91.89   At airports without an operating control tower, all turns are made to the left unless markings indicate otherwise; FAA departure patterns also apply.

91.90 (a)   Operating within a Group I TCA requires a two-way radio with appropriate frequencies, ATC clearance, and a transponder with an encoding altimeter. A private pilot's certificate is required to land at or take off from an airport with a Group I TCA.

91.91   Special flight restrictions are issued as *Notices to Airmen (NOTAMs)*.

   10. FAR Part 91, Visual Flight Rules.

91.105 (a)   Cloud clearance and flight visibilities:

      Surface to 1200 AGL:

         Controlled airspace: 3 miles visibility and 500 feet below, 1000 above, and 2000 feet horizontal cloud clearance.

         Uncontrolled airspace: 1 mile visibility and clear of clouds.

      1200 AGL to 10,000 MSL:

         Controlled airspace: 3 miles visibility and 500 feet below, 1000 above, and 2000 feet horizontal cloud clearance.

         Outside controlled airspace: 1 statute mile and the same cloud clearance as for controlled airspace.

      More than 1200 AGL and at or above 10,000 feet MSL: 5 statute miles and 1000 feet above and below with 1 mile horizontal cloud clearance.

91.107   Special VFR weather minimums that apply in a control zone: clear of clouds, visibility 1 statute mile, and daytime only.

91.109   VFR cruising altitudes more than 3000 feet AGL:

      Below FL 18: on magnetic courses of 0° to 179°: odd thousand foot MSL altitudes plus 500 feet; on courses of 180° to 359°: even thousand foot MSL altitudes plus 500 feet.

      FL 18 to FL 29: on magnetic courses of 0° to 179°: any odd flight level plus 500 feet; on courses of 180° to 359°: any even flight level plus 500 feet.

   11. FAR Part 91, Subpart C, Maintenance, Preventive Maintenance, and Alterations.

91.163   The owner/operator is primarily responsible for maintaining the aircraft in an airworthy condition. Only authorized persons can perform maintenance and alterations.

91.165	Maintenance and inspections are the owner's or operator's responsibility.
91.167	No passengers may be carried until a repair or alteration has been checked and entered in the aircraft log. There are two logs, one for the airframe and one for the engine.
91.169 (a)	Annual inspections are required for all aircraft.
91.169 (b)	100-hour inspections are required for all aircraft operated for hire (including flight instruction).
91.169 (c)	Progressive inspections may be authorized to replace (a) and (b).
91.173	Records of inspections, alterations, total airframe time, overhauls, and so on must be maintained by the owner or operator.

12. Part 830, National Transportation Safety Board: Accidents.

830.1	Accidents must be reported.
830.5	The operator shall notify the NTSB immediately.
830.10	Aircraft wreckage, cargo, and all records must be presented.

DISCUSSION QUESTIONS AND EXERCISES

The following true-false questions and short essays concentrate on what the FAA tests on the Private Pilot Written Examination.

1.   T F An airport traffic area extends from the surface to 12,000 MSL and for a radius of 5 miles from the control tower.

2.   T F Calibrated airspeed is indicated airspeed corrected for position and installation error.

3.   T F The ceiling is defined as the height above the ground of the lowest clouds.

4.   T F Transition areas are examples of controlled airspace.

5.   T F Indicated airspeed refers to pitot-static airspeed corrected for airspeed system errors.

6.   T F Flights in prohibited areas must be cleared by ATC in a manner identical to that of flights in other control zones.

7.   What does each of the following acronyms mean?

    a. AGL

    b. ATC

c. CAS

d. DME

e. IAS

f. IFR

g. MSL

h. NDB

i. TAS

j. Vx

k. Vy

l. VFR

m. VHF

8. T F To act as pilot-in-command, you must have your pilot certificate and medical certificate in your possession.

9. T F Temporary certificates are typically good for six months from the day on which they were issued.

10. T F Student pilot certificates are issued without an expiration date.

11. T F The logging of flight time is recommended but not required by FARs for student pilots.

12. T F Biennial Flight Reviews are recommended but not required for private pilots once every two years.

13.   T F To act as a pilot-in-command of a single-engine airplane carrying passengers, you must have made three takeoffs and landings in the past 30 days in the same category and class of aircraft.

14.   T F Student pilots can carry passengers on local flights but not on cross-country flights, unless authorized by a CFI.

15.   T F To act as pilot-in-command you must have your current and appropriate pilot certificate and medical certificate in your possession.

16.   T F Student pilots cannot carry passengers.

17.   T F Obtaining weather information is mandatory only for cross-country flights that may encounter weather below IFR or marginal VFR minimums.

18.   T F Alcohol cannot be consumed more than 8 hours before you perform duties as a crewmember of a civil aircraft.

19.   T F Each passenger is responsible for knowing how to fasten and unfasten safety belts.

20.   T F Minimum fuel reserves for a VFR flight of more than two hours' duration is 45 minutes.

21.   T F Simulated instrument flights require the presence of an appropriately rated safety pilot.

22.   T F Group I and II TCAs both require two-way radio communication.

23.   What aircraft documents must you carry on board the airplane? They are represented by the letters ARROW.

24.   Supplemental oxygen is required for the minimum flight crew of a civil aircraft if the flight exceeds 30 minutes above a certain minimum cabin pressure altitude. What is this altitude? What is the minimum cabin pressure altitude at or above which the minimum flight crew must use oxygen continuously? At what minimum cabin pressure altitude must *every* occupant of the aircraft be provided with supplemental oxygen?

25.   Who has the right-of-way in the following circumstances?

a. aircraft of the same category converging on your right

b. two aircraft approaching head-on

c. one aircraft overtaking another

d. aircraft on final approach

26.   T F If two aircraft are on final approach, the aircraft at the lower altitude has the right-of-way.

27.   T F The speed limit in a TCA below 10,000 feet MSL is 150 knots (180 mph).

28.   T F Supplemental oxygen is required of all crewmembers for any flight if over 30 minutes at 10,000 MSL or higher.

29.   T F Acrobatic flight is prohibited over congested areas, below 3000 feet, and when visibility is less than 1 mile.

30.   T F Position lights are required for night flight but not for taxiing an aircraft from one place to another on the airfield.

31.   T F Except in an emergency or if in violation of FARs, the pilot must comply with ATC instructions when flying in an ATA unless he/she obtains an amended clearance.

32.   T F Aircraft must always be operated at an altitude that would allow an emergency landing without undue hazard to people and property on the surface.

33.   T F Over sparsely populated areas, you must stay at least 1000 feet away from people or structures.

34.   What are the minimum safe altitudes (except for takeoffs and landings) and horizontal clearance from obstacles required for operations over a congested area? Over a sparsely populated area?

35.   T F For flights below 18,000 feet MSL, the altimeter must be set to a station within 50 miles of the route of flight.

36.   T F Flight plans are mandatory for VFR flights over 200 miles.

37.   T F Flight plans are mandatory on any cross-country flight in which the pilot-in-command is a student pilot.

38.   A tower clears you to "taxi to" the active runway. Between you and the active runway are several other intersecting runways. How will you proceed?

39.   T F At airports without control towers, turns are typically made to the left unless markings (for instance, a segmented circle) indicate otherwise.

40.   T F To land at or take off from an airport within a Group I TCA, the pilot must possess at least a private pilot's certificate and have at least 20 hours of instrument flight instruction.

41.   List the basic VFR flight visibilities and distance from clouds required (both within and outside controlled airspace) for flights:

    a. at 1200 feet or less AGL

    b. at more than 1200 feet AGL but less than 10,000 feet MSL

c. at more than 1200 feet AGL and at or above 10,000 feet MSL

42.   T F Special VFR minimums that apply in a control zone include visibility of at least 3 miles and clear of clouds.

43.   T F An altitude of 9500 feet MSL would be an appropriate VFR cruising altitude if you were flying a magnetic course of 120° (southeast).

44.   T F The owner/operator is primarily responsible for maintaining the aircraft in an airworthy condition.

45.   T F The agency to whom airplane accidents must be reported is the National Transportation Safety Board.

46.   T F A private pilot may not act as pilot-in-command for compensation or hire, but he/she may share operating expenses of a flight with passengers.

REVIEW QUESTIONS

1.   *Ceiling* as defined by Federal Aviation Regulations means the height above the earth's surface of the
   a. highest layer of clouds that is reported as "broken," "thin," or "obscuration"
   b. lowest layer of clouds that is reported as "broken," "overcast," or "obscuration"
   c. lowest layer of clouds that is reported as "scattered," "broken," or "thin"
   d. lowest reported "obscuration" and the highest layer of clouds that is reported as "overcast"

2.   To act as pilot-in-command of a single-engine nosewheel-equipped airplane, regulations require recent experience before carrying passengers. To meet this requirement you must, within the preceding
   a. 60 days, have made at least three takeoffs and three landings to a full stop in any single-engine airplane
   b. 60 days, have made at least five takeoffs and five landings to a full stop in an aircraft of the same category as the one you will be flying
   c. 90 days, have made at least three takeoffs and three landings in an aircraft of the same category and class as the one you will be flying
   d. 90 days, have made at least three takeoffs and three landings to a full stop in an aircraft of the same category, class, and type as the one you will be flying

3.   If official sunset is 1830 MST and you do not meet the recency of experience requirements for a night flight carrying passengers, you must land at or before what time to comply with regulations?
    a. 1730 MST
    b. 1800 MST
    c. 1830 MST
    d. 1930 MST

4.   Your current and appropriate pilot and medical certificates must be in your personal possession
    a. any time you are acting as pilot-in-command or in any other capacity as a required pilot flight crewmember
    b. only when acting as pilot-in-command
    c. only when you are acting as pilot-in-command while passengers are aboard
    d. only when acting as pilot-in-command for compensation or hire

5.   Which of the following statements is true regarding private pilot privileges and limitations? A private pilot may
    a. act as pilot-in-command of an aircraft carrying *only* property for hire if the flight is in connection with a business
    b. act as pilot-in-command demonstrating an aircraft to a prospective buyer if the private pilot has logged at least 100 hours of flight time in the aircraft being shown
    c. act as pilot-in-command of an aircraft carrying passengers for compensation if the flight is in connection with a business or employment
    d. share the operating expenses of a flight with the passengers

6.   If you have made a change in your permanent mailing address, you may not exercise the privileges of your pilot certificate after 30 days from the date you moved unless you
    a. forward your certificate to the FAA Airmen Certification Branch and request reissuance
    b. forward your certificate to the local General Aviation District Office (GADO) for a change of address
    c. notify the FAA Airmen Certification Branch in writing of your change of address
    d. request your local General Aviation District Office (GADO) to issue you a temporary pilot certificate

7.   Assume that your private pilot certificate was issued on March 15, 1978. Unless you complete a proficiency check for another pilot certificate, rating, or operating privilege, to act as pilot-in-command of an aircraft you will be due for a flight review no later than
    a. March 15, 1979

    b. March 31, 1979
    c. March 15, 1980
    d. March 31, 1979

8.   To act as pilot-in-command of an aircraft carrying passengers during the period beginning one hour after sunset and ending one hour before sunrise, a pilot must, within the preceding 90 days, have
    a. flown a minimum of three hours
    b. made five takeoffs and five landings to a full stop in the category and class aircraft to be used
    c. made five takeoffs and five landings to a full stop in the same make and model of aircraft to be used
    d. made three takeoffs and three landings to a full stop in the category and class aircraft to be used

9.   During flight, which of these aircraft documents is required to be aboard?
    a. airframe and engine logbooks
    b. owner's manual
    c. registration certificate
    d. weight and balance handbook

10.   Regulations require that seat belts be fastened about passengers
    a. during all periods of flight
    b. only during flight in turbulent flight conditions
    c. only during takeoffs and landings
    d. only when advised by the pilot-in-command to do so

11.   In addition to other preflight action for a VFR cross-country flight, regulations specifically require the pilot-in-command to
    a. check each fuel tank visually to ensure that it is always filled to capacity
    b. determine runway lengths at the airports of intended use
    c. file a flight plan for the proposed flight
    d. perform a VOR equipment accuracy check before the proposed flight

12.   When two aircraft are approaching each other head-on or nearly so, which aircraft should give way?
    a. If the aircraft are of different categories, an airship would have the right-of-way over an airplane.
    b. If the aircraft are of different categories, an airship would have the right-of-way over a helicopter.
    c. Regardless of the aircraft categories, a glider has the right-of-way over all engine-driven aircraft.
    d. Regardless of the aircraft categories, the pilot of each aircraft shall alter course to the right.

13.   Which statement is true concerning an emergency locator transmitter (ELT) aboard an airplane?
    a. An operable ELT is required on all training airplanes operated within 50 miles of the point of origin of the flight.
    b. ELT battery replacement is required after each ten hours of cumulative use.
    c. Tests of the equipment should be conducted during the first five minutes after every hour.
    d. When activated, an ELT transmits on the frequencies 118.0 and 122.3 MHz.

14.   When operating an aircraft at cabin pressure altitudes above 12,500 feet MSL up to and including 14,000 feet MSL, supplemental oxygen shall be used
    a. at no required time by a private pilot
    b. during the entire flight time at those altitudes
    c. while at those altitudes for 15 minutes
    d. while at those altitudes for more than 30 minutes

15.   During flight, which of these aircraft documents is required to be aboard?
    a. airframe and engine logbooks
    b. FAA-approved and current aircraft flight manual or aircraft operating limitations
    c. owner's manual
    d. weight and balance handbook

16.   Who is responsible for determining whether an aircraft is in condition for safe flight?
    a. the maintenance inspector
    b. the maintenance man who maintains the aircraft
    c. the owner of the aircraft
    d. the pilot-in-command

17.   The airworthiness certificate of your airplane remains valid
    a. as long as the aircraft has a current registration certificate
    b. as long as the aircraft has not had major damage
    c. as long as the airplane is maintained and operated as required by Federal Aviation Regulations
    d. from the date of its issuance

18.   When two or more airplanes are approaching an airport for the purpose of landing, the right-of-way belongs to the airplane
    a. at the lower altitude, but it shall not take advantage of this rule to cut in front of or to overtake another
    b. that has the other to its right
    c. that is either ahead of or to the other's right regardless of altitude
    d. that is the least maneuverable

19. Approaching a VOR station while flying southwest at 8500 feet MSL, you see a multiengine airplane at the same altitude converging from your left, headed northwest toward the VOR. According to regulations, which pilot should give way and why?
    a. The multiengine airplane should give way since your airplane is to its right and you have the right-of-way.
    b. The pilot of the multiengine airplane should give way since the airplane is not flying at a proper VFR cruising altitude.
    c. You should give way since the other airplane is to your left and has the right-of-way.
    d. You should give way since your airplane is slower and more maneuverable than a multiengine airplane.

20. Unless otherwise authorized, no person may operate an aircraft below 10,000 feet MSL at an indicated airspeed of more than
    a. 156 knots (180 mph)
    b. 200 knots (230 mph)
    c. 250 knots (288 mph)
    d. 300 knots (345 mph)

21. An aircraft should not be operated in acrobatic flight when
    a. below 3000 feet AGL
    b. the flight visibility is less than 5 miles
    c. the flight visibility is less than 10 miles
    d. over any congested area

22. A clearance to "taxi to" the active runway means a pilot has been given permission to taxi
    a. on taxiways to the active runway without crossing any intersecting runways
    b. to and hold in takeoff position on the active runway
    c. to the active runway and to take off
    d. via taxiways and across intersecting runways to, but not on, the active runway

23. Aircraft operating at night, in the air or on the surface, must display lighted position lights during the period from
    a. 30 minutes after sunset to 30 minutes after sunrise
    b. 30 minutes before sunset to 30 minutes after sunrise
    c. one hour before sunset to one hour after sunrise
    d. sunset to sunrise

24. No person may operate an aircraft in acrobatic flight when
    a. below 2000 feet AGL
    b. over an open-air assembly of people
    c. the flight visibility is less than 5 miles
    d. the flight visibility is less than 7 miles

25.   According to regulations, which statement is true regarding acrobatic flight or the use of parachutes?
   a. An intentional maneuver not necessary for normal flight involving an abrupt change in the aircraft's attitude is considered acrobatic flight.
   b. For acrobatic flight, the visibility must be at least 5 miles and the ceiling must be 3000 feet or more.
   c. Parachutes are always required for all occupants of an aircraft when spins are practiced.
   d. Parachutes are not required when a private pilot carrying a passenger performs a power-on stall in a nose-up attitude of 40 degrees relative to the horizon.

26.   Closing a VFR flight plan at the completion of a flight is
   a. accomplished by any government agency through teletype service
   b. advisable but is not required by regulations
   c. automatically accomplished by the control tower or FSS personnel when the aircraft lands at its destination
   d. required by regulations

27.   When flying below 18,000 feet MSL in an aircraft without radio equipment, cruising altitude must be maintained by reference to an altimeter that was
   a. adjusted to 29.92 inches of mercury
   b. periodically reset to the elevations of en route airports
   c. set to the elevation of the departure airport
   d. set to zero elevation prior to takeoff

28.   To operate an aircraft over any congested area, a pilot should maintain an altitude of at least
   a. 500 feet above the highest obstacle within a horizontal radius of 500 feet
   b. 500 feet above the highest obstacle within a horizontal radius of 1000 feet
   c. 1000 feet above the highest obstacle within a horizontal radius of 2000 feet
   d. 2000 feet above the highest obstacle within a horizontal radius of 1000 feet

29.   An "alternating red and green" ATC light signal directed to an aircraft in flight is a signal to the pilot of that aircraft to
   a. abort the landing
   b. exercise extreme caution
   c. give way to other aircraft and continue circling
   d. return for landing

30.   During operations *outside controlled airspace* at altitudes of more than 1200 feet AGL but less than 10,000 feet MSL, the minimum "horizontal distance from clouds" requirement for VFR flight is
   a. 500 feet

b. 1000 feet
c. 1500 feet
d. 2000 feet

31.   According to Federal Aviation Regulations, VFR flight in controlled airspace above 1200 feet AGL and below 10,000 feet MSL requires a minimum visibility and vertical cloud clearance of
a. 3 miles, and 500 feet below or 1000 feet above the clouds in controlled airspace
b. 3 miles, and 1000 feet below or 2000 feet above the clouds at all altitudes within and outside of controlled airspace
c. 5 miles, and 1000 feet below or 1000 feet above the clouds at all altitudes
d. 5 miles, and 1000 feet below or 1000 feet above the clouds only in the continental control area

32.   The basic VFR weather minimums for operating an airplane under a ceiling within a control zone are
a. 500-foot ceiling and 1 mile visibility
b. 1000-foot ceiling and 3 miles visibility
c. 2000-foot ceiling and 1 mile visibility
d. clear of clouds and 2 miles visibility

33.   During VFR operations at altitudes of more than 1200 feet AGL and at or above 10,000 feet MSL, the minimum flight visibility requirement is
a. 1 statute mile
b. 3 statute miles
c. 5 statute miles
d. 7 statute miles

34.   Regarding operation within a Group I terminal control area (TCA), which of the following statements is true?
a. An IFR flight plan must be filed to fly within a Group I TCA.
b. Private pilots are not permitted to fly within a Group I TCA.
c. The aircraft must have an operable VOR receiver, two-way communications radio, and a 4096 mode transponder.
d. The pilot must have an instrument rating.

35.   To operate an airplane within a control zone at night under special VFR, the pilot is required to
a. be instrument rated
b. have an instructor aboard
c. have logged more than 500 hours as pilot-in-command
d. remain 500 feet below the clouds

36.   A *special VFR* clearance authorizes the pilot of an airplane to operate VFR while within a control zone
    a. at or below cloud base with a flight visibility of 1 mile or less, provided he remains below 1000 feet above the surface
    b. if clear of clouds and the visibility is at least 1 mile
    c. when the ceiling is less than 1000 feet and visibility less than 1 mile if he does not exceed maneuvering speed
    d. with no minimum visibility requirements if clear of the clouds

37.   The basic VFR weather minimums for flights within controlled airspace below 10,000 feet MSL requires the minimum visibility and distance under the clouds to be
    a. 1 mile and clear of clouds
    b. 1 mile and 500 feet
    c. 3 miles and 500 feet
    d. 3 miles and 1000 feet

38.   During operations *within controlled airspace* at altitudes of more than 1200 feet AGL but less than 10,000 feet MSL, the minimum "distance above clouds" requirement for VFR flight is
    a. 500 feet
    b. 1000 feet
    c. 1500 feet
    d. 2000 feet

39.   During operations *within controlled airspace* at altitudes of more than 1200 feet AGL but less than 10,000 feet MSL, the minimum "distance below clouds" requirement for VFR flight is
    a. 500 feet
    b. 1000 feet
    c. 1500 feet
    d. 2000 feet

40.   You can determine if an aircraft has had an annual inspection and has been returned to service by referring to the
    a. appropriate notation in the aircraft maintenance records
    b. appropriate notations on a repair and alteration form
    c. issuance date of the airworthiness certificate
    d. relicensing date on the airworthiness certificate

41.   If an alteration or repair may have appreciably changed an airplane's flight characteristics, the airplane must be test flown and approved for return to service by an appropriately rated pilot prior to being operated
    a. away from the vicinity of the airport
    b. by anyone who is not at least a commercial pilot

    c. for compensation or hire
    d. with passengers aboard

42.   The responsibility for ensuring that an aircraft is maintained in an airworthy condition is *primarily* that of the
    a. certified mechanic who signs the aircraft maintenance records
    b. maintenance shop
    c. owner or operator of the aircraft
    d. pilot-in-command of the aircraft

43.   Appropriate VFR cruising altitudes should be maintained when operating in level cruising flight during
    a. all special VFR operations
    b. all VFR operations in controlled airspace above 2000 feet above the ground
    c. all VFR operations in uncontrolled airspace above 2000 feet above the ground
    d. VFR operations at more than 3000 feet above ground level

44.   The selection of VFR cruising altitudes should be made on the basis of the magnetic
    a. course when more than 3000 feet above sea level
    b. course when more than 3000 feet above the surface
    c. heading when more than 3000 feet above sea level
    d. heading when more than 3000 feet above the surface

45.   Of the following incidents, which would require an immediate notification to the nearest National Transportation Safety Board field office?
    a. an in-flight generator failure
    b. damage to a landing gear as a result of a hard landing
    c. flight control system malfunction or failure
    d. minor damage to an aircraft with no intention of flight, sustained during ground operations with the engine functioning

46.   After an annual inspection has been completed and the aircraft has been returned to service, an appropriate notation should be made on the
    a. aircraft maintenance records
    b. airworthiness certificate
    c. instrument panel inspection sticker
    d. repair and alteration form or operating placards

47.   The last annual inspection was performed on your aircraft December 1, 1978. The next annual inspection will be due no later than
    a. December 1, 1979
    b. December 31, 1979
    c. 100 flight hours following the last annual inspection
    d. 12 calendar months after the date shown on the airworthiness certificate

ANSWERS

Discussion Questions and Exercises

1. F; it extends up to but does not include 3000 feet AGL and for a 5-mile radius.
2. T.
3. F; the clouds must be reported as broken, overcast, or obscured.
4. T.
5. F; this is called calibrated airspeed.
6. F; flights are prohibited in prohibited areas.
7.a. Above ground level.
   b. Air traffic control.
   c. Calibrated airspeed.
   d. Distance measuring equipment.
   e. Indicated airspeed.
   f. Instrument Flight Rules.
   g. Mean sea level.
   h. Nondirectional beacon.
   i. True airspeed.
   j. Best angle-of-climb airspeed.
   k. Best rate-of-climb airspeed.
   l. Visual Flight Rules.
   m. Very high frequency.
8. T.
9. F; 120 days.
10. F; they expire at the end of the month 24 months after they were issued.
11. F; they are required.
12. F; they are required.
13. F; the past 90 days.
14. F; student pilots cannot carry passengers.
15. T.
16. T.
17. F; it is mandatory on all IFR and cross-country flights.
18. T.
19. F; it is the responsibility of the pilot-in-command to inform passengers how to fasten and unfasten their seat belts.
20. F; the minimum is 30 minutes for any VFR flight.
21. T.
22. T.
26. T.
27. F; it is 250 knots (288 mph).
28. F; from 12,500 to 14,000 MSL; above 14,000, it is required for crewmembers all the time; and above 15,000 everyone must have it.
29. F; below 1500 AGL and when visibilities are less than 3 miles.
30. F; they are required for any night operation.

31. T.
32. T.
33. F; 500 feet.
35. F; the station need only be within 100 miles, if one exists.
36. F; they are optional, but highly recommended!
37. F; they are optional, but highly recommended!
39. T.
40. F; a private pilot's certificate is required to land at or take off from an airport within the horizontal and vertical limits of a Group I TCA. A two-way radio, a transponder, and an encoding altimeter are required for all operations within a Group I TCA.
42. F; visibility must be at least 1 mile.
43. T; magnetic course of 0° to 179°: odd thousand plus 500; magnetic course of 180° to 359°: even thousand plus 500.
44. T.
45. T.
46. T.

Review Questions
1. b; this defines *ceiling;* the clouds must cover more than 50 percent of the sky.
2. c; the landings do not have to be a full stop.
3. d; night flight requirements for carrying passengers are from one hour after sunset until one hour before sunrise.
4. a; you must carry both documents.
5. d; private pilots cannot carry passengers or property for compensation or hire, but they may share operating expenses with their passengers.
6. c; you need only notify the certification branch in writing.
7. c; Bienniel Flight Reviews are good for exactly two years.
8. d; landings must be to a full stop.
9. c; this is required to be aboard.
10. c; only passengers are required to wear them, and then only during takeoffs and landings.
11. b; runway lengths and a study of the weather (both current conditions and forecasts) must also be considered.
12. d; both pilots should turn to the right to avoid collision.
13. c; ELTs are mandatory equipment; batteries should be replaced after one cumulative hour of use; they transmit on 121.5 and 243.0 Hz; battery expiration date is marked on the outside of the transmitter.
14. d; above 14,000 MSL, the pilot shall use supplemental oxygen, and above 15,000 all passengers shall use it, too.
15. b; these are required.
16. d; he/she is the one about to fly it and who shall determine whether it is in a condition safe for flight.
17. c; self-explanatory.

18.   a; self-explanatory.
19.   a; self-explanatory.
20.   c; the "speed limit" in ATAs is 156 knots (180 mph).
21.   d; visibility must be 3 miles and the minimum altitude is 1500 feet AGL.
22.   d; "taxi to" means exactly that.
23.   d; night lights are required from sunset to sunrise.
24.   b; see question 21 above.
25.   a; self-explanatory.
26.   d; filing a flight plan is optional (but highly recommended) for VFR flights; closing them once they are filed is mandatory.
27.   c; self-explanatory.
28.   c; self-explanatory; over sparsely populated areas an aircraft may not be operated closer than 500 feet to people or obstacles.
29.   b; review the ATC light signals in Chapter 7.
30.   d; self-explanatory.
31.   a; self-explanatory.
32.   b; self-explanatory.
33.   c; self-explanatory.
34.   c; self-explanatory.
35.   a; self-explanatory.
36.   b; self-explanatory.
37.   c; self-explanatory.
38.   b; self-explanatory.
39.   a; self-explanatory.
40.   a; self-explanatory.
41.   d; self-explanatory.
42.   c; self-explanatory.
43.   d; self-explanatory.
44.   b; self-explanatory.
45.   c; you are also required to report in-flight fires, the failure of a crewmember to perform normal flight duties as a result of an in-flight injury or illness, an overdue aircraft believed to be involved in an accident, and aircraft involved in an accident. Accidents must be reported to the NTSB immediately.
46.   a; self-explanatory.
47.   b; self-explanatory.